THE SELLER'S LIABILITY FOR THE NON-CONFORMITY OF GOODS TO THE CONTRACT OF SALE OF GOODS UNDER THE OHADA UNIFORM ACT ON GENERAL COMMERCIAL LAW:

COMMON LAW PERSPECTIVE

GALDA VERLAG 2019

ROLAND DJIEUFACK

THE SELLER'S LIABILITY FOR THE NON-CONFORMITY OF GOODS TO THE CONTRACT OF SALE OF GOODS UNDER THE OHADA UNIFORM ACT ON GENERAL COMMERCIAL LAW:

COMMON LAW PERSPECTIVE

GALDA VERLAG 2019

Bibliografische Information der Deutschen Nationalbibliothek
Die Deutsche Nationalbibliothek verzeichnet diese Publikation in der Deutschen Nationalbibliografie; detaillierte bibliografische Daten sind im Internet über http://dnb.ddb.de abrufbar.

ISBN 978-3-96203-068-1 (Print)
ISBN 978-3-96203-069-8 (E-Book)

Originally presented as the author's thesis at the University of Dschang,
Dschang, Cameroon, 2014

ABSTRACT

This study assesses the seller's duty of conformity of goods in a contract of sale under the OHADA Uniform Act on General Commercial Law. It highlights the fact that even though the duties of the seller are encapsulated in the concept of '*conformity*' under the Act, it raises confusion and uncertainty in determining the seller's liability for non conforming goods. This concept today is not efficient as business practices by sellers are to an extent characterised by deception, false pretense, misrepresentation and false promise. Sellers usually in their commercial transactions with commercial buyers do not deliver goods which correspond to the specifications agreed under the contract of sale. The justification for this has been an alarming outcry of consumer buyers of goods complaining about their vulnerability to deficient goods they receive directly from the commercial buyers. From this standpoint, this study is based on the assumption that the provisions of the OHADA Uniform Act on General Commercial Law are not effective enough to afford protection to commercial buyers of goods in their business with the seller. Thus, this work has as general objective to ascertain the extent to which the OHADA law effectively constrain sellers to ensure the conformity of the goods they sell to commercial buyers of goods as to the specifications of the contract of sale of goods.

Adopting an in depth content analysis and critical evaluation of primary and secondary data, the study concludes that there should be an effective implementation of the laws in place with a view to ensure that sellers adequately fulfil their contractual obligations as agreed in a contract of sale of goods. This will eventually cause them in supplying goods of conformity to the contractual specifications which will go a long way to afford satisfaction to consumers who are the end users of the goods sold to them by the commercial buyers. It will equally call on the sellers of goods to press on manufacturers of goods to be more cautious in ascertaining the quality of their goods during the production phase. All this is achieved by invariably weaving into the text nearly all important Cameroonian, foreign cases and other statutes on this subject.

RESUMÉ

Cette étude analyse l'obligation de conformité imposée au vendeur dans le contrat de vente des marchandises régi par l'Acte Uniforme OHADA portant sur le Droit Commercial Général. Cette étude souligne que malgré le fait que les obligations du vendeur dans l'Acte Uniforme se trouvent résumé par le concept de '*conformité*', ce dernier suscite confusion et incertitude pour la détermination de la responsabilité du vendeur pour non conformité des marchandises. Ce concept n'est pas efficace puisque de nos jours les pratiques commerciales sont dans une certaine mesure caractérisées par la fraude, l'escroquerie, la mauvaise foi et les fausse promesses, etc. Par conséquent, une telle situation ne garantit pas une grande protection à l'acheteur-commerçant dans leur relation commerciale avec les consommateurs. La preuve découle d'incessantes plaintes des consommateurs des marchandises du fait de leur vulnérabilité face aux marchandises défectueuses qu'ils reçoivent directement des vendeurs. De e point de vue, la thèse est basée sur l'hypothèse selon laquelle les dispositions de l'Acte Uniforme sur le Droit Commercial Général ne sont pas suffisamment efficaces pour conférer une protection aux acheteurs commerçants. Ainsi, l'objectif général de ce travail vise a déterminer l'étendue de l'obligation imposée par le législateur OHADA aux vendeurs d'assurer aux acheteurs la conformité des marchandises telle que prévue dans le contrat de vente. En procédant a une analyse minutieuse du contenu des textes et a une évaluation critique des information primaires et secondaires, ce travail propose qu'il soit mis sur pied une réelle application des textes en vue de permettre au vendeurs d'effectivement accomplir leurs obligations convenablement au spécifications du contrat de vente. Ceci pourrait éventuellement les pousser a livrer les marchandises conformes telles que stipulées au contrat et par la procurer satisfaction aux consommateurs qui sont au bout de la chaine du processus de vente. Une telle mesure aura pour effet d'inciter les vendeurs de mettre la pression sur les fabricants à plus de vigilance concernant la conformité de leurs produits pendant la phase de fabrication. Ce résultat sera obtenu en compulsant dans le texte la quasi-totalité des jurisprudences importante recenses sur la question au Cameroun et à l'étranger.

DEDICATION

To My Elder Brother

GAIMA Martin of Blessed Memory

ACKNOWLEDGEMENT

I owe a debt of gratitude to my academic supervisor; Professor **Martha S. Tumnde**, whose constant advice provided me with invaluable insights on this subject. I am also grateful to Professors **Claire Moore Dickerson**, **Ingeborg Schwenzer** and **Joseph Nzalie Ebi** for their extraordinary mentoring during my years of research on this study.

I sincerely thank the officials of the International Institute for the Unification of Private Laws (UNIDROIT) in Rome, Italy, Tulane Law School New Orleans, USA and the OHADA Permanent Secretariat, Yaoundé, Cameroon for awarding research grants which provided me with remarkable materials in edifying this study.

Finally, I earnestly thank my parents, Clement and Madeleine Gaima, my siblings—Noel, Michel, Patrice and Françoise, for supporting me emotionally and otherwise.

I however take responsibility for all the errors, omissions and shortcomings in this work.

TABLE OF CONTENTS

THE SELLER'S MATERIAL DUTY OF CONFORMITY

THE SELLER'S FUNCTIONAL DUTY OF CONFORMITY

SELLER'S DUTY TO GUARANTEE AGAINST THIRD PARTY RIGHTS

THE PASSING OF PROPERTY AND RISK IN GOODS

LIMITS OF THE SELLER'S LIABILITY FOR NON-PERFORMANCE

PREFACE

This work is a reflection of my experiences as a student, teacher and researcher on Commerial law. The publication of a book in English dealing with an aspect of Sale of goods under the OHADA law is topical. This work adopts a panoramic view of the OHADA Uniform Act on General Commercial Law, with focus on contract of sale of goods. It critically eamines the current provisions of the Act dealing with the seller's duty of conformity of goods as to the specifications of a contract of sale of goods. It adapts a comparative approach to the understanding of the OHADA law by weaving into the text the English law approach on this subject.

The Organisation for the Harmonization of Business Law in Africa, known by its French acronym, OHADA, is a system of business-related laws, designed to reduce transaction costs, promote transparency and predictability in business ventures. Its laws are directly applicable in 17 countries with more than 250 million people. Regrettably, adequate implementation of OHADA laws in member States remains the issue of concern, especially in Common Law jurisdictions. The main objective of this book is therefore to raise and discuss relevant issues that impede the smooth implementation of these laws. The intention of the author is to familiarise practitioners and other stakeholders with the laws on Sale of goods put in place by OHADA and to contribute towards promoting investment, economic growth and social development.

This work is expected to fill a vacuum in the Cameroonian literature on Commercial law. The book is written for both common law and civil law trained legal practitioners, students, teachers, and business men.

Roland Djieufack
The University of Bamenda

December 2018

LIST OF STATUTES

CAMEROON

Decrees

LIST OF CASES

AFRICA

CAMEROON

ENGLAND

FRANCE

UNITED STATES OF AMERICA

COMMONLY USED ACRONYMS AND ABBREVIATIONS

AGOA	*African Growth and Opportunity Act*
APP	*Appeal*
All N.L.R	*All Nigerian Law Reports*
BCA	*Bamenda Court of Appeal*
B2B	*Business to Business*
B2C	*Business to Consumers*
CC	*Code Civil*
CIV	*Civil*
CCLR	*Cameroon Common Law Report*
CASWP	*Court of Appeal South West Province*
All ER	*All England Reports*
CISG	*United Nations Convention on Contracts for the International Sale of Goods*
CCJA	*Common Court of Justice and Arbitration*
CEMAC	*Communauté Economique et Monétaire de l'Afrique Centrale*
CO	*Company*
DEA	*Diplôme d'Etudes Approfondies*
Ed	*Edition*
HCSW	*High Court South West*
NO	*Number*
UAGCL	*Uniform Act Relating to General Commercial Law*
UN	*United Nations*
UN-DROIT	*International Institute for the Unification of Private Law*
OHADA	*Organisation pour l'Harmonisation en Afrique du Droit des Affaires*
UCC	*Uniform Commercial Code*

UA	*Uniform Act*
USA	*United States of America*
OAPI	*Organisation Africaine pour la Propriété Intellectuelle*
PARA	*Paragraph*
WIPO	*World Intellectual Property Organisation*
IP	*Intellectual Property*
IPR	*Intellectual Property Right*
NWLR	*Nigerian Weekly Law Reports*
No	*Number*
LTD	*Limited*
LGDJ	*Librairie General de Droit et de Jurisprudence*
K.B	*Kings Bench*
P.U.A	*Presses Universitaires d'Afrique*
P	*Page*
PP	*Pages*
SGA	*Sale of Goods Act*
Q.B	*Queens Bench*
Vol.	*Volume*
V.	*Versus*

1

GENERAL INTRODUCTION

Background to the Study

The utter confusion prevailing on the subject of warranty has been deplored in some literature over the years and the multiple irregularities, uncertainties, and difficulties encountered in this field, though varying, cannot be denied. The origin of the doctrine of warranty has nowhere been very ancient. The implied warranty of quality or fitness for particular purpose was first developed in Anglo-American jurisprudence in the early 19th century.[1] This was universally characterised by the slogan, *caveat emptor*; the thing is sold as it is, let the buyer beware; who does not open his eyes may open his purse.[2] The principle persisted, due to the predominance of cash-and-carry bargains in the legal minds even in periods when sales contracts were in fact made without delivery or payment or both. In the English development as it is known from the beginning of the seventeenth century, Lord Ellenborough established implied warranty of merchantability in terms of resaleability in 1815 for the first time when the sizeable section of the English population was employed in commercial navigation and manufacturing in any agricultural and mining work. Prior to this time, particularly in the seventeenth century, commerce and trade were subjected to intolerable abuse and fraud.[3] In fact,

1 George G. Bogert & Eli E. Fink, Business Practice Regarding Warranties in the Sale of Goods, (1930–1931) 24 *Illinois Law Review*, pp. 400–417, p. 401.

2 Ernst Rabel, The Nature of Warranty of Quality, (1950) vol. 24 (3) *Tulane Law Review*, pp. 273–287, p. 274.

3 George G. Rogert, Express Warranties in Sales of Goods, (1923–1924) 33 *Yale Law Journal*, pp. 14–32, p. 15.

17th century onwards, doctrine of *caveat emptor* was given a new lease of life because of the influence of an emergent individualism and notions of *laissez-faire* which strongly opposed medieval regulation of quality by guilds, church and the state. Abuses of trade regulations became so wide-spread in England that the people gradually revolted against the rules and decided that it might be better to let each customer shift for himself. By the 17th century, there was general complaint of intolerable abuse and fraud in the application of administrative and trade regulations in England.

It was in this popular frame of mind which emerged the adage, "*Let the buyer beware*", embalmed by the writers in the Latin phrase *caveat emptor*. The ideology of *caveat emptor* was popular with the common folk. It denoted to them that they could stand their own ground with tricks of the merchants. The doctrine of *caveat emptor* was best calculated to excite that caution and attention which all prudent men ought to observe in making their contracts.

As a principle of legal relationship between buyer and seller, *caveat emptor* is today a pretty sick horse.[4] It is not so much the buyer as it is the manufacturer and the seller who must beware, on penalty of damages. The rise and fall of this Latin phrase, which had attained the status of an ancient maxim, has brought damaging effects to the buyer in his relationship with fraudulent sellers. The total absence of any express warranty by the seller did not afford much protection to the buyer over the goods he bought from the seller. In some cases, the exceedingly low grade or quality of the article sold to the buyer explained the failure to warrant by the seller. In many cases, sellers were in fact very liberal in making adjustments to reliable customers since sale was customarily by description or sample and the implied warranty thus obviates the necessity of any express warranty.[5] The doctrine of *caveat emptor* had a strong influence and retarded the development of not only implied but also express warranties. In England, implied warranty of merchantability had remained a strong legal tool in favour of the buyer.

In spite of administrative and trade regulations which cause the decline of trade and commerce, it gave impetus for the development of the concept of implied warranty of merchantability. The concept of implied warranty for the fitness for the buyer's particular purpose got developed and was recognised as something separate and distinct from that of merchantable quality. From its inception, breach of warranty was a tort. Action was passed on breach of

4 Charles T. Leviness, *Caveat Emptor* versus *Caveat Venditor*, (1943) 7 (7) *Modern Law Review*, pp. 177–200, p. 177.

5 George G. Bogert & Eli E. Fink, *Express Warranties in Sales of Goods*, Op. cit., p. 403.

assumed duty and the wrong was considered to be a form of misrepresentation in the nature of deceit. The tort element served as a sound argument for those who intend to extend implied warranties of quality from the buyer to the ultimate consumer in the absence of privity of contract between the two.

Warranty is a '*civil*' obligation says Professor Llewellyn: '*Its purpose, like that of any civil obligations, is at once to police, to prevent and to remedy.*'[6] Warranty, as it is understood in English means "*almost the whole range and scope of the seller's duty with regard to the quality of the goods.*"[7] Under civil and common law, the sellers' responsibility for quality is similar. Both systems provide protection against fraudulent concealment and allow the buyer to bind the seller with familiar commercial promises and warranty. In both the systems, expansion of responsibility is a welcome feature. The common law by contrast, experienced a relapse to the principle of *caveat emptor*, so that the break had to begin anew in the last century. Common law was supporting the principle of *caveat emptor* which had shown to be inefficient. Before 1893, English Law on implied warranty was in an unsettled stage. There was considerable confusion and uncertainty with regard to the nature of sellers' liability for defective goods and title.[8] *Caveat emptor* was often applied in cases of defective goods as well defective title. Even under the English Sale of Goods Act (SGA) 1893,[9] no attempt to define the concept of '*merchantable quality*' was made, and the matter was left entirely to case law. This made lawyers and judges to use their legal ingenuity in interpreting the contours of this concept. But despite this, the phrase did service for some eighty years without any statutory definition ever emerging. To many, it appeared to be less appropriate in modern times when applied to consumer sales and widely to a variety of transaction of goods between businessmen.[10]

Trade and commerce continued to play a central role in the development of the concept of implied warranty. The idea of quality has become more important in the present-day world where the consumer-buyer of goods is

---

6 Llewellyn, K. N., On Warranty of Quality, and Society, (1936) 34 (5) *Columbia Law Review*, pp. 689–744, pp. 689–744, p.712.

7 Samuel J. Stoljar, Conditions, Warranties and Descriptions of Quality in Sale of Goods, (1952) 15 *Modern Law Review*, pp. 425–445, p. 425.

8 Rajendra Kumar Nayak, *Consumer Protection Law in India—An Eco-Legal Treatise on Consumer Justice*, (Sweet & Maxwell Ltd., London 1991) p. 133.

9 This is an English Statute which has been replaced in the UK by the Sale of Goods Act 1979. This new Act which operates in England is inapplicable in Cameroon because of the cut-off date imposed by Section 11 of the Southern Cameroons High Court Law 1955, which forbids all post 1900 Statutes from application in that part of the territory. Much reference to this Statute will be referred to under this work.

10 P. S. Atiyah et al., *The Sale of Goods*, (11th edition Pitman, London 2005) p. 164.

guided by the fact that the development of a modern nation is based on increase in products of reputable sellers to expect responsibility for defective goods sold to the commercial buyers. This notion of the consumer accompanied with responsibility has best influenced upon sellers in running their business in order to ensure conformity of the goods they sell to commercial buyers. An enduring legacy of globalisation is the widespread of sophisticated goods which through the medium of cross-border trade, involves the flow of those goods across national frontiers. The saleability of those goods for the commercial buyer rests on laws in place in ascertaining the conformity of the goods as to the stipulations in the contract of sale of goods.

The importance of '*conformity*' today as a result of the ineffectiveness of the *caveat emptor* rule occupies a considerable place in modern sales law. The contract of sale of goods covers such an extraordinary wide range of transactions that it seems necessary to set out a single standard of quality appropriate to guarantee the conformity of goods for commercial concerns. As a result it could be said that the seller's duty of conformity today also to a greater extent comes into operation by operation of the law rather than independent of any intention to agree upon the seller's terms.

Today, sales law is proceeding in the direction to protect the buyer and its expectation with regard to the quality of the commodity and also that the seller is responsible for the qualities relating to the goods which the buyer is entitled to expect in the light of all surrounding circumstances including the purchase price. In fact, this view is being strengthened with the function of warranty law which is to establish a balance between price and quality.

Accordingly, the warranty protection has been made available to the commercial buyer under the OHADA Uniform Act on General Commercial Law on the basis of the conformity requirement unlike their common law counterparts who put at the disposal of the buyer implied and express warranties. The Uniform Act on General Commercial Law has worked out a unified treatment of the complete sales responsibility of the seller under the duty of conformity. The chief function today is to enable the parties to tailor the sales contract to their individual needs. This is particularly to expand the sales obligation in order to include aspects not covered by the express warranty of a buyer from a fraudulent seller.

It must be noted therefore that the harmonisation of business law in Africa is situated in this same line of reasoning. This is the case of the Organization for the Harmonisation of Business Laws in Africa (better known by its French acronym OHADA).[11] To this effect, pursuant to Decree No. 96/177 of 5th September 1996, the President of the Republic of Cameroon ratified the Treaty, thus incorporating it into Cameroonian law. By virtue of Article 10 of the OHADA Treaty, its Uniform Acts are of direct applicationand take precedence over national laws of the Member States[12] in the same way as European Union Regulations are directly applicable in EU Member States. Also, Article 45 of the Cameroon Constitution as revised by Law No. 96–06 of 18th January 1996, gives precedence to international laws or conventions over national laws.

The primary objective of this treaty was to provide a secure legal and judicial environment for business to operate in.[13] This was to be done through the elaboration and adoption of simple modern and common rules adapted to their economies, by setting up appropriate judicial procedures and by encouraging arbitration for the settlement of contractual disputes.[14] To effectively carry out the piece-meal harmonisation of the business laws of member states, the Organisation operates through a number of institutions.[15] In furtherance of this objective, nine Uniform Acts have been adopted till date.[16]

---

11 This French appellation refers to Organisation pour L'Harmonisation en Afrique du Droit des Affaires.The Treaty setting-up OHADA was signed at Port-Louis, Mauritius Island on 17th October 1993, as revised at Quebec, Canada, on 17th October 2008. The revisions became effective on 21 March 2010. As of July 7, 2010, the West African members of OHADA are Benin, Burkina Faso, Cote d'Ivoire, Guinea, Guinea-Bissau, Mali, Niger, Senegal, and Togo, and the Central African members of OAHDA are Central African Republic, Chad, Cameroon, Comoros, Congo, Equatorial Guinea, and Gabon. See http://www.ohada.org and http://www.ohada.com. On February 22, 2010, the Democratic Republic of Congo's president ratified the country's adoption of the OHADA treaty. By the treaty's terms, a country becomes a member sixty days after the note has been deposited in Senegal. OHADA Treaty, art.52, para. 3.

12 Martha Simo Tumnde, Cameroon offers a Contextual Approach to Understanding the OHADA Treaty and Uniform Acts, in *Unified Business Laws for Africa, Common Law Perspectives on OHADA* (ed. Claire Moore Dickerson), (2nd edition , IEDP, London 2012) pp. 64–65; Paul-Gérard Pougoué & Yvette Rachel Kalieu Elongo, *Introduction Critique a l'OHADA*, (P.U.A., Yaoundé 2010) p. 62.

13 Nanette Pilkington, The Secuity of Transactions and Investment in Africa, pp. 28–41, p. 28–30, culled from the Proceedings of the OHADA Seminar held at the University of Buea, Buea, Cameroon, 18–19 September 2003 on the theme: The Applicability of the OHADA Treaty in Cameroon.

14 The rules adopted are known as Uniform Acts.

15 The Conference of Head of States and of Government, Council of Ministers, Permanent Secretariat, Regional Training Centre for Legal Officers (ERSUMA), The Common Court of Justice and Arbitration (CCJA).

16 The following Uniform Acts are already applicable in Member States: Commercial Companies and Economic Interest Groupings, Law of Securities, Simplified Recovery Proocedures and Measures of Execution, Collective Proceedings for Wiping-off Debts, Arbitration Law, Accounting Law, Law of Co-operatives. Carriage of Goods by Road. Two other Uniform Acts have been enacted and adopted by the Council of Ministers but are still inapplicable, to wit; Consumer Law and Contract Law.

Our interest being sale of goods contract, we shall examine the Uniform Act on General Commercial Law,[17] with respect to the provisions governing the relationship between the seller and the commercial buyer of goods under a contract of sale. This new Uniform Act was adopted in Lome, Togo in December 2005, which replaces the former one of 1997. So far, nine Uniform Acts, including the Uniform Act on General Commercial Law have been enacted. In fact, in this area of the law, that is, sale of goods, the OHADA law has superseded certain previous national legislation of contracting States.[18] This is the case, for example, in Cameroon where certain portions affecting sales agreement of Law No. 90–031 of 10th August 1990, regulating economic activities in Cameroon have been replaced by the current provisions of the OHADA Uniform Act on General Commercial Law.

The focus on the OHADA business law is to test its functionality in achieving the predictability of business transactions within the contracting states.[19] The approach should be two-pronged. The OHADA law can constrain formal-sector actors, principally the seller transacting with commercial buyers in a sale agreement, and constrain that formal-sector actor (seller) an absolute liability in ensuring goods of conformity in accordance with the terms of the contract of sale, including the interests of local consumers, who are the end-users of those goods.

Statement of the Problem

The effectiveness of sellers' responsibility in ensuring the conformity of the goods to the terms of their contract of sale under the Uniform Act on General Commercial Law is hardly satisfactory in affording protection to commercial buyers of goods within the context of a sale of goods contract. There is usually at some point a considerable confusion and uncertainty as to who to blame for the non-conformity of the goods to the terms of the contract of sale. Business malpractices by sellers today include deception, false

[17] Hereinafter referred variously as 'UAGCL' or 'Uniform Act'. This is known in French as OHADA, Acte Uniform portant sur le Droit Commercial Général, found in the Official Gazette of OHADA, No. 23, of 15th February 2011. It is also available at http://www.ohada.com/textes.

[18] Paul-Gérard Pougoué, Jean Claude James, Yvette Rachel Kalieu, et al., in *Ecyclopedie du Droit OHADA*, (Lamy, Paris 2011) pp. 36–37.

[19] Nzalie Joseph Ebi, Reflecting on OHADA Law Reform Mission: Its Impact on certain aspects of Company Law in Anglophone Cameroon, (2002) (6) *Annales de la Faculté des Sciences Juridiques et Politiques*, Université de Dschang, pp. 97–119, p. 102.

pretense, false promise, misrepresentation, concealment of facts which pose a great challenge to the law. Commercial buyers are increasingly the victim of a diverse and bewildering array of unscrupulous selling and deceptive business practices in a market overt[20] which this thesis sets out to explore. By extension, this causes hardships to commercial buyers in their business relationship with consumers. In fact, these frauds undermine the consumer's confidence in the entire business community, thus injuring the goodwill of honest commercial buyers. As a result of this, this thesis will examine the seller's liability for the non-conforming of the goods as to the contract of sale of goods that may give a preliminary indication of whether the seller in practice ensures conformity of goods to the terms of the contract of sale.

Contracts are ubiquitous in modern business, often governing almost every aspect of a commercial transaction. This is particularly true of transactions involving the sale of goods between professional business parties: seller and commercial buyer as governed by the Uniform Act on General Commercial Law. As a standard part of this contract, quality plays a critical role in allocating risk and determining the final sale price. Warranties are a standard part of most commercial transactional contracts, with both buyers and sellers choosing to make and demand quality goods.[21] Basically, they are often in the interests of both the buyer and the seller. The seller's obligation to supply goods of good quality can serve many functions but its purpose is usually to ease the mind of a contracting party-(buyer) and assure the purpose of the sales contract.

For buyers, a seller warranty lends credibility to a product and reduces risks related to a possible product defect. On the other side of the transaction, the seller will typically give assurances to the buyer about the quality of the goods, which usually appear in the form of warranties. These warranties assure commercial buyers that they are not exposing themselves to false or misleading representations of goods. All of this is expected commercial behaviour, and makes a good deal of sense. Unexpectedly, however, these legal measures set out in the OHADA Uniform Act on General Commercial Law are not usually applied incongruently by sellers in many local markets. There is usually an adverse selection problem commonly referred to as by one

20 The market system in major cities in Cameroon which are publicly patronised at regular hours and acknowledged as markets qualify to be described as a market overt. However, it is generally admitted at common law that "market overt" is a legally constituted market, open on hours of sunrise and sunset and where goods for sale are openly displayed to any stand-by or passerby.

21 Kabir Masson, Paradox of Presumptions: Seller Warranties and Reliance Waivers in Commercial Contracts, (2009) 109 *Columbia Law Review*, pp. 1–32, p. 1.

author as the "*lemons problem*".[22] In order to complete their deal that might be difficult to close otherwise sellers often signal to the buyer that their product is good, but rather is not of good quality (so called "*lemons*").

Applicability of these measures set out in the Uniform Act has changed dramatically, resulting in an asymmetry in the law: sellers' implied conditions of conformity of goods are presumptively enforceable, but the buyer's protection from this duty is presumptively swindled. As a result of this, this thesis will examine the seller's liability for the non-conformity of the goods as to the terms in the contract of sale of goods.

Misrepresentation over the quality of goods in the current market is a serious problem in a developing country like Cameroon. This is usually characterised by dishonesty of facts over the quality of the goods being sold. The commercial buyer's problem, of course, is to identify quality. The presence of sellers in the local markets who are willing to offer inferior goods tends to drive the market of some specific brand of goods out of existence—as is the case of bad automobiles or building construction materials. It is this possibility that represents the major costs of dishonesty- for dishonest dealings tend to drive honest business dealings in some goods out of the market. There may be potential buyers of good quality products and there may be potential sellers of such products in the appropriate price range; however, the presence of dishonest sellers who wish to pawn bad wares as good wares tends to drive out the legitimate business, causing scarcity. The cost of dishonesty, therefore, lies not only in the amount by which the buyer is cheated; the cost also must include the loss incurred from reducing the size of the legitimate business of certain goods out of the market thereby affecting the country's economy.

A further exploration of the problem centres on the considerable evidence that quality variation is greater in underdeveloped than developed countries. Standardisation and quality control are still underdeveloped in most countries signatories to the OHADA treaty, such as Cameroon.[23] For instance, the need for quality control of export-import goods can be taken as one indicator for the influx of bad quality goods in the Cameroonian markets as an example.

---

22 See for example, George A. Akerlof, The Market for 'Lemons': Quality Uncertainty and the Market Machanism; (1970) 84 (3) *The Quaterly Journal of Economics*, pp. 488–500, p. 489. (using automobiles to demonstrate how warranties in private market places exist to combat 'lemons problems'. By way of explanation, this has been used to illustrate how most cars traded will be the 'lemons', and good cars may not be traded at all. The 'bad' cars tend to drive out the good because they sell at the same price as good cars since it is impossible for a buyer to tell the difference between a good and a bad car; only the seller knows).

23 Growth and Employment Strategy Paper; Refernce Framework for Government Action over the period 2010–2020 for Cameroon.

The importation rules in Cameroon like in other member States are not as efficient in ensuring the certification of goods into the country. There is still some laxity on the part of government institutions to strongly supervise the quality of goods in the markets. The magnitude of the problem of defective products may be better appreciated by bearing in mind the potential problem of product dumping from jurisdictions with stricter safety laws.[24] It is not inconceivable for unscrupulous foreign manufacturers to target the markets of developing countries with products that fail to meet the safety requirements of their home countries by charging low prices for those products in the developing countries. Products which have been banned or which had failed to get government approval in the developed countries are often dumped in developing countries.[25] Consequently, the local markets have been flooded with new products from different origins. This state of affairs is clearly evident with the proliferation of Chinese goods in the local markets.[26] This situation has some significant consequences on the purchasing public because these imported goods fail to meet the expected standards of buyers due to the laxity of the government in ensuring the quality control of those products.

Another problem which corroborates the effects of lack of conformity of goods as to the terms of the contract of sale is uncertainty in our markets. One obvious institution is guarantees in market overt settings. Most consumer durables have guarantees to assure the buyer of some expected standard quality. Often too, new products are associated with old brand names. This is to deceptively assure the prospective buyer of the quality of the products.

---

24 Samgena D. Galega, Strict Liability for Defective Products in Cameroon? Some Illuminating Lessons from Abroad, (2004) 48 (2) *Journal of African Law*, pp. 239–270, p. 253–254.

25 This is common with vendors in an open market in most Cameroonian cities, who are by the side of the roads, peddling medicines, pharmaceutical products, and many other kinds of produce, including telephone sets and household utensils. Almost certainly in the informal sector of the Cameroonian economy are the shopkeepers who, from the stalls that line the streets, sell second-used clothes, hand-made furnitures, small electronic equipments from abroad. Also included is the caterer or tailor whose business is in the formal sector but who, who from the back room hidden from tax collector and government agents from the Ministry of Trade and Commerce, run a dress shop or sell electronic items already used from abroad to sell to trusted customers. All these nano-entrepreneurs deliberately run away from formal government authority because as one principal reason, due to the defective state of the goods they sell and the absence of business license. See Claire Moore Dickerson, 'Informal-Sector Entrepreneurs, Development and Formal Law: A Functional Understanding of Business Law', (2011) 59 *American Journal of Comparative Law*, pp. 159–226, p. 180.

26 It is commonplace to find a high incidence of Chinese goods in shops and streets of most towns. Preference of these goods by commercial buyers is because of their cheap prices and easy affordability. However, the local consumers continue to complain about the poor quality of these goods in terms of durability. Suchgoods include from clothings, shoes electronics and electrical equipments.

As a consequence, false brand-name goods do not only indicate the quality of the goods but by extension is detrimental to the business of commercial buyers. In many cases the commercial buyer and consequently the ultimate consumer are defrauded and mislead by the contractual guarantees made by sellers. Generally, sellers' fraud is related to products and services bought by the commercial buyer which are simply not supplied, or products and services supplied but found for one reason or another to be unsatisfactory. It gives the local commercial buyers and also the consumers a means of retaliation if the quality does not meet expectations. For the commercial buyers and of course the consumers will then curtail future purchases. One observation consistent with our approach is the cosmetic sector of the economy.

It is alarming that in most markets today there is rampant fraud in the selling business of some commodities. The feature of the tort of passing-off[27] is commonplace in some markets of some Cameroonian big cities. There has been a rampant illegal activity that consists of filling up empty containers of products (perfumes and other cosmetics and liquor bottles) with deficiencies in quantity supplied to reselling buyers. Government has attempted isolated measures to contain these unfair practices but the degree of the practices largely outweighs the efforts.

Research Questions

Flowing from the problem are the main and specific questions:

Main Research Question:

To what extent does the OHADA Law constrain sellers to provide goods to commercial buyers that are in conformity with the specifications of the contract of sale?

Specific Questions:

The following specific questions were formulated to guide the conduct of this research:

[27] This is an economic tort, which relates to the selling of goods under such a name, mark, description or otherwise in such a manner as to mislead the public into believing that the goods or merchandise belongs to another person.

- Do the provisions of the current Uniform Act on General Commercial Law adequately guarantee the quality of goods sold by the seller?
- What is the meaning of conformity?
- What is the buyer's perception and response to unsatisfactory sales?
- Do remedies exist to avail the commercial buyer of the seller's non-conformity of goods?
- Is the seller always to be blamed for lack of conformity?

Hypothesis

This thesis has main and sub- hypotheses:

Main Hypothesis:

This work is based on the assumption that although some legal measures or requirements have been put in place by the OHADA Uniform Act to afford protection to commercial buyers of goods, those safeguards seem to be inadequate in assuring the quality of goods supplied to the commercial buyers in their business with the seller.

Sub-Hypotheses

HO 1: The provisions of the OHADA Law do not adequately guarantee the quality of the goods by the seller.

HO 2: The notion of conformity is not adequately articulated upon by the OHADA law.

HO 3: Buyers perceive and respond negatively to unsatisfactory sales.

HO 4: Formal law provides remedies which can avail a commercial buyer in the event of the seller's non-conformity.

Research Objective

This work has general and specific objectives:

General Objective

The general objective of this work is to investigate the extent to which the OHADA Law can constrain sellers in ensuring conformity of the goods they sell to commercial buyers to the terms of their contract of sale.

Specific Objectives

To achieve this broad objective set out above, the work will look at the following specific objectives:

- To clearly examine the provisions of the law governing the expansive seller's duty of conformity.
- To clearly articulate the meaning of conformity.
- To assess buyer's perception and responses to unsatisfactory purchase.
- To examine remedies available to commercial buyers.
- To propose recommendations.

Research Methodology

This research invariably adopts the legal empirical research method, which is better adapted to address the salient legal issues raised. This research essentially used a content analysis of both primary and secondary materials in the relevant domain. The research adopts a critical and analytical approach in interpreting the provisions of the OHADA Uniform Act on General Commercial Law, and of national and international instruments regulating the sale of goods contracts.

This work embarked on the collection and analysis of primary data in the form of statutes, decided cases from the local courts, decisions of the Common Court of Justice and Arbitration in Abidjan and the Supreme Court in England, as well as foreign cases touching on issues of sale of goods.

In addition, extensive use has been made of secondary sources of literature on the subject. The researcher used content analysis of journals, periodicals, textbooks, conference proceedings and policy documents relevant to this work, which were found in the libraries of the Universities of Buea, Dschang, Douala and Yaoundé II–Soa in Cameroon.

Visits were also made to libraries abroad, such as the libraries of the International Institute for the Unification of Private Laws (UNIDROIT) in Italy, the Common Court of Justice and Arbitration in Abidjan, Cote d'Ivoire, the Tulane Law School and The John Marshall Law School in U.S.A. Extensive use was equally made of electronic libraries and internet sources such as Westlaw, heinonline and JSTOR.

The researcher conducted systematic interviews with businessmen in the market cities of Douala and Yaoundé, and consumer associations, legal practitioners, and government officials engaged with the regulation of commercial activities within the country. This gives first hand impression about their perception of problems inherent in the business relationship with sellers and buyers. The responses from the unstructured interviews constitute one of the primary sources of materials for the work. The interviews were effected in English or French depending on the interviewee's preferences.

Conceptual and Theoretical Framework

This section shall in the main dwell on the core concepts and theories which underpin this research.

Freedom of Contract Theory

The classical theory of contract is based on the idea of freedom of contract which was an offspring of the *laissez-faire* economic theory championed by Adam Smith. Hence, the will of the contracting parties become the source of their mutual rights and duties which the contracting parties hold with respect to one another. The essential teaching in this respect and in connection to this research study is the principle of economic freedom under a contract of sale of goods. According to Adam Smith[28], everyone has the economic freedom to act on his or her self-interest in order to achieve his economic desires. Consequently, in their relentless effort to achieve this economic desire, they are guided by an invisible hand, which ensures that while seeking to promote their self-interest, they incidentally promote the public interest as well although they did not set out to do so.[29]

[28] Wealth of Nations, (Vol.1, Dent 1910) p. 421

[29] S. Todd Lowry, Bargain and Contract Theory in Law and Economics, (1976) 10 (1) *Journal of Economic Issues*, pp. 1–22, p. 13.

Certainly, there is a paternalistic ground for legal rules to regulate and protect the very interest of the contracting parties as well as the consuming public at large.[30] This concept of legal paternalism is instrumental to this thesis in that under a contract of sale, the seller's duty of conformity is embodied in a magnitude of implied rules contained in articles 255 et seq. of the Uniform Act on General Commercial Law to ascertain the quality of goods to the commercial buyer.

This study seeks to argue that the freedom of traders of goods to enter into a contract of sale for the supply of quality goods in conformity with the contract terms in the market is much dictated too by the demands of consumers in insisting for quality goods. Hence, in spite of the freedom of the parties in their contract of sale, such measures under the OHADA Uniform Act by extension, tend to be protective to consumers, (who are the end-users of those goods), and the economy of the state. Arguably, this research is working on the premise that the idea of freedom of contract is today a pretty sick horse, because of socio-legal and economic considerations among the economic actors. This relates to the fact that the expansive duties imposed on the seller in satisfying the preferences of the commercial buyer under their business contract, are also by analogy serve as measures to protect the development of a country by requiring sellers to do legitimate business with commercial buyers.

Interest Theory

Exponents of the interest theory, such as Ihering and Bentham[31] argued in favour of the idea that individuals have interests which frequently conflict. This theory demonstrates that a claim-right is an interest protected by a duty. To identify the person to whom I owe my duty (the holder of the correlative claim-right), we need to work out whose interest is protected by my duty. The interest theorists happily concede that when duties do not protect individual interest, they are regarded as protecting collective interests. Hence, interest theorists regard the correlativity of claim-rights and duties as strict and universal: for them, all claim-rights entail duties, and all duties entail claim-rights.

---

30 Michael J. Trebilock, *The Limits of Freedom of Contract* (Havard University Press, 1993) pp. 149–151.

31 N.E. Simmonds, *Central Issues in Jurispudence, Justice, Law and Rights* (2nd edition, Sweet & Maxwell, London) 2002, pp. 304–307.

This theory is central to this study in that the expansive seller's duties to supply goods in conformity with the terms of the contract of sale as contained in article 255 of the Uniform Act on General Commercial Law stand as a fact to protect the interest of commercial buyers of goods. The breach of these duties by the seller to provide conforming goods is an injury to the interests of commercial buyers and entitles the latter to claim remedies. Hence, the seller's duty is correlative to the commercial buyer's claim-right to damages in so far there is evidence that the seller has failed in its contractual duty of conformance.

Economic Theoretical Perspective

Two kinds of theories are going to be examined here: the theory of price and marginal utility and the information theory and welfare perspectives.

The Theory of Price and Marginal Utility

The needs and wants of buyers remain at the centre of our economic system. An individual decides freely on how to spend his or her income. The concept of money naturally proceeds from the idea that the recipient has the right to choose what he or she will buy with it from the range of goods and services which are available to the buyer and the restrictions on the individual's freedom of choice are less obvious than they may be in other respects.[32]

In a contract of sale of goods, the issue of price largely determines the quality of goods in the market. Similarly, the commercial buyer would achieve that objective by adjusting his income for each goods or service in accordance with the price of the goods offered by the seller. The utility of the goods to the commercial buyer is for resale and thus, the price is of consequence to his business and customers. Inevitably, if local consumers are unable to freely bargain because of high prices of goods in the marketplace, the demand is likely to be virtually insatiable for the commercial buyer and other non-market methods must therefore be used in deciding who is to buy them. The philosophy behind this action is based on Jeremy Bentham's jurisprudence on utilitarianism, which advocates for the "*welfare*" of individuals.[33] His argument is constructed from the viewpoint of rational interest which explains that

---

[32] Ibid., p. 324.

[33] N.E. Simmonds, *Central Issues in Jurispudence, Justice, Law and Rights*, Op. cit., p. 19.

every person would prefer a set of rules that advances its preferences at the expense of everyone; but the best it can hope for is a set of rules that serves the aggregate welfare.

There is an economic view that just as producers want to earn maximum profit in the same way the seller or buyer equally wants to gain maximum from the goods which he buys as per the price in order to derive maximum satisfaction from the money he spends.[34] Therefore, the pattern of money expenditure varies with the range of goods and their prices in the market. The individual buying these goods expect them to be of satisfactory quality and be useful to him. In effect, price control of certain goods must be checked, should be the concern of the government in curtailing the excessive freedom of businessmen in the augmentation of prices of goods.

Information Theory and Welfare Perspective

This research deals with the issues addressed both from the information asymmetries and the welfare perspective. The information theory or signal theory relates to product warranty policy. It emphasises warranty terms which provide information to users of goods about the merchantability of the commodity in the market. This theory regards the '*market*' for information about products.[35]Manufacturers or producers are required under this theory to draft warranties in simple and readily understood language in order to reduce the difficulty of comprehending warranty content. It also requires the disclosure of all important provisions conspicuously and to display warranties prominently so that they are available for buyer inspection prior to purchase of the product. Under this theory it is rather costly for the buyer to determine precisely product reliability at the time of purchasing through direct inspection. A buyer may view warranty as a '*signal*' of product reliability which to some extent is related negatively with the cost of warranty coverage.

Though this theory is advanced to deal specifically with consumer product warranty, it is also of interest to professional traders under a contract of sale in the light of the principle of policy and the law. This is because the responsibility for defective goods rests upon the seller who is the person who distributed the goods to the public. The commercial buyer cares because he will be

---

34 In conventional supply and demand analysis, it is assumed that in most contexts more goods or services will be supplied at higher than lower prices and that fewer goods or services will demand at higher prices than lower prices.

35 G. J. Stigler, The Economics of Information, (1961) 69 *Journal of Political Economy*, p.213.

selling those products to the retail buyer. Circumstances may arise where the seller or commercial buyer buys with an intention of further processing or fabricating the goods or seller may also be a producer or manufacturer of a good sold to the retail buyer. In this situation, the latter needs to be informed on the warranty content of the goods available to him for inspection prior to delivery for the interest of his business. Therefore, on the basis of this, the commercial buyer is entitled to protection of his interest within the scope of seller's responsibilities.[36]

In the welfare perspective model, it is supported by Paretian welfare justifications for private exchanges.[37] The organising assumption of this model is that one party to a contract is substantially less well informed about some aspect of the contract subject-matter than the other party. The Paretian justification further argues that both parties to an exchange are rendered better off by it—in terms of the subjectively perceived impact of the exchange on their respective utility functions—or they would not have entered into it. But if at least one party inaccurately perceives or evaluates the impact of the exchange on her utility, we can no longer be confident that the exchange will in fact render both parties better off. Proceeding from this argument, the author contends that to encourage appropriate circumspection on the part of sellers in claims they make about goods they are selling whose histories they are not fully informed of, the law would be justified in providing the buyer with relief. Such a conduct on the part of the sellers in their transaction induced by fraudulent representation of the goods they sell is unlikely discourage buyers generally in the long–run to buy goods.

Human Rights and Ethical Theories

Legal and Rights Perspective

Commercial buyers as well as consumers have the right to make an informed choice over the kind of goods they buy or consume. This issue raises legal and ethical questions. The legal basis for this relates to the fact that it is an inalienable human right for any ordinary commercial buyer or consumer to make an informed judgment of what he chooses to buy. To a commercial buyer, this right is important to the resaleability of the goods as

---

[36] Robert C. Brown, The Liability of Retail Policies for Defective Food Products", (1939) 23 *Minnesota Law Review*, pp. 585–611, p. 585.

[37] Michael J. Trebilock, *The Limits of Freedom of Contract*, Op. cit., pp. 103–110.

this is what he expects under his contract of sale with the seller with a view to satisfying the demands or needs of his customers. The commercial buyer cares because he does not want to be saddled with a product which may injure the health, religion and life of his customers. Article 25 (1) of the 1948 Universal Declaration of Human Rights[38] provides inter alia that:

> *everyone has the right to a standard of living adequate for the health and well-being of himself and of his family including food... Arguably, inherent in the right to food is the right to choose which food to eat.*

As a matter of fact, individuals might wish to know whether the food they buy has been genetically modified (GM) with animal contents either because they are vegetarians or for religious reasons. They could justify their demands to know and make appropriate choice by virtue of the provisions of Articles 1(1) and 18 (1), (2) and (3) of the United Nations International Covenant on Civil and Political Rights.[39] While examining the role of the consumer in GM food regulation, it is argued that no GM regulation is complete if visibility is not given to the consumer's right to know the GM components of their food, even if such food had passed public health or environmental safety muster.[40] This argument is premised on the proposition that consumer empowerment in this respect is as much a human right as an ethical or moral imperative. The central argument is that the consumer should be empowered through the labelling of products. From this standpoint, commercial buyers of goods are under the duty to have knowledge of the type of products that is free from any defect in its packaging and labelling in order to satisfy their customer's demands.

Additionally, most countries have constitutional and legal provisions guaranteeing the consuming public's right of choice directly or indirectly. For instance, the Cameroon Constitution[41] in its preamble adheres to the development, use, enjoyment and disposal of goods by every individual. It

---

38 The United Nations 1948 Universal Declaration of Human Rights, available at <http:#www.hrweb.org/legal/udhr.html>(last accessed on 27th April 2010).

39 Article 1(1) of this Covenant provides that 'all people have the right of self-determination'. By virtue of that right they freely determine their political status and freely pursue their economic, social and cultural development. This is available at < http:#www.hrweb.org/legal/cpr.html> Article % 2017.2 (last accessed on April 2010)

40 Taiwo A. Oriola, Consumer Dilemmas: The Right to Know, Safety, Ethics and Policy of Genetically Modified Food, (2002) *Singapore Journal of Legal Studies*, pp. 514–573, p. 522.

41 Law No. 96–06 of 18th January 1996 to amend the Constitution of 2nd June 1972, available at <http://confinder.richmond.edu:admin:docs:cameroon.pdf> (downloaded on October 19, 2010).

could be agreed that it is on the basis of this that the consumers in Cameroon keep on pressing the commercial buyers to provide them with quality goods in order to make informed choices in the markets.

Ethical Perspectives

The right to know and make informed purchase decisions also has ethical implications. One of the ethical theories used to assess quality of goods is the ethical theory of "*consequentialism*", which is also founded on moral theory. An individual is morally required to perform a particular action or do a certain specific thing only if it would result in a greater good and benefit to the world than if he had chosen to perform one of the alternative actions.[42] How do we assess if genetically modified food labelling policy, for example, would be more beneficial or lead to the greater good of the society than non-genetically modified food labelling policy and vice versa? The easiest way to do this would be through a consensus, and let the people decide which would be more beneficial: a labelling or non-labelling policy?

Viewed from the foregoing perspective, it would be morally wrong and unethical to make definitive business rule regarding price or labelling or packaging without consulting the stakeholders whom the decision was supposed to benefit.

Significance of the Study

The importance of this study cannot be over emphasised. It touches on a socio-legal and economic issues which are very topical in the business world. Sellers and commercial buyers are at daggers-drawn over the raison d'être of enhancing ethical behaviour in business transactions. The business world is moving now from *caveat emptor* to caveat venditor.

This research will be quite edifying to law students with interests in the OHADA Sales Law, merchants, legal practitioners, sociologists, as it will contribute to the existing legal literature in this area of the law, thus stimulating thoughts for a way forward in the quest to bring more clarifications for law reform. The research will establish equality and certainty in the business of sale of goods.

---

42 see Robert Streiffer, *Ethical Behaviour in Modern Biology*, Course Overview for 2001 at the Department of Philosophy, University of Wisconsin-Madison, available at <http:#www.bitech-info.net/biothics_corse.html> (last accessed in June 2009).

This research suggests and develops new approaches to the provisions of the OHADA Uniform Act on General Commercial Law as it focuses on the relationship between the seller and the commercial buyer in an effort to appreciate the impact that the OHADA Uniform Act on General Commercial Law may have on the protection of consumers. The work will go a long way to raise the awareness of consumers and will obviously advocate for the application of the draft Uniform Act on Consumer Law. This work will definitely contributes to the understanding of the provisions of the OHADA Uniform Act on General Commercial Law.

Justification of the Research

Research on the seller's liability for the non-conformity of goods as to the terms of the contract of sale is timely. It is justified for addressing the pertinent issues of buyers' dissatisfaction over the poor quality of goods in the market. It comes at a time when consumers are exposed to poor quality of goods in the local markets.

Furthermore, this research will go a long way in raising the awareness of sellers and producers of goods within the OHADA territories. In fact, it reiterates the principle of '*caveat venditor*' (let the seller beware) because it argues that the seller can also be deceived in a market transaction with producers. Eventually, the seller is bound to take responsibility for the products he sells that are not in conformity with the specifications of the contract of sale as required by the commercial buyer.

Literature Review

There is abundant literature on the OHADA law. In this light, Charles Mba-Owono,[43] clearly articulates the distinction between the non-conformity of the goods and hidden defects of the goods. He asserts that hidden defects in goods do not provide satisfaction to the commercial buyer. He opines that the seller has the duty under the Uniform Act on General Commercial Law not to offer goods with hidden defects which render the goods useless to the commercial buyer. According to him, notwithstanding the seller's duty to deliver goods of good quality, it is a contractual duty for the seller

[43] Non-Conformite et Vice Cachés dans la Vente Commerciale en Droit Uniforme Africain, (2002) 41 *Juridis Périodique*, pp. 107–127.

to also guarantee that the goods the goods in the contract are free from any hidden defects which may then improper for use by the commercial buyer.[44] In fact, the seller's duty to guarantee should be an extension of his duty of conformity. By observation, the Uniform Act does clearly demarcate between hidden and latent defects of goods which makes it difficult at times to attribute liability to the seller for the non-conformity of the goods as a result of a hidden defect.[45] The proof of hidden defects by the commercial buyer is difficult to establish. However, this researcher is of the opinion that the proof should be based on the functionality of the goods due to the defect(s) which is an important aspect to the commercial buyer.[46] Regrettably, the position of the law has changed on this subject with the new Uniform Act in place, for the author's analyses were from the old provisions of the Uniform Act.The issue of non-conformity and hidden defects of goods is no longer a separate duty of the seller but rather it has been made an integral part of the seller's duty of conformity under the amended OHADA Uniform Act on General Commercial Law. The author's work has not been so extensive in ascertaining the seller's liability for the non-conformity of goods in relation to other legal aspects, such as the transfer of title, passing of risk and the remedies offered by the Uniform Act to the buyer for the seller's breach of conformity. Consequently, these are also important issues which this thesis intends to explore in identifying the seller's liability under a contract of sale.

Furthermore, the author did not examine the expansive duty of the seller and what facts in a case are considered part of the '*goods*' for the purposes of the seller's duty of conformity under the Uniform Act.He rather focuses only on the seller's duty to deliver goods free from any hidden defect(s).

Josette Nguebou[47], presents a critical analysis of the general provisions of the old Uniform Act on General Commercial Law. On the aspect of sale of goods, she carefully points that it is of no essence to impose the seller diverse duties contained in separate legal rules. She underscores the fact that, the duties of the seller are protective of the interests of the commercial buyer and it is necessary to package the obligations of the seller in a unique approach: to deliver goods of conformity.[48] According to the author, the seller's liability of conformity of goods under the Uniform Act can be assessed by measuring

[44] Ibid., p. 114.

[45] Ibid., p. 113.

[46] Ibid., p. 115.

[47] *Le Droit Commercial Général dans l'Acte Uniforme OHADA*, (P.U.A., Collection Droit Uniforme, Yaoundé 1998).

[48] Ibid., p. 70.

from different aspects: the contract stipulation and the seller's warranty of the goods being sold to the commercial buyer. She acknowledges that apart from the contract stipulations, other measures could be used to ascertain the quality of the goods; national or international standard norms relating, for example, to the packaging of goods.[49] The author's analysis were purely general and did not reveal an in depth knowledge specifically on the seller's liability for the non-conformity of goods which this thesis sets out to explore from the current provisions of the amended Uniform Act. This thesis suggests that the seller's duty to deliver goods of conformity is fundamental in any sales agreement and must not only be appreciated from the contract of sale as agreed by the parties but other practical issues need to be revealed in order to test the applicability of the law.

Jean-René Gomez[50], while also contributing to the existing knowledge of the OHADA law, acknowledges the seller's obligations under the OHADA Uniform Act on General Commercial Law to be threefold: delivery obligation, duty of conformity and the duty to guarantee. The author makes an in depth interpretation of these three obligations by insisting that they are interwoven. He posits that the seller's duty of conformity can be measured from the material and functional elements of the duty.[51] The implication is that the author is of the view that the duty of conformity is appraised from the content of the contract between the parties and from the utility of the conforming goods to the commercial buyer. Though this is a thorough exposition of a litany of facts of the law as they are, the author has not been so much concerned in showing the limits of the seller's duty of conformity with respect to the goods under the contract of sale governed by the Uniform Act.

Kamwe Mouaffo M.C.[52] notes in the course of exploring the notion of conformity in a sales contract under the former Uniform Act on General Commercial Law, that the seller's duty of conformity has been given considerable attention. She appreciates the fact that the OHADA legislator has extended the seller's duty of conformity by essentially including the elements of labelling and packaging.[53] She further acknowledges the fact that even though the notion of conformity supports the general principle

---

49 Ibid. p. 71.

50 Un Nouveau Droit de la Vente Commerciale en Afrique, (1998) *Penan*, pp. 145–203; Also available on the OHADA website : www.ohada.com

51 Ibid., pp. 171–176.

52 *L'obligation de Conformité dans la Vente Commerciale en OHADA*, (D.E.A., Dissertation, Faculty of Law and Political Science,University of Dschang, 1999).

53 Ibid., p. 2.

of party autonomy expressed in the Uniform Act, regard should also be given to domestic and international standards of goods to be of acceptable conformity.[54] The author's work has not been so extensive in ascertaining the seller's liability for the non-conformity of goods in relation to other legal aspects, such as the transfer of title, passing of risk and the remedies offered by the Uniform Act to the commercial buyer in the event of the seller's liability of non-conformity of goods. These are also important issues which this thesis intends to explore in identifying the seller's liability under a contract of sale.

P. S. Atiyah, John Adams and Hector Macqueen[55] observe that the seller's duties under a contract of sale are embodied in implied terms geared to protect the buyer, that is, both commercial and consumer buyers of goods. They argue that those statutory implied terms as contained under the English Statute—Sale of Goods Act 1973—requiring goods to be of merchantable quality appear less appropriate in modern times when applied to consumer sales. They posit that the contract of sale of goods covers such an extraordinarily wide range of transactions that it seems impossible that a single standard of quality could be formulated which is appropriate to all kinds of goods, extending from consumer durables to agricultural produce, and to goods for resale.[56] The authors then advocated for an effective change of the nomenclature which was laid down by the Sale and Supply of Goods Act 1994 to now mean satisfactory quality[57] in order to give buyers a substantial degree of protection. Consequently, the seller's duties as regard quality under the concept of merchantability could not possibly cope with the wide variety of problems, giving way for the seller to escape liability.

This present research is in consonance with the views of these authors in that it gives guidelines as to what is expected of the seller in his duty of conformity under a contract of sale of goods under the OHADA Uniform Act on General Commercial.In fact, under this duty, the seller is expected to tender goods which are not only saleable but satisfactory as to the terms of the contract of sale. As a difference, this thesis situates its analysis specifically in the context of a contract of sale as governed by the OHADA Uniform Act on General Commercial Law. The focus is on the relationship between a seller and the commercial buyer and not generally on consumer sales as opposed to the work of the previous authors.

---

[54] Ibid., pp. 14–15.

[55] *The Sale of Goods*, Op. cit.

[56] Ibid., pp. 164–166.

[57] Section 14 (2) SGA 1994

Roy Goode[58] devotes much attention to the rules of law governing commercial and consumer buyers of goods under English law. He acknowledges the fact that the seller's duties in a contract of sale f goods have been imposed by law as statutory implied terms. His perception of the seller's duty under the concept of satisfactory quality is not fixed or immutable but changes with commercial and consumer attitudes.[59] According to him the standard in testing the seller's duty must be drawn from the description, price and other relevant circumstances under which the goods are sold.[60]

Samgena D. Galega[61] in his article x-rays the problem of defective products which beset the local markets in Cameroon. The author deplores the fact that the Cameroonian legislator has not introduced strict delictual liability for unsafe products as is the case in several countries in the world. Arguably, he supports the fact that Cameroonian consumers are thus vulnerable, when compared with their counterparts in strict liability jurisdictions and suggests the way forward for Cameroon.[62] The author argues vehemently that the liability for the quality of goods should lie on those in the best position to exercise prudent safety and quality decisions relating to products. This is to suggest that manufacturers should systematically manage risks within their enterprise. Moreover, it is arguable that the imposition of strict liability on manufacturers would merely extend to ultimate consumers' rights, which immediate purchasers already have against their retail buyers.[63]

The work of this author is central to the definitional problem which this thesis sets out to demonstrate. His work is a persistent cry for the improvement of the quality of goods which continuously flood the market. Though his argument is based on the introduction of a strict liability rule under Cameroonian law for the advancement of consumers' interests, the approach of this thesis is to examine the effectiveness of the measures developed by the OHADA Uniform Act on General Commercial Law in constraining sellers of goods to offer quality goods to commercial buyers. Arguably, the thesis supports the fact that the effectiveness of these rules, if proven, will advance commercial buyers' interests and by extension cater for the rights of consumers who are the end-users of the goods they receive from the commercial buyers.

58 *Commercial Law*, (3rd edition, Penguin Books, 2004).

59 Ibid., p. 134.

60 Ibid., pp. 304–305.

61 *Strict Liability for Defective Products in Cameroon? Some Illuminating Lessons from Abroad*, Op. cit.

62 Ibid. p. 239.

63 Ibid. p. 252.

Mevoungou Nsana Roger[64] shares the view that a seller in the first place is a producer of goods and the essence is not to produce but to sell. From this standpoint, he asserts the fact that the seller's duty must consist principally to fulfil his engagement under a contract of sale. He therefore attempts a thorough discussion of the different duties imposed by the Uniform Act on General Commercial Law. Consequently, he acknowledges the fact that the breach of the seller's duty of conformity is a fundamental breach which impinges on the interest of the buyer under the contract of sale.[65] In spite of the discussions on the various obligations of the seller as discussed in this article, the author has not made an attempt to spot out the liability of the seller of the non-conformity of the goods from different perspectives resulting from a contract of sale such as, during the passing of title and risk. His main focus has been on the duties of the seller as governed by the Uniform Act.

Akuété Pedro Santos and Jean Yado Toé,[66] present an in depth knowledge on the interpretation of the entire provisions of the former OHADA Uniform Act on General Commercial Law. In the course of their critical analysis, the authors are concerned by the quality of goods that the seller is under the duty to deliver to the commercial buyer. On their discussion on the seller's duty to guarantee against hidden defects,the scholars argue that such a duty further seeks to make sellers who stand behind the goods they sell to be further responsible not only to commercial buyersbut to qua-buyers as well. This justification arises from the seller's absolute duty to guarantee against hidden defects, which according to the authors can be described as an indirect extension of the seller's duty to consumers over the quality of goods.[67] This is a relevant observation to this thesis as it identifies one of the objectives of this thesis which is the empowerment of consumers through the regulation of the seller's duty to offer quality goods to the commercial buyer in their commercial dealings.

Delimitation of Study

This research deals purely with commercial sale of goods between professional traders, that is, seller and commercial buyer in consonance with

64 Les Obligations du Vendeur de Marchandises dans l'Acte Uniforme OHADA, (2000) 1 (2) *Revue Africaine des Sciences Juridiques, Faculte des Sciences Juridiques et Politiques,* Université de Yaoundé II, p. 6–19.

65 Ibid., p. 9.

66 *OHADA Droit Commercial Général,* (Bruylant, Collection Droit Uniforme Africain, Bruxelles 2002) .

67 Ibid., pp. 397–398.

the provisions of the OHADA Uniform Act on General Commercial Law.[68] It therefore does not to an extent deal with consumer sales but has as an objective to indirectly advocate for consumers' interests by principally dealing with the business relationship between the seller and the commercial buyers of goods.

The research identifies some specific problems affecting the quality of goods in the local marketplace which commercial buyers are exposed to. In order to do so, this research intends to limit its scope to two major towns of Cameroon, namely, Douala and Yaoundé, which play host to large form of businesses operating within the formal sector of the economy such as, commercial companies and professional traders.

Also, the researcher is conversant with the Cameroonian realities and the existing laws in place making it possible to identify easily the existing problems on the ground and to carry out some feasible studies. It is equally the more reason why the researcher made systematic interviews with businessmen in these towns because of their market strength and proximity. Practically, the research will chose a commercial buyer, and then its own supplier(s), to obtain first-hand information based on their business relationship.

In fact, the researcher will make references to certain international legal instruments, English Law and Civil Law on matters of sale of goods for purposes of comparison, clarification, or specifically to suggest some reforms.

Organisation of the Book

The study has nine chapters as follows:

- Chapter One opens up with a general introduction, which presents the research background as well as presenting the problem which the research seeks to address.
- Chapter Two focuses on the elements of a sale of goods contract under the UAGCL.
- Chapter Three discusses the seller's material duty of conformity.
- Chapter Four dwells on the seller's functional duty of conformity.
- Chapter Five examines the seller's duty of conformity in respect to third party rights over the goods supplied to the commercial buyer.
- Chapter Six discusses the seller's liability for the transfer of property and risk over the goods sold to the commercial buyer.

---

[68] Article 234 UAGCL.

- Chapter Seven explains the limits of a seller's liability, with focus on instances where the seller is exonerated from liability under the UAGCL.
- Chapter Eight examines the remedies available to a commercial buyer in breach of the seller's non-performance.
- Chapter Nine ends up with a general conclusion which makes some recommendations.

Definition of Keywords

Contract of Sale, Conformity, Commercial Buyer, Consumer, Goods, Liability, Seller.

Contract of Sale

This is a contract by which the seller transfers or agrees to transfer property in goods to the buyer for money consideration; called the price.[69] In the context of this thesis, this research is limiting its discussion to the commercial contract between a seller and a commercial buyer as governed under by UAGCL.

Conformity

From a legal standpoint, it could be understood to mean being in accordance with contractual obligations. The seller's duties under the OHADA Uniform Act are encapsulated under this concept obliging the seller to deliver goods to the commercial buyer in conformity with the agreed contract terms.

Commercial Buyer

This is a party under a contract of sale who is involved in the buying-and-reselling business. This concerns professional traders such as wholesalers. The Uniform Act on General Commercial Law identifies such persons as "*commerçant*" whose businesses are registered with the Commercial Registry[70] and have an accounting book.[71] A commercial buyer may be a physical person or a commercial company.

[69] P. S. Atiyah et al., *The Sale of Goods*, Op. cit., p.6.
[70] Book II of the UAGCL.
[71] Article 13 UAGCL.

Consumer

This is a person who purchases goods for his or her private use or consumption.

Goods

Goods may be basically moveable or tangible objects being acquired for business purposes. These are objects which form the subject-matter of contracts of sale. This research is concerned with tangible goods being purchased for resale, which does not necessarily mean for industrial use. It is the intended use and not the actual use which is decisive. This research is concerned with manufactured goods sold by a seller to a commercial buyer, for the purpose of having the commercial buyer resell to consumers. Thus, the "*intended use*" is resale. This is so even though the goods will ultimately end up being used by consumers. The premise of this definition stems from the spirit of the Uniform Act on General Commercial Law, which has as purpose to cover transactions of sale of tangible goods between traders.[72]

Liability

This denotes the legal responsibility which rests on a contracting party (seller) under a contract of sale to properly perform his duties towards a commercial buyer. Failure in doing so gives way to remedies.

Seller

A person who sells or contracts to sell goods. We are concerned here with a professional seller in the capacity of a trader involved in the regular selling of large scale commodities.

---

72 Article 235 & 236 UAGCL.

2

ELEMENTS OF A CONTRACT OF SALE OF GOODS

Introduction

In contracts of sale of goods governed by the Uniform Act on General Commercial Law, the duties of the seller are principally governed by the notion of '*conformity*'. This duty is expansive, imposing an absolute liability for defects that exist when risk passes to the buyer, regardless of the fault. But before that is imposed on the seller, there must be an agreement between the buyer and the seller in order to establish a contractual commercial relationship. Contract formation[73] is an important aspect as far as contract for a sale of goods is concerned. This is because it is at this level that parties freely express themselves on how their transaction should look like be it at the regional or global levels. Another pertinent issue is that there has to be a valid and legally enforceable agreement for a sale to be envisaged. What makes such enforceability in addition to the elements of a contract are mutual assent though the test usually to be applied is not what each party in fact had in mind but what each ought reasonably to have assumed from the language and conduct of the other,[74] the legal capacity[75] of the parties, intention to be

[73] Nsie E., La Formation de la Vente Commerciale en Afrique (1999) 829 *Penant*, p. 5.

[74] *Smith v. Hughes* (1871) LR 6 QB 597; *Reardon Smith Ltd v. Hansen-Tangen* [1976] 3 All ER 570; *The Hannah Blumenthal* [1983] 1 All ER 34; *The Leonidas D* [1983] 3 All ER 737. This is otherwise where one party's understanding of the contract was known to the other, even though not matching his own *Hartog v. Colin and Shields* [1939] 3 All ER 566.

[75] see now Minors' Contract Act 1987, which repealed the Infants Relief Act 1874, leaving the enforceability of contracts entered into by minors to be governed exclusively by common law rules and by the provisions of the 1987 Act relating to ratification. See G. H. Treitel, *Law of Contract* (11th edition , Sweet & Maxwell, London 2003), ch. 13; Cheshire, Fifoot and Furmston, *Law of Contract* (14th edition, Butterworths, 2001), ch. 13.

legally bound,[76] consideration[77] and the form[78] of the contract.

Contract of sale of goods is by far the most common type of contracts and often concern goods of a utilitarian nature, with a clearly defined purpose. People enter into agreements every day to buy goods for a variety of reasons. The most obvious, of course, is to enjoy and acquire their ownership and use them for different purposes. But in commercial transactions, traders, not being consumers, are not interested in the goods as such, but rather only in the profit that can be made, or the loss that can be avoided, by reselling them.

Most, if not all, contracts, whether they involve goods, real property or services, are necessarily economic activities. This is a fortiori true of the types of contracts which are the subject of this thesis: contract of sale of manufactured goods purchased for resale. Importantly, the utility of these types of goods for the commercial buyer may be influenced by a broad range of factors. The buyer may choose particular goods based on their brand or reputation. The environmental and social practices involved in their manufacture may also be significant. Moreover, consumer tastes and preferences matter to the commercial buyer, as the brand of goods in the markets may rise and fall.

In order to have an understanding of facts in which these complex transactions occur, it is appropriate that a thesis of this kind addresses some fundamental rules to be fulfilled for the effective conclusion of a sales contract. It is of interest to look at what the UAGCL provide as to the conclusion of a sale contract. It is also important to point out that some elements are not expressed in the Uniform Act but are indirectly stipulated.

The Contract of Sale Goods Defined

As a general principle, the law relating to a contract of sale is an aspect of the general law of contract. A contract of sale is first and foremost a contract,

[76] There are certain situations in which people find it convenient to fudge the question whether a legal commitment is intended, in order to be able to do the deal. The typical case is the so-called letter of comfort, which may or not generate a contract, depending upon the intentions of the parties as determined in the terms of the contract of comfort. Inevitably, agreement is bought at the price of uncertainty. see For example, *Kleinwort Benson Ltd v. Malaysia Mining Corp. Bhd.* [1989] 1 All ER 785 (letter of comfort held not to be contractual); and, for a similar finding in relation to a letter of intent, *British Steel Corp v. Cleveland Bridge and Engineering Co Ltd* [1984] 1 All ER 504. By contrast, in *Wilson Smitheett & Cape (Sugar) Ltd v. Bangladesh Sugar & Food Industries Corp.* [1986] 1 Lloyd's Rep 378, the letter of intent was held to be contractual.

[77] see Paul Mitchell and John Phillips, Contractual Nexus: Is Reliance Essential?, (2002) 22 (1) *OJLS* 115.

[78] Statute of Fraud 1677, section 4.

that is, a binding consensual transaction based on agreement to buy and an agreement to sell.[79] It appears therefore that it cannot be examined in isolation from its very context.

The Uniform Act does not expressly define what constitutes a '*contract of sale.*' However, it can be established indirectly from the provisions of the Act setting out the duties of the seller[80] and of the buyer.[81] According to those provisions, the contract of sale is a contract by which one party (seller) is obliged to deliver the goods, and to transfer property on the goods, to the other party (buyer) at an agreed price.[82] This denotes the fact that a sales contract is a reciprocal exchange of goods which one party binds itself to transfer against the price. This is a clear confirmation found under Article 250 para.1 UAGCL; the main obligations of the seller is to deliver the goods, hand over any documents relating to the goods. Under Article 262 UAGCL, the main obligations of the buyer are to pay the price and take delivery of the goods.

For more clarification, a contract of sale is defined in Section 2 of the Sale of Goods Act as:

> *... a contract by which the seller transfers or agreesto transfer property in goods to the buyer for money consideration, called the price.*

Also, in the French Civil code, a sales contract is merely between two parties, one party who is under the obligation to deliver the contract goods and the other one who is under the obligation to pay the price.[83]

To be concise, we can state the general proposition that the Uniform Act follows the positions at Common Law and the Civil code, by holding that for sales contract to exist, the goods, must be definite that is, must exist, be movable, be capable of being determined,[84] and legal.[85] At Common Law these requirements are also observed.

The root definition in the above definitions contains a number of ingredients, which are pointers in perceiving the essential requirements and

---

79 Atiyah et al., Op. cit., p. 6.

80 Article 250 (Conforming goods)

81 Article 262 (to purchase)

82 Ibid (refers to buyer's obligation to pay the price)

83 La vente est une convention par laquelle l'un s'oblige à livrer une chose, et l'autre à la payer: see Civil Codes (CC) of Cameroon, Article 1582 CC; Côte d'Ivoire, Article 1582 CC; France, Article 1582 CC.

84 Cameroon, Article 1129 CC; Côte d'Ivoire, Article 1129 CC.

85 Cameroon, Article 1128 CC; Côte d'Ivoire, Article 1128 CC.

nature of a sales contract.

We are concerned here with the principal duty of the seller to deliver goods of conformity under a contract of sale as formulated under the UAGCL, the heart of the seller's contract obligation[86] of conformity. Therefore, to identify the ambit of '*conformity*', it is relevant to identify the '*goods*' that are the object of the OHADA Uniform Act on General Commercial Law.

Formation of a Contract of Sale

For parties to have a legal contract, some requirements are indispensable. Among others are: mutual assent, legal capacity, consideration, mistake, misrepresentation.

Mutual Assent

Commerce is concerned with the exchange of goods and services, and the legal framework of '*exchange*' is provided by the law of contract.[87] The formation of sales contracts under the Uniform Act is largely subject to the Common law principles of offer and acceptance. As contracts are normally consensual, the parties must be in agreement with each other as to its terms. This agreement is manifested through offer and acceptance. The parties must have agreed on the essential terms in order to establish a contract. This translates the prevailing traditional principle of freedom of contract whereby contracting parties are called upon to fix the terms of their own bargain.The UAGCL is silent on the specific point relating to the freedom of contract. Therefore, in accordance with its provision, the rule on the autonomy is largely subject to general principles of contract law.[88]

Offer

Depending on the circumstances, the course of dealing and usages might require additional information for the offer to become definite. This is for

[86] This duty is governed by Article 255 para.1 UAGCL. See also, Larry Dimatteo et al., The Interpretive Turn in International Sales Law: An Analysis of Fifteen Years of CISG Jurisprudence, (2004) 24 *Northwestern Journal of International Law and Business*, pp. 299–392, p. 292, commenting on Article 35 CISG which also spells out the seller's duties.

[87] Robert Bradgate, Op. cit., p. 35.

[88] Article 237 UAGCL.

instance the case where time of delivery might be of essence, the place of shipment or sometimes the offer might be required to provide information on the goods such as the type, brand, or the performance. Failure for a proposal to be definite in this respect does not constitute an offer.[89]

To be definite, an offer, as per the UAGCL, must spell out the goods, expressly or implicitly determine the quantity and price of the goods. If this is determined, the proposal must provide for guidelines which help in fixing them.[90] It should be noted that the UAGCL[91] and the Common law rules agree that an invitation to treat be distinguished from an offer.[92]It is an invitation for someone to make an offer in respect to the particular goods or services. Thus, it cannot be accepted to form a legally binding contract. The latter position therefore brought a clear distinction between an invitation to treat and an offer. Hence, an invitation to treat is an invitation for someone to make an offer in respect to the particular goods or services and thus cannot be accepted to form a legally binding contract. In Carlill v Carbolic Smoke Ball Company,[93] the defences of the company was that there was no intention to be bound. It never intended to be serious and therefore had no intention to be legally bound.[94] Invitations to treat and offers should be differentiated from a declaration of intention, which is a statement that offers will be invited in the future.[95] Similar to the common law position, an invitation to treat is not an offer under the UAGCL.[96]In the CCJA's decision,[97] the court confirmed the decision of the Djamena's Court of Appeal based on the fact that terms intended for a binding agreement do not constitute an offer if the offeror intends to provide additional information relevant to the offer in a later date. It was held that the offeror in this case did not intend to be bound as per the UAGCL.[98]

---

89 Akuété Pedro Santos & Jean Yado Toé, *OHADA Droit Commercial Genéral*, Op. cit., p. 375.

90 Article 241 para. 1 UAGCL.

91 Article 241 para. 2 UAGCL.

92 *Carlill v. Carbolic Smoke Ball Company* (1893) 1 QB 256.

93 (1893) + QB 256

94 Stephen A. Smith & P.S. Atiyah, *Atiyah's Introduction of the Law of Contract*, (6thedition, Clarendon, Oxford 2005) p. 37.

95 Brian A. Blum, *Contracts, Examples and Explanations*, (4th edition, Aspen Publishers, New York 2007) p. 60.

96 Article 241 para. 2 UAGCL.

97 CCJA Arret No. 064/December 22, 2005.

98 Article 247 UAGCL.

An offer in the UAGCL will be treated as having reached the offeree[99] when it is made orally to him or delivered by the other means to him personally or to his place of business or postal address.[100] In other words, any means of communication without exception seems to have been included in this provision.

Acceptance

Acceptance is defined as the final and unqualified expression of assent to the terms of an offer.[101] According to the UAGCL, a statement by or any other attitude or conduct from the offeree indicating that he assents to an offer constitutes acceptance.[102] Subject to no condition as to form,[103] the declaration of acceptance must be made simple, that is without reservation or condition, in such a way that upon acceptance the contract is concluded.[104] Hence, the contract is concluded at the moment the acceptance of an offer becomes effective.[105] Unless the proposal prescribes the manner in which it is to be accepted; and if the proposal prescribes a manner in which it is to be accepted, and the acceptance is not made in such manner, it will be treated as not effective and there will be no acceptance.

Under the UAGCL, the means of communication to render the offer and acceptance effective is not restricted. What matters is that the acceptance must reach the offeror.[106] In most cases of verbal offer, acceptance is required to be made immediately unless otherwise agreed by the parties.[107] Also, it can be made within the time limit set by the offeror which starts running from the time the offeree receives the offer.[108]

It is a general rule that silence or the absence of action does not as a rule amount to acceptance.[109] This is also a general rule stated in the leading

[99] Within the domain of sales law, an 'offeror' will mean any person (or persons) who takes the first step in the formulation of a sales contract, while the 'offeree' will mean the person (or persons) to whom the offer is addressed.

[100] Article 243 UAGCL.

[101] G.H.Treitel, The Law of Contract, Op. cit., p.18.

[102] Article 244 para. 1 UAGCL.

[103] Article 244 para. 2 UAGCL.

[104] Akuété Pedro Santos & Jean Yado Toé, *OHADA Droit Commercial Général*, Op. cit., p. 377.

[105] Article 244 UAGCL.

[106] Article 242 UAGCL.

[107] Article 244 para. 1UAGCL.

[108] Article 246 UAGCL.

[109] Article 243 para. 2 UAGCL.

case of *Felthouse v. Bindley*.[110] Though acceptance is free from requirement as to form, this rule is aimed at protecting the offeree from the offeror who might want to impose silence as a condition of acceptance. It is however clear from the wording of the provisions of the UAGCL that this rule is subject to limitation. For instance, it is a practice and usage in sales contracts that upon delivery, the goods must be rejected if not accepted. The defence of silence will be inappropriate for example in this case if the offeree has eventually used the goods upon receipt. Also, practice and usages between the parties in a contract may also be treated as acceptance if the offeree remains silent.[111]

It follows that declaration of acceptance can also be performed by conduct, behaviour or by the mere implied act of the offeree indicating acceptance.[112] For instance, the use of materials sent by the offeree is a clear indication that the offer has been accepted, the payment of the price is an act indicating acceptance as well.

Legal Capacity of Commercial Persons Engaged in Business

Capacity is very important as far as the conclusion of a sale contract is concerned. Capacity means the ability to perform legally binding acts. The parties must possess the legal capacity before entering into a contract of sale.

The UAGCL subjects the practice of commercial activities to a class of individuals.This is because the practice of business warrants a certain degree of maturity and experience. This is why the UAGCL expressly prohibits minors from delving into such business. The UAGCL stipulates that for a person to engage in trading as a regular occupation, he must be legally fit.[113] This means that such a person must be of the required age and free from any legal restrictions. The UAGCL restricts certain persons to undertake commercial activities due to the complexity of business especially with minors. A minor does not have the legal capacity to have the status of a commercial person or engage in trading, he can only do this if he becomes emancipated.[114]

---

[110] [1862] 11 C.B (N.S) 869 and reaffirmed in [1863] New Rep. 401.

[111] Article 243 para. 2 UAGCL.

[112] Article 244para. 2 UAGCL.

[113] Article 6 UAGCL.

[114] Article 7 UAGCL; See Djieufack Roland, *The Nature of Agency Relationship under the OHADA Uniform Act on General Commercial Law: A Comparative Study*, (D.E.A. Dissertation, Faculty of Law and Political Science, University of Dschang, 2004) p. 5

A minor at Common law is he who has not yet attained the age of 18.[115] As a result of this deficiency on the part of the minor, he is at the mercy of the adult contracting party who often than not, take advantage of the minor's inexperience to exploit him by inserting onerous terms in the contract. The question of capacity of corporations is equally excluded from the ambit of the Act.[116]Capacity to buy and sell is regulated by the general law of contract related to capacity to enter into an agreement. The SGA 1893 contains limited provisions on contractual capacity. Section 2 of the 1893 Act deals only with purchase of '*necessaries*', leaving all other matters arising in connection with capacity to buy and sell, and matters of property to the ordinary law of contract.

It is with a view of protecting the minor that the general principle of law is to the effect that contracts entered into by minors are generally voidable and therefore, are not binding upon the minors. However, sub-sections 4 and 5 of Section 2 of the 1893 Act provide an exception to this general rule. That Section provides to the effect that where necessaries[117] are sold and delivered to a minor or to a person who by reason of mental incapacity[118] or drunkenness is incompetent to contract, he must pay a reasonable price for them. Accordingly, the incapacitated person must pay a reasonable price for necessaries that are sold and delivered. This raises three major points:

First, '*necessaries*' are defined in general terms by the above section as, '*goods suitable both to the condition in life of the minor*' or other incapacitated person and to his actual requirements at the time of the sale and delivery. The definition has been particularly hard to apply in the case of minors. The question whether goods are necessaries is a mixed question of law and fact, so that there must be some evidence on which a finding to that effect can be made.[119] It is the seller who carries the burden of proving that the goods are necessaries[120] and given the nature of the test, it will often be a difficult burden to discharge. The seller will have to show that the goods are necessaries, having regard not only to the condition in life of the minor, but also to the minor's existing provision of goods of that kind.[121]

---

[115] The Family Reform Act 1969 reduced the age from 21.

[116] see *Palmer's Company Law* (ed. by G.K. Morse and others), (Sweet & Maxwell, London) p. 2–3.

[117] Section 2 of the 1893 Act defines "necessaries" as goods suitable to the condition in life of a person.

[118] see also sections 1, 2, and 3 of the Mental Capacity Act 2005.

[119] *Ryder v. Wombwell* (1868) LR 4 Ex. 32.

[120] Ibid.; *Nash v. Inman* [1908] 2 KB 1.

[121] *Nash v. Inman, supra*. For the difficulties of a seller who lacks knowledge, see *Johnstone v. Marks* (1887) 19 QBD 509. For details of nineteenth century case law showing the consumer needs of sons of the nobility, see G.H. Treitel, *The Law of Contract*, Op. cit., pp. 495–496.

Secondly, the section above applies only to necessaries '*sold and delivered*'. Where the goods have not yet been delivered, or have been but the property has not yet pass to the buyer, the common law applies and does not give a clear answer to the question whether the seller and/or buyer are bound.[122] Since the minor lacks capacity to contract,[123] there is no reason to give the protection of a binding contract to a seller who can help himself by refusing to deliver, or by taking proceedings for the recovery of goods, in which he has reserved the general property, against a minor unlawfully retaining possession. Nor is there any reason to give the minor a right to compel further performance of the contract by demanding that the seller delivers the goods or convey the property in them.[124]

Thirdly, the contractual price is displayed by the reference to a reasonable price, that is, consistent with the price recoverable on a restitution basis under the old count of goods sold and delivered.[125] It is not necessarily predicated upon a binding contract. The above section does not include the count of goods bargained and sold, applicable where the property had passed but delivery has not yet been made. A seller dealing with a minor in these circumstances is protected by the unpaid seller's right of retention in section 39 and the right of resale in section 48.[126] Such a seller does not need the protection of a personal action as well.

Section 2 of the 1893 Act can therefore be rationalised as minimal legislative intervention designed to avert an unjustified enrichment of the minor. It would take a modern rationalisation of law to interpret it as a partial codification of the law dealing with the enforcement of contracts against minors.

As in English law, those wishing to involve in commerce under the Uniform Act come in different guises. An individual wishing to engage in business may act on his own or a wide variety of business organisations are possible, most being legal or '*moral*' persons, that is, having a legal personality in their own

[122] see *Nash v. Inman, supra*; *Roberts v. Gray* [1913] 1 KB 520 (services).

[123] The position of mentally incapable buyers is different. If the seller is unaware of the mental disorder, he need not rely on s. 2 but may enforce the contract at Common law: *Baxter v. Portsmouth* (1826) 5 B & C 170. Otherwise the contract may be avoided by the mentally incapable party: *Imperial Loan Co v. Stone* [1892] 1 QB 599. A drunkard is liable on a contract at Common law unless his unless his condition is so extreme as to be known to the other party: *Gore v. Gibson* (1843) 13 M & W 623.

[124] see Jason Chuah, *supra*, at p. 16.

[125] Ibid.

[126] To be examined later under remedies for breach of contract by parties.

right, distinct from that of the natural persons involved.[127] Those who involve in doing business under the OHADA Uniform Act on General Commercial Law must *prima facie* be considered to be *commerçants*,[128] and their acts are deemed to be commercial acts subject to the rules of French commercial law.[129] In English there is no equivalent defined term.As Article 2 of the Uniform Act puts it:

> *Est commerçant celui qui fait de l'accomplissement decommerce par nature sa profession*[130].

There is obviously circularity in the definition but this has not led to practical difficulties in delimiting the scope of a trader's commercial acts by '*nature*' (*actes de commerce par nature*) as identified under the Uniform Act. Probably the nearest equivalent in English law to '*un acte de commerce*' is the notion of '*acting in the course of a business*'.[131] The word '*profession*' translates the fact that a trader must engage in a business. '*Business*' includes a profession and the activities of certain professions are not permitted under the Uniform Act.[132] The term is a wide one and denotes any regular activity of a business character carried out by a person on its own account. '*In the course of a business*' has a broad meaning. It is not necessary that the transaction should be one of a type conducted with regularity by the seller.[133] From the text of the Uniform Act, it could involve, for example, a dealer in sales of goods or sales by an agent.[134]

Asthe characterisation of a person as a commercial person depends on the nature of the particular activities in which it is engaged under the OHADA Uniform Act, registration of the business in the Commercial Registry is also an

---

[127] Specifically, the businesses of these organisations are governed by the Uniform Act on Commercial Companies and Economic Interests Groups of OHADA. These are profit-making organisations. The general term used in French law is société such as, société anonyme (SA), société en commandite simple (SCS), société en nom collectif (SNC), société a responsabilité limitée (SARL),and Groupements d'Intérêts Economiques (GIE).

[128] Article 1 UAGCL.

[129] Slyvain SorelKuate Tameghe, in *Encyclopedie du Droit OHADA*, (ed. by Paul-Gerard Pougoue et al.), (Lamy, Paris 2011) p. 3; Paul-Gérard Pougoué & Foko Athanase, *Le Statut du Commercant dans l'espace OHADA*, Yaoundé, (P.U.A., Collection vademecum, Yaoundé) pp. 19–21.

[130] A trader is a person who carries out commercial acts in nature as its profession

[131] Brice Dickson, *Introduction to French Law*, (Pitman Publishing , London 1994) p.170.

[132] Article 9 UAGCL; see Anoukaha François, L'incompatibilité d'exercise d'une activité commerciale dans l'espace OHADA: le cas du Cameroun (2001) 1 (5) *Annales de la Faculté des Sciences Juridiques et Poltiques*, Université de Dschang,p. 6.

[133] Roy Goode, *Commercial Law*, Op. cit., p. 300–301.

[134] Slyvain Sorel Kuate Tameghe, *Encyclopedie du Droit OHADA*, Op. cit., p. 23.

important factor. This seems to be a permission or admission to commercial professions. The Uniform Act has created a central register[135] to supplement the registers kept at the national courts.[136] The impact of registration differs depending upon whether the name registered is that of an individual or of a company.[137] Registration of the former has merely a declaratory effect: it raises a rebuttable presumption that the acts of that individual are commercial in nature[138]. If the individual is not registered, he cannot rely upon his status as a commercial person *vis-à-vis* other persons but retains the duty to fulfill the obligations which lie upon it as a person. For companies' registration has a constitutive effect: it is only then that the company acquires legal personality.[139]

Likewise, any incidental acts which a trader undertakes in the context of his or her trade or profession are nevertheless classified as commercial acts (*actes de commerce par acessoire*). It is in this concept of '*commercial acts*' (*actes de commerce*) that the key to the scope of French commercial law is to be found, for commercial law is essentially about acts and the *commerçants* who engage in them.[140] Some acts under the Uniform Act are considered commercial by virtue of their nature that is, taking account of what is done and by whom (*actes de commerce par nature*).[141] Certain acts are automatically deemed to be commercial because of the form of the act itself or of the organisation involved: actes de commerce par la forme.[142] In addition, acts which normally if they are done as an ancillary part of a commercial activity are known as actes de commerce par accessoire.

Besides that, the OHADA Uniform Act on General Commercial Law now covers a special category of traders known in French as "*entreprenant*". There is still some doubt as to what may be the equivalent to this in English. For the sake of convenience, '*entrepreneur*' will be used in this work. A closest meaning can be derived from the literal meaning given to who an entrepreneur is: "someone who uses money to start business and make business

[135] Article 76–78 UAGCL.

[136] The organisation of this registry is contained in Book III UAGCL.

[137] This is contained in Book II Chapter 1 of the UAGCL.

[138] Article 3 UAGCL.

[139] Article 59–69 UAGCL.

[140] John Bell, et al., Op. cit., pp. 432–433; SlyvainSorel Kuate Tameghe, *Encyclopedie du Droit OHADA*, Op. cit., pp. 2–4.

[141] Article 3 UAGCL. These acts purposefully constitute a participation in the circulation of wealth (such as, goods and services).

[142] Article 4 UAGCL. The clearest examples covered by the Uniform Act are the bill of exchange, negotiating instrument and a warrant.

deals".[143] This is a natural person who when sales pass a threshold, will lose that status and, when eligible, acquires that status of a commercial person.[144] The determining factor in circumscribing an entrepreneur's activities will be done particularly to taxes and the obligation to pay social charges in accordance with the national laws of OHADA member States.[145] In other words, it all depends on the income of the individual. This current dispensation is contrary to the spirit of harmonisation as championed by the OHADA Treaty as its principal objective.[146]

By virtue of Article 30 of the Uniform Act, an entrepreneur is:

> *L'entreprenant est un entrepreneur individuel, personnephysique qui, sur simple déclaration prévue dans le présent Acte Uniforme, exerce une activité professionnelle civile, commerciale, artisanale ou agricole.*

The above text suggests that it is a natural person who undertakes a commercial or civil act, artistic or agricultural activity. It entails therefore that the acts carried by an entrepreneur can be categorised to be '*acte de commerce par nature*'or '*acte de commerce par accessoire*' because acts which would normally be regarded as civil (that is not commercial) will be categorised as commercial if they are done as an ancillary part of a commercial activity.[147] This entails that if any person who is prohibited by the Uniform Act to exercise a trade may fall under this head if he engages in a commercial activity provided it is not incompatible with the rules of his profession.[148]

143 *Macmillan English Dictionary for Advanced Learners*, International Students Edition, Macmillan Publishers Limited, 2002, p. 462.

144 Martha Simo Tumnde, Cameroon offers a Contextual Approach to Understanding the OHADA Treaty and Uniform Acts, in *Unified Business Laws for Africa, Common Law Perspectives on OHADA* (ed. Claire Moore Dickerson), Op. cit., p. 66; Paul-Gérard Pougoué, Jean Claude James, Yvette Rachel Kalieu, et al., in *Ecyclopedie du Droit OHADA*, Op. cit., p. 49.

145 Article 30 para. 7 UAGCL. Such a measure usually scares away some entrepreneurs of this category for fear of paying taxes upon disclosing their business activity to the government. Thus, they usually carry out their different activities hiddenly in most towns of Cameroon. This is even further evidenced by the non-declaration oftheirbusiness activities at the Commercial Registry. However, based on exchanges which the researcher had with some of these individuals in the city of Douala, the problem stems from lack of information and illiteracy. It also concerns the remote geographical zone where some of these persons are found. Some do migrate from town to town. see Kanchop Thierry Noel, *Le Secteur Informel a l'Epreuve du Droit des Affaires OHADA*, Memoire de D.E.A., Universite de Dschang, 2008, pp. 82–83.

146 Paul-Gérard Pougoué, Jean Claude James, Yvette Rachel Kalieu, et al., in Ecyclopedie du Droit OHADA, Op. cit., p. 49.

147 Donald Harris and Denis Tallon, *Contract Law Today, Anglo-French Comparisons*, (Clarendon Press, Oxford 1991) p. 15.

148 Article 9 UAGCL.

Consideration

The UAGCL does not expressly define consideration. But, it is deduced from the duties of the parties. The seller agrees to transfer goods to the buyer who in return pays for them. The buyer is further expected to take all necessary steps for the effective payment of the price.[149] Under the Uniform Act, a contract of sale cannot be concluded without the specification of price.

The doctrine of consideration is peculiar to the Common law system. Generally, consideration is something of value in the eyes of the law. It follows that a valuable consideration can be some right, interest, profit or benefit accruing to one party or some forbearance, detriment, loss or responsibility, given, suffered or undertaken by the other.[150] Whether through doctrine or case law, the appropriate definition of consideration seems to lay emphasis on the value of what is exchanged between the parties.[151] At Common law, it does not matter whether the value is too small or too high. What matters is the mere value of the consideration, no matter how small it is, as it was held in *Thomas v. Thomas*[152] when analysing the adequacy of the consideration.[153]

Consideration can also be described differently in sale of goods, for instance, as the price of the promise, as it was held in the case of *Dunlop Pneumatic Tyre Co. v. Selfridge Ltd.*[154] In such case, the House of Lords decided that a promise can be enforceable if it is bought for a price required; consideration here was the price.

In practice, the doctrine of consideration is divided into two categories: Executory and Executed consideration. In a sale of goods transaction, it will be described as "*executory*" when a promise is made in return of a counter promise and it will be executed when made against the performance of an act.[155]

While executed and "*executory*" considerations are valid considerations, common law treats past consideration as an absence of consideration. In Re McArdle,[156] the promise was not binding on children and the consideration was past. The Court of Appeal in this decision took in consideration that the

---

149 Article 264 UAGCL.

150 *Currie v. Misa* (1975) LR 10 Exch 153, 162).

151 Hugh Beale et al., *Cases, Materials and Text on Contract Law*, (Hart Publishing, 2002) p. 141.

152 (1842) 2 QB 851

153 Michael Furmston, *Law of Contract*, Op. cit., p. 106 ; Nicholas B, *The French Law of Contract*, Op. cit., p. 113.

154 [1915] A.C 847 p 855.

155 Michael Furmston, *Law of Contract*, Op. cit., p. 97.

156 [1951] Ch. 669.

children promised to repay the expenses of the plaintiff after the work was completed.

Under Civil law, where a contract arises from an agreement, it is understood to be as a result of the consensus of the minds of the contracting parties, Common law departs from a promise supported by consideration.[157] Therefore, consideration at this stage appears to be relevant because a promise is not a contract unless converted into an agreement upon acceptance.[158] The promises lead then the parties to bargain. This might be the reason why consideration might be considered a consensus of intentions, a consensus of two promises. In a comparative perspective, with regard to onerous French contracts for instance, a promise amounting to consideration may fall within the criteria of "*la cause*". Thus, in a sales contract situation, the buyer's obligation to pay for the price will be treated as follows; the consideration supporting the contract and "*la cause*" of the seller's obligation to transfer the property of the goods. Consequently, in a sales contract, the cause of the seller remains the delivery of the goods and that of the buyer, why he wants the goods.[159] Based on this example, in a substantive note, what may amount to consideration under English Law, will likely be regarded as cause under French civil law.

In the case of the formation of the contract of sale of goods under English law, the consideration consists of rendering of mutual promise and most importantly the payment of the price. Only promises supported by a legal consideration (price) are legally binding. Generally speaking, the central function of the doctrine of consideration is to prevent people from making gratuitous promises, and the purpose of the law of consideration is to distinguish between gratuitous and non-gratuitous promises. The price is money which has to be paid for the purchase of something.

Just as the CISG,[160] the issue of price under the UAGCL can be inferred from the mutual exchanges of goods on the one hand for price on the other. Article 263 of the Uniform Act stipulates that:

> *A sale may not be validly concluded without a specification of the price in the contract of sale, unless the parties referred to the price generally charged at the time of conclusion of the contract in the commercial sector considered for the same goods sold under similar circumstances.*

[157] Nicholas B., *The French Law of Contract*, Op. cit., pp. 39–65;

[158] *Carlill v. Carbolic Smoke Ball Co.* (1893) 1 QB 257, AC.

[159] Henri & Leon Mazeaud et al., *Obligations, Théorie Générale, Leçons De Droit Civil*, (9 ed., Montchrestien, 1998) p. 271–272.

[160] Article 55 CISG.

The wording of the above article shows that price is a determining factor in the formation of a contract of sale. It represents a consideration on the part of the seller while transfer of title is for the buyer. There is however, the possibility for concluding contracts without specifying the price by making reference to the price generally charged at the time of the contract.[161] From the consumer's point of view, price is usually defined "*as what the consumer must give up to purchase a product or service*".[162] Even though the parties in their contract are free to debate on the price of the object to be sold, they are prices of certain commodities which have been statutorily fixed by the government, at times in, relation to the trade usage and practice. In practice, sellers usually have discriminatory prices of goods they sell their marketplaces. The prices of some goods do not represent the real value of such goods, a situation which may put commercial buyers into difficulties *vis-à-vis* their customers in particular. However, through the enactment of price control legislation, sellers of certain commodities are under a statutory duty to respect price arrangement. In this regard, a seller has a duty to deliver goods in conformity price imposed by the government. Price control in Cameroon attests this fact. Price control began in Cameroon, with the Law No. 63/LF/27, of the 19th June 1963, which established a regime of price control.

The substantial provisions on price control in the country consist essentially in placing goods under three different categories, and in attributing to each category a particular method of determining prices.[163] These categories are (a) essential goods (such as foodstuffs and other necessaries), (b) heavy and bulky goods (building materials, for example), and (c) luxury goods (jewellery for instance). Different profit margins are allowed to the sellers of these goods. The base-line for the determination of the profit margins is the gross cost of the goods in question, in the case of imported goods, their cost, insurance, freight and other warehouse and transport charges, and in the case of home-produced goods, the manufacturers' or producers' prices.[164] Furthermore, different profit margins apply depending on whether the seller

[161] Edie Diable Pascal, *Contract of Sale of Goods under the OHADA Uniform Act on General Commercial Law, The Common Law and the CISG: A Comparative Study*, (Masters Dissertaion, Faculty of Law and Political Science, University of Dschang, 2011) p. 45.

[162] J. Paul Peter & Jerry C. Olson, *supra*, p. 496.

[163] Arrêté No. 0196/MINCOMMERCE du 13 April 2007 portant fixation de la liste des produits et services dont les prix et tarifs sont soumis a la procédure d'homologation préalable.

[164] Arrêté No. 100/MINDIC/DPPM du 12 Décembre 1988 fixant les éléments constitutifs du prix de revient et les marges bénéficiaires applicable aux produits importés, aux produits de fabrication locale et aux prestations de services.

is a wholesaler or retailer.[165]

In addition to these general provisions, specific legislation has been enacted to deal with particular businesses. Ministerial Order No. 14/MINEP/DPPM, of March 4th regulates the sales of pharmaceutical products. Another Order, No. 006/MINDIC/DC/82 deals with activities related to the automobile industry.

Mistake

Mistake is a ground for annulment of agreement only where it rests on the very substance of the thing which is the object thereof.[166] The general rule in most Civil law countries is that, mistake is not a ground for nullity of agreement. However, it is not a ground for annulment where it only rests on the person with whom one has the intention of contracting, unless regard to or for that person was the main cause of the agreement.[167]

However, the code sets aside, as exceptions, two grounds of mistake causing that nullity; mistake on the substance and mistake on the contracting person.[168]

With regard to mistake on the substance, contrary to the interpretation given in Common law courts, civil law courts have given a very wide and flexible interpretation which contradicts with the restrictive and narrow interpretation given.

Regarding mistake on the substance, the court's interpretation is that it includes qualities of the thing which go to its substance; la qualité substantielle de la chose.[169] In addition, some scholars emphasise on the accuracy of the provision of the Civil Code when it states that "*thing*", that is,the object of the contract, as per the Civil Code,[170] should be understood as the object of the obligation of either party as opposed to the object of the agreement.

A substance can be of objective quality when the mistake is on the consent, in the sense that without the mistake, the party would have consented to the agreement.[171] The objective quality of the substance can be related to the goods, the subject matter of the contract. For instance, a party contracted for particular goods that he saw at the time of the contract, but he got delivered

---

165 Details are spelt out in Decree No. 69/DF/409 of October 2, 1969.
166 Article 1110 (1) Civil code.
167 Article 1110 (2) Civil code.
168 Article 1110 (2) Civil code.
169 For instance decision in Cass Civ. 1re, 28.6.1988, D.1989.450
170 Article 1110 Civil code.
171 Cass, Civ. 1re, 13 Janv. 1998, Bull. Civ. I, No. 17.

something different. The substance can also refer to the objective quality when a bona fide purchaser buys goods for a personal purpose and the party made a fundamental mistake on an element on the object which lead to the choice. The substance can also be subjective whenever the determining quality of the value of the goods purchased is affected. This is the case of an original paint of Picasso against a new original copy. Here the substance lies on the authenticity of the goods contracted for.[172]

Mistake as to the person arises when there is an error on the person. For the ground of mistake to be established here, it should not only be the person with whom the other party intended to contract with but "*the consideration of this person shall be the principal cause of the agreement*".[173]It is thus worthy to know the determining motive for the party to enter into the contract; "*motif principal*".[174] In other words, without it, the party would never have entered into the agreement. According to the French Civil Code, a contract can only be void on this ground if the contracting party of the agreement is the principal cause of the mistake.[175]

All these elements have potentials of leading to the annulment of an agreement based on this ground. [176] Hence, the mistake shall fall either on the essential quality of the person,[177] his consent[178] or the person should be excusable, as is the case with mistake on the substance.[179]

For a contract concluded *intuitu personae*, a purported mistake on the person will cause nullity if it rests on the essential quality of that person.[180] Mistake as to the person as described above under civil law is closely similar both in theory and practice to mistake that negates consent at Common law. The slight difference lies in the interpretation given to mistake in the respective legal systems. While Civil law courts and doctrine have given a wider and flexible interpretation of the civil code provision, Common law remains on

172 Cass, Civ. 1re, 5 Fevr. 2002 Brossard aff. Tableau de Liège,

173 Nicholas B., *The French Law of Contract*, Op. cit., p. 95

174 As used in the French legal jargon.

175 B. Starck, et al., *Droit Civil et les Obligations*, Op. cit., para. 478, p. 176

176 Jacques Ghestin, *La Formation du Contrat*, Op. cit., p. 177–178.

177 Ibid.; B. Starck, et al., *Droit Civil les Obligations*, Op. cit., p. 500.

178 Cass. Civ. 1re, January 4,1980, Saint-Jean, the nationality of a contracting party does not on itself annull a contract if the seller cannot proof that such consideration is part of the contract terms, B. Starck, et al., *Droit Civil les Obligations* (Litec 6 ed. 1998) at 176

179 Cass. Soc. July 3, 1990, Bull. Civ., No. 329, p. 197; J.C.P., 1990, IV, p. 334.

180 Article 1110 (2) Civil code; An arbitral agreement is null if one party was ignorant of that fact that the chosen arbitrator was the counselor of his opponent; Cass. Civ. 2e, 13 Avr. 1972, Bull. Civ. II, No. 91.

a restrictive and narrow approach.[181] For instance, at Common law, there is simply no contract if A intends to contract with B but rather does it with C. In *Sowler v. Potter,*[182] Judge Trucke L.J. applied what he called "*the French Rule*" of mistake in deciding on the matter.

As pointed above, at Common law, mistake includes[183] common mistake, mutual or unilateral mistake. Under common mistake, basically, both parties are mistaken on the subject matter. Most often, common mistake occurs when the subject matter of the contract ceases to exist, has never existed or is unknown to the contracting parties; they are mistaken as per the decision in *Bell v. Lever Bros.*[184] This decision is in line with Section 6 of the Sale of Goods Act 1893.

Common mistakes are often determined within the meaning of *res extincta, res sua.*[185] Under *res extincta*, the subject matter does not exist or had perished at the time of the contract *Couturier v. Hastie.*[186]In this case, both the buyer and the seller consented to the agreement. The contract was held void as there was no subject matter at the time of the contract. This decision was arrived at in the Nigerian case of *Tabs Assurance Ltd v. Awurie Industries (Nig.) Ltd.*[187] where the subject matter of the insurance ceased to exist well before the insurance contract was concluded. The court made it clear in this case that it is immaterial whether or not the fact was unknown to the parties.

Under *res sua*, neither of the parties is aware of the fact that the seller has no title. In some cases, the buyer is the owner of what the seller is about to sell to him as it was decided in the leading case of *Bell v. Lever brothers Ltd.*[188] In the Nigerian case of *Abraham v. Chief Oluwa,*[189] when the owner of the subject in this case got to realise that he purchased his own property, he brought an action for the contract to be set aside and claimed refund of the purchase money on the ground of mutual mistake. The court decided in his favour and declared the contract void. Aside from the above mentioned instances, it should be pointed out that *res extincta, res sua*, common mistake will also

181 Mostly due to interpretationof case law and doctrine as developed on the issue; Nicholas B., *The French Law of Contract*, Op. cit., pp. 96–97.

182 (1940) 1KB 271

183 Although the content remain similar in substance, legal authors classify the mistake in diverse way. In Uganda for instance, there mistake nullifying the consent, mistake that negative consent before looking at mistake at equity.

184 (1932) AC 161 at 217.

185 J. Ademola Yakubu, *Law of Contract in Nigeria*, (Malthouse Press Limited, 2003) p. 134.

186 (1856) 5 HLC 673;

187 (1995) 4 NWLR (Pt.388) 223.

188 (1932) A.C 218.

189 17 NLR 123.

occur in many other ways so long as it affects either the quality or the subject matter of the contract, both parties believing so. In *Bell v. Lever Bros*[190], the House of Lord, on the majority opinion, held that there was no mistake at law to render the contract void. To them a contract will be void on the ground of mistake whenever the quality is essentially different from the thing it was believed to be.

Even on mistake related to the substance of the subject matter, the decision cannot always be similar. In *Solle v. Butcher*[191]the court held that there was a mistake and due to the social context of the occurrence of the facts, the identity of the flat which had gone under serious improvement with considerable changes, the court held the lease not void at Common law. In *Bell v. Lever Bros*,[192] regarded as the leading authority on mistake, it was drawn as a general rule that although mistake as to the quality of the subject matter cannot give rise to mistake at law, Lord Atkin in his reasoning pointed out that such a mistake will not assent parties unless both parties are mistaken as to the existence of the quality which makes the thing without the quality essentially different from the thing as it was delivered to be.[193]

Under mutual mistake, both parties make the mistake but with the difference that the mistake is based on a mutual fundamental misapprehension of the parties of every intention. In such a circumstance, the parties are contracting out of mistake.[194] To determine mutual mistake, courts use the objective test, that is, if a contracting party assumes the existence of the contract, the contract will be thereof enforced by the court no matter the motive or the subjective intention of the parties. Generally, what matters to the court is the appearance of the factual situations; the intention of the parties is immaterial in the determination of the objective test.

However, if the external factor does not point to the existence of a contract or to any element taken into account under the objective text, the court will then declare the contract void on the ground of mutual mistake.[195] In the case of *Wooh v. Scarth*,[196] an authoritative case on mutual mistake, it was held that there was no mistake at law as no one could enter into a lease contract of just £63 per annum.

[190] (1932) AC 161 at 217.

[191] (1950) 1 K 671 at p. 692, I.E. Sagay, *Nigerian Law of Contract*, (Spectrum Law ed., Spectrum Books Limited 2007) p. 270.

[192] (1932) AC 161 at 217

[193] (1932) AC 161 at p.218

[194] J. Ademola Yakubu, *Law of Contract in Nigeria*, Op. cit., p. 141

[195] *Cornish v. Abington* (1859) 4H N 549 at 556.

[196] (1858) 1 F. & F. 293.

In this case, the defendant offered in writing to let a place to the plaintiff at £63 per annum. After a conversation with the defendant's clerk, the plaintiff accepted by letter, believing that the £63 rental was the only payment under the contract. In fact, the defendant had intended that a £500 premium would also be payable and he believed that his clerk had explained this to the plaintiff. The defendant refused to complete and the plaintiff brought an action for specific performance. Though the court refused the order specific performance the defendant nevertheless was liable in damages.[197] This position of the English court was reinstated in the Nigerian case of *S. Nasser & Sons Nig. Ltd v. Lagos Executive Development Board.*[198] In addition, the court in this case held that the burden of proving mutual mistake lies on the alleging party.[199]

Under unilateral mistake,[200] one of the two contracting parties enter into contract under mistake. The other party knows or ought to know that the mistake is being orchestrated when entering into the contract. As a result, the contract is void. In determining unilateral mistake, courts use a subjective approach. Therefore, what matters is the intention or belief of the party mistaking. Also, courts trace out whether the other party cause such a mistake or ought to have known as a reasonable man the circumstances of the fact in order to prevent the mistake. In the case of *Abdul Yusuf v. Nigerian Tobacco Company,*[201] the court of appeal stated that this case was a typical case on unilateral mistake.

In this case the defendant engaged the plaintiff's lorry to haul tobacco from various parts of Western Nigeria to their cigarette manufacturing factory at Ibadan. The plaintiff commenced the carriage for four weeks when he was stopped by the defendants. The defendant claimed that the normal freight rate for the carriage of their tobacco was half penny per 100 mile and not half penny per lb, per miles, and that the latter figure appeared on the contract as a result of a typing error. The defendant then invited the plaintiff to have the contract rectified as half a penny per 100 lb, but the plaintiff refused and rather sue the defendant for breach of contract, claiming damages, based on the freight he would have received. The defendant adduced evidence to the effect that the usual rate was half a penny per 100 lb and he also claimed that the plaintiff must have known of the error, but had decided to take advantage of it. On appeal the defendant succeeded and the court was of the opinion

---

197 *Cornish v. Abington* (1859) 4H N 549 at 556.

198 (1959) F.S.C 242, S.C.

199 Ibid.

200 Unilateral mistake also includes mistake as to the person as discussed above.

201 Western States Court of Appeal Suit No. CAS/39/74 decided on Nov. 14, 1974 at 256.

that the benefit of the plaintiff would have been unreasonable (£1800 per day) and any reasonable person would have found the correction of the mistake introduced by the defendant as reasonable.

Misrepresentation

A representation is a statement made by one party to the other, before or at the time of contracting, with regard to some existing fact or to some past event, which is one of the causes that induces the contract.[202]It is an unambiguous false statement of fact which induces the other party to enter into a contract.[203] In fact, a representation relates to some existing fact. A representation that something will be done in the future cannot either be true or false at the moment it is made. It at least implies that the alleged intention does indeed exist, and if this is not true there is a clear misrepresentation of an existing fact. Essentially, the representation renders a contract voidable unless it was intended to cause and has in fact caused the representee to make the contract. It must have produced a misunderstanding in his mind, and that misunderstanding must have been one of the reasons which induced him to make the contract. It must be carefully noticed that once it is shown that a representation was calculated to influence the judgment of a reasonable man, the presumption is that the representee was so influenced and thus creates liability.

When Civil law countries use "*manoeuvres*" to determine fraud, common law uses the word "*misrepresentation*". The distinction of these two terms may somctimcs lcad to the conclusion that the term fraud is narrower to a Common law lawyer than to a civil law lawyer. In Nigeria, the ingredient of misrepresentation is defined as per the decision in *Udogwu v. Oki*[204] where it was held that it is made up of facts, past or present as distinct from statement of opinion, intention or of law. However, depending on the person, a statement of opinion will not amount to misrepresentation.[205] In the Civil code "*dol and violence*" are used. According to the Civil Code, fraud is a ground of nullity of a contract where the schemes "*manoeuvres*" used by one of the parties are such that it is obvious that, without them, the other party would not have

202 Cheshire and Fifoot, *The Law of Contract, London*, (7th edition, Butterworths, 1969) p. 234.

203 Evan McKendrick, *Contract Law, Text, Cases and Materials*, (2nd edition,Oxford University Press, 2005) p. 659.

204 (1990) 5 NWLR (Pt 153) at 721

205 *Edgington v. Fitzmaurice* (1885) 29 Ch. D 549 at p. 483.

entered into the contract.[206] It may not be presumed, and must be proved. Duress, on the other hand, although not defined in the Civil Code, occurs in circumstances where there is no valid consent, where the consent was given only by mistake, or where it was extorted by duress.[207] However, the Common law legal system in majority treats fraud under misrepresentation, in particular under fraudulent misrepresentation.[208]

It should be noted that in some civil law systems, particularly those under the French legal system, it has been proved that there is only a slight difference between fraud and mistake. What constitutes fraud is a mistake that has been induced by schemes that is, "*manoeuvres*".[209] Once a mistake as such which has been induced occurred, the avoidance of mistake is not an option anymore as the mistake will be treated as fraud at law thereby nullifying the transaction.[210] In short, what matters in determining the scheme is not the act but the intention.[211] At common law, although innocent and negligent misrepresentations do not produce legal effect,[212] fraudulent misrepresentation does.[213]

With regard to duress, although not defined by the civil code, it is rather more discussed therein than fraud.[214] However, to establish that consent has been obtained by duress, the civil code has not been accurate enough on the question.[215] Case law has made it clear that consent may be obtained by all means: moral,[216] physical, or by any other sort of threats.[217] Therefore, it does not matter whether or not the contracting party contributed in the threat.[218] At common law duress is no more restricted to actual or physical violence or unlawful constraint; it has been extended to threats on goods by their

206 Article 1116 Civil code.

207 Article 1109 Civil Code.

208 This Common law rule emanates from the leading case of *Derry v. Peek*, 14 app. Cass. 337; 58 L.J. Ch. 864.

209 Schemes is not only limited to deception, it also includes any falsehood provided the requisite intent is present.

210 Hugh Beale et al., *Cases, Materials and Text on Contract Law*, Op. cit., p. 337.

211 Nicholas B., *The French Law of Contract?*, Op. cit., p. 101; Hugh Beale et al., *Cases, Materials and Text on Contract Law*, Op. cit., p. 337 .

212 Unless they are tainted with mis take Hugh Beale, Op. cit.

213 *Derry v. Peek* (1889) 14 app. Cass. 337; 58 L.J. Ch. 864.

214 Articles 1109; 1111; 1112; 1113; 1114; 1115 Civil code

215 Hugh Beale, et al., *Cases, Materials and Text on Contract Law*, p. 432–3; Nicholas B., *The French Law of Contract*, Op. cit., p. 106–107 ; Article 1112 (1&2) Civil code.

216 Moral pain as compared to physical pain, Cass. Com., 28 mai 1991, Bull, Civ. IV, No. 180; Dependence on a secret society as in Cass. Civ., 3re, 13 Jan. 99, Bull. Civ. III, No. 11.

217 Threat for prosecution is the result might be higher.

218 Nicholas B., *The French Law of Contract*, Op. cit., p. 106.

detention as above mentioned.

Fraud, "*dol*" under French law is satisfied when the following three elements are met: there must have been deception, which must have determined the consent and the intention to deceive from the other party.[219] Firstly, deception might be a false statement, a lie or an untrue statement on its own. All these constitute fraud.

This similarly goes with the duty of disclosure which was not required from the onset. As schemes "*manoeuvres*", due to the evolution in case law, it is considered a fraud if a party keeps silent on what he knows and the other party does not know, though he should know.[220] Fraud therefore must have been induced.

Initially, it is a result of a mistake caused by the "*manoeuvre*" or practice inducing a contracting party to enter into contract. It follows that "*manoeuvre*" or practice does not cause fraud but the mistake that induces. It does not therefore matter whether the mistake causes the nullity of that transaction. What matter here is the schemes that led to mistake for fraud to be established.[221]

Secondly, the fraud committed must have determined the consent: referred to as the dol principal by some writers.[222] As opposed to *dol principal*, incidental dol or *dol incident* does not affect the validity of the contract but rather gives rise to damages. However, the other party at this instance must have suffered from the incidental fraud.[223]Lastly, the fraud must have emanated from the contracting party to be satisfied.[224]

Unlike in the Civil law system, fraudulent misrepresentation at Common law occurs only when false statement of fact amounts to fraud. The House of Lord in *Derry v. Peek*[225] made it clear that if the party honestly believed that he was given the true statement of that fact, he will not be liable under fraudulent misrepresentation and therefore, his statement will not constitute fraud at law. However, for the test of fraudulent misrepresentation to be satisfied, the party

[219] Hugh Beale, et al., *Cases, Materials and Text on Contract Law*, Op. cit., p. 337.

[220] Hugh Beale, et al., *Cases, Materials and Text on Contract Law*, Op. cit., p. 337; In the same manner, Law No. 92–60 of 18th January 1992 made it mandatory the disclosure of all information to consumer; Cass. Com., 28 juin 2005, Bull. Civ. IV, No. 140; Case for instance of a seller who fails to inform the buyer that the goods have been seized in Cass. Civ. 1re, 19 mai 1958.

[221] Cass. Civ., 1re, 10th July 1995, D., 1997.20.

[222] Nicholas B., *The French Law of Contract*, Op. cit., p. 101.

[223] Cass. Civ. 3e, 1er mars 1977, D., 1978 .91, n. Cher. Larromet ; n.p.8.

[224] Hugh Beale, et al., *Cases Materials and Text on Contract Law*, Op. cit., pp. 336–337; Cass. Civ. 1re, 21 fevr. 1995, Bull. Civ. I. No. 91.

[225] Op. cit.

must have knowledge of the fact that his representation is untrue.[226]

As is the case under a contract of sale, misrepresentation widely rests on the seller's implied duty of warranty. It is here that the buyer gets what he ordered from the seller or in most cases what the seller purports to deliver in his business to the buyer.

The attitude of our producers is that they must rush their products to the market, to be first with the most and cheapest for the biggest profit. In this scramble the business community is being both cheated and injured. Buyers often are subjected to the fraudulent, deceptive and unfair trade practices which are inter-related with the breaches of contract, misunderstanding and dishonest selling practices. It is a matter of great concern for the business community in general and the government in particular that the non-consumer and consumer buyers pay such a heavy penalty for social and economic ignorance or lack of adequate defence. The primary problem in Cameroon, for example, is perceived as the problem of cunning and predatory businessmen who design to play fraud and deceive innocent buyers.

Fraud in common parlance is somewhat a comprehensive word that embraces a multitude of delinquencies differing widely in turpitude, the types of conduct that give rise to an action of deceit at Common law. In the view of the Common law "*a charge of fraud is such a terrible thing to bring against a man that it cannot be maintained in any court unless it is shown that he had a wicked mind*".[227] This was influenced by the decision of the House of Lords in the leading case of *Derry v. Peek*[228] that an absence of honest belief is essential to constitute fraud. If a representor honestly believes his statement to be true he cannot be liable in deceit, no matter how ill-advised, stupid, credulous or even negligent he may have been. Fraud was given an elaborate meaning by Lord Herschell as making a false representation '*1-knowingly, or 2-without belief in its truth, or 3-recklessly, careless whether it be true or false*'. The lowest common denominator of fraud is thus the making of a statement, which happens to be false, without believing it to be true.[229] In testing the honesty of the representor's belief, his statement must not be considered according to its ordinary meaning, but according to its meaning as understood by him. Mere silence as to a fact likely to affect the willingness of a person to enter into a contract is not fraud.

---

226 *Derry v. Peek*, (1889), Op. cit.

227 Cheshire Fifoot & Furmston, *Law of Contract*, Butterworths, Op. cit., p. 246.

228 *supra*.

229 Michael Bridge, *The Sale of Goods*, Op. cit., p. 358.

The reselling businesses of commercial buyers today are faced with fraudulent practices. Consequently, consumer buyers of these goods are equally affected. The connotation of business or consumer fraud is inclusive of deception, false pretense, false promise, misrepresentation or knowing concealment, suppression of facts. Although buyers' problems with regard to fraud have long been a matter of great public importance for the consumers, courts and governments, these problems are presently graver in nature than before.

Businessmen are increasingly victims of a diverse and bewildering array of unscrupulous selling and deceptive business practices. This mal-practice adversely affects the marketplace allocation of economic resources by causing a buyer to purchase a product or service different from that which he believes it is getting.

Generally, the fraud on buyers is related to the products and services contracted and paid for which are simply not supplied, or products supplied but found for one reason or another unsatisfactory. It is current today to find false or falsely disparaging or misleading statements about certain products being sold in the market. Such a practice constitutes a fraud which rather deceives or misleads buyers of those goods.

Fraudulent, deceptive and unfair trade practices to which buyers are subjected may be ethical and legally clear-cut in theory, but they are extremely difficult to define and to distinguish from other kinds of business conduct. One compromising factor in fraud is the element of intent. In that situation, it may be considered as a breach of contract and certainly may not amount to fraud. This misrepresentation is innocent where the seller believes his assertion to be true. The word "*innocent*" in this context, means "*innocent fraud.*" In many disputes, there appear to be no breaches of contract, but when they are analysed, they reveal as fraudulent act. In that situation, misunderstanding or breaches of contract and fraudulent and deceptive practices need to be categorised to determine the problems of the transaction. In other words, it is difficult to define and draw lines between fraudulent and acceptable business practices. The classic fraudulent practice could be illustrated in an appropriate way. A sewing machine seller advertised for sale at the amazing low price of 300 000 FCFA. When the buyer goes to buy the machine, he is shown a sewing machine worth 300 000 FCFA and explains its deficiencies and then urges that the sewing machine worth 400 000 FCFA is far superior, and of much better quality and service. In view of the superior quality, the buyer concludes that the seller is right and decides to buy on his advice. The buyer discovers later that the seller has in stock more machines of the value of 400 000 FCFA and only three machines of the value of 300 000 FCFA. In such stock situation, the seller is trying to promote his sale of the costly machine which is more in stock than the machine of the lesser value which is few in the stock. This is a pattern of business practice which has been accepted and leads to difficult classification.

The term sale of goods by description according to Channell, J., in *Varley v. Whipp*[230] "*applies to all cases where the buyer has not seen the goods, but relying on the description alone*". False description renders the goods substantially different resulting to failure of consideration. The test to determine whether the goods conform to the description essentially relies on the representation given by the seller to the buyer, for the latter to rely on. In fact, this includes any statement which may be essential to the identity of the goods as contracted for as their quality, or fitness, place of origin or mode of packaging. Parties usually at least use some description or symbols to determine the characteristics relating to a particular product.

A trade description is defined so as to embrace a wide range of attributes of goods, including their composition, method of manufacture, performance, fitness for purpose, physical characteristics, and history. A statement that a ten year old car performs well should not be interpreted with the same rigour as the same statement made in relation to a two year old car.[231]

Another problem concerns clauses attempting to limit or exclude the seller's liability for misrepresentation for things done or said by an agent acting on his behalf. This question is more likely to arise, for example, where the seller's agent has given an opinion as to the suitability for use of the goods being sold, and the seller later claims that the agent had no authority to give such an opinion. Knowledge of the agent's authority and the notices of the clauses must be treated in accordance with ordinary principles of contract law. In most cases, the seller excludes his liability by shifting the burden on the other party-customer to make further inquiries on the representation of the agent.

A more troublesome area is when the contract is for the supply or sale of a specified identified product which is well-known in the market. Arguably, sale by description and hence warranty of merchantable quality should be confined to cases where description is essential to the identification of the product sold. In the absence of any kind of identification or description it will be difficult to recognise the product.

230 [1900] 1 Q.B. 513.

231 Section 2 Trade Descriptions Act 1968.

It is obvious that a description may form an essential part of a contract for the sale of a particular product which is identified by its trade name, by its gradation and other identifications. The description has to be treated as an express warranty of the product and the product will be known in the market by its name and trade mark, for example, a Philips radio will be identified by the trade mark or trade name to the well-known radio manufacturer Philips. When the goods are bought in the presence of the buyer, and the seller, and the buyer agrees to buy with the available information of the product, and he knows of the full description of the same, then no dispute or difference in principle arises. The dispute will arise in a case when the buyer goes to a hardware shop and asks for a bag of cement and the seller be fools him or even by mistake sells something else in a packet with a counterfeited trade mark. Here the buyer does not get what he wants because even though the seller had promised that the product in the package was bound to be cement and nothing else, and that the product must be reasonably fit for ordinary use to which generally cement is put. The basic question is what the buyer has ordered and the seller has promised to deliver.

It should be stressed that in some instances the buyer may have had time to examine the specific goods before purchase but not have knowledge of its hidden defects by accepting the goods. In this regard the seller's skill or judgment is necessary to reveal the fitness or merchantability of the product. The warranties must be assured by the seller on the basis of its superior knowledge concerning the qualities of the product which he is selling in the market. The buyer relies on the fact that the seller is not the manufacturer of the goods but a dealer in the selling of those goods and could disclose possible knowledge about the product. Therefore, there is reliance or complete guarantee could be expected impliedly or expressly by the seller. In other words, the seller holds the true facts of the goods he sells. The reliance in relation to the cause of action to constitute any form of misrepresentation may not be dependent upon the sale reliance or any kind of inducement to act on behalf of the seller may be enough to constitute a misrepresentation or fraud on behalf of the seller.[232] As a justification for this, the buyer buys a product from the seller. He is aware of the fact that the latter though not the maker of the goods, is nevertheless in the business of selling products of the kind to be purchased and whatever he buys is based on the advice and disclosed information which the seller provides to him. The buyer thinks that

[232] Rajendra Kumar Nayak, *Consumer Protection Law in India, An Eco-Legal Treatise on Consumer Justice*, Op. cit., p. 156.

the information provided to him is reliable and the seller has enough past experience in dealing in such goods.

The principle is a familiar one, and enters into everyday business of men. Common honesty is expected of businessmen in their dealings with one another, without any stipulation for it. The fact is that a seller must deliver goods in conformity with the terms of the contract of sale. Any relation to the seller's knowledge of the characteristics of the goods is not the assumption and he may not know the quality of the content of the products in its package. Then the question that arises is what does the buyer expect and the seller understands him to expect and to receive in a retail sale? Is it the label or package or name of the product that the seller is concerned to deliver to the buyer? It is not necessary only on the part of the seller to deliver what the buyer had ordered. The law implies that the seller in a contract of sale warrants his goods to be of conforming quality and fit for ordinary use even when they are sold in sealed containers. Under such circumstances, it would be absurd to permit a vendor to fulfill his contract by delivering a product of the kind contracted for, as it would be to permit him to fulfill it by delivering an article of a totally different kind, such as sugar instead of salt.

It is common that a buyer may buy a commodity from a seller who does not have a title or authority to sell the commodity. It could be in an event where the commodity may have been stolen or hired, etc. In that eventuality, the dispute will centre around the real owner. The action against such a fraudulent seller may be in many cases quite illusory because either he will not be traceable or may not be in possession of any assets. The Uniform Act in its Article 260 provides that the seller must warranty that the goods shall be free from any charge or encumbrance in favour of any third party.

The Sale of Goods Act, in section 12 (1), implies a non-acceptable condition in contracts of sale and the seller has the right to sell an item or in case of an agreement to sell, will have that right when property is to pass. In *Rowland v. Divall*,[233] an important English case where four months after the sale it was discovered that the car was stolen and the Court of Appeal held that the buyer was entitled to get back the full purchase price withoutany amount taken into account for use since there has been a total failure of consideration.

On the other hand, buyers have every right to agitate for the inconvenience caused to them due to the defective sale. In many cases title is defective; the real dispute will be between the seller or owner and the third party consumer. The basic rule of English law as stated before is that a person cannot give a

[233] [1923] K.B. 500.

better title to a commodity than what he has. It should be noted at the outset that goods must be '*sold*' by the apparent owner or agent. Consequently, if the property does not pass under the contract of sale concluded by that person, no title will be transmitted to the purchaser. This was the decision in *Shaw v. Commissioner of Police of the Metropolis*,[234]where the owner of a car gave possession of it to a rogue on unusual agency terms, taking a post-dated cheque for a substantial sum that was subsequently dishonoured. The rogue agreed to sell the car to the plaintiff purchaser from whom he received a banker's draft for payment in the agreed amount, the third party '*rightly*' conceding in the present case that the property in the car was not to pass until the rogue received payment under the draft. The rogue attempted to present the draft for payment to a bank where he had shortly before opened an account, but that bank declined to pay cash against the draft and the rogue disappeared. It was most unlikely that the rogue would be called in. The plaintiff's only loss, therefore, was the loss of bargain. It would have been extraordinary if the plaintiff had been held entitled to retain a valuable car for nothing, and the court recoiled from a result that would have offended its sense of justice.

The same thing applies in cases of obvious representation given that the seller has power to do so. Most cases on sale of goods concern apparent owners or agents of a class who sometimes deal on their own account and sometimes for an undisclosed or unnamed principal. This finds meaning in estoppel by representation.[235] The estoppel may take the form of a representation (words) or conduct. The starting point with estoppel by conduct is the proposition that the mere transfer of possession of goods or the indicia of title does not create an estoppel that the person in possession is the owner, for possession is consistent with a variety of transactions from bailment to outright sale, not all of which involve the transfer of the general property.[236]

Another most pertinent question which arises is that, who bears the loss if a commodity is lost or destroyed before it is delivered to the buyer? In Cameroon, the business community does not take such fraudulent practices and offences as seriously as other types of deviations. For example, a consumer buyer buys a washing machine which is stolen or destroyed by fire before the seller actually delivers same to the commercial buyer. The general rule is that if there is no special term or reference in the contract, in that eventuality risk

---

234 [1987] 3 All ER 405.

235 Djieufack Roland, *The Nature of Agency Relationship under the OHADA Uniform Act on General Commercial Law and Common Law: A Comparative Analysis*, Op. cit., p. 30.

236 Michael Bridge, *The Sale of Goods*, Op. cit., p. 420. see the case of *Farquarson Brfos. and Co. v. King and Co.* [1902] AC 325.

follows the property.[237] Consequently, it is an accepted phenomenon that it is only when the property in the goods must have transferred to the real owner, that the person is responsible for any kind of loss arising out of destruction or injury or deterioration of the goods, irrespective of whether delivery had been effected or not.

Another problem is that of misleading advertising of goods. In commercial agreements, it is common enough to advertise goods by flamboyant reports of their efficacy and to support these by promises of a more or less vague character if they fail to produce such results. Advertisements may relate to the packaging, labelling or trademarks of the goods in the markets. This seems to be detrimental to the practice of fair competition.[238] The buyer, induced to buy on the basis of such promises, may sue the seller for misrepresentation if he later finds out the true facts of things.

A difficulty with information requirement is the exact type of information that requires protection. In many instances, the law does not query certain types of information as when puffery is used. In Cameroon, a typical advertisement presents a washing soap—'*Savon May*', as having ''*quality, freshness and pleasure*''. What exactly does this represent to an average consumer when bought from a commercial buyer? Does it imply durability or a high performance level of product? This sort of information is not only meaningless; it is also designed to cajole the consumer to go for one brand of washing soap in lieu of another brand similar to it in all material particulars. In this sphere of things, the local consumers are left with the difficulty to estimate the gradiation of the quality of the goods within a class of similar products. Consequently, this seems to be an imperfect informational requirement defeating the very essence of a fair competition within a market place. It also pushes manufacturers to market low-quality goods at high prices.[239]

Furthermore, certain information on the products would seem misleading in informing the consumer about the usage of the goods. For instance, manufacturers (especially of complex goods like pharmaceuticals and machinery) are often required to adequately warn consumers of unforeseen hazards associated with the use of their products. In *Vacwell Engineering Ltd. v. B.D.H. Chemicals Ltd.*,[240] for instance, the defendants supplied some chemicals

237 Article 275 UAGCL.

238 René Njeufack, Temgwa, *La Protection de la Concurrence dans la CEMAC*, (Thèse de Doctorat, Faculté des Sciences Juridiques et Politiques, Université de Dschang 2005).

239 Alvine Longla Boma, Consumer Protection: A Cameroonian Protection, (2011) 8 (2) *The African Law Review*, pp. 47–62, p. 53.

240 [1971] 1 Q.B. 88.

in glass ampoules to the plaintiffs. The ampoules had as warning, *"harmful vapour"*. When the product came into contact with water, it exploded and killed a scientist working for the plaintiffs. The court ruled that the warning was inadequate and the defendants were liable.

The Categorisation of a Contract of Sale under the Uniform Act

The categorisation of a contract of sale under the OHADA Uniform Act on General Commercial Law is very restrictive. The preoccupation of the Act relates to contracts for the acquisition of goods for business purposes which can be identified as B2B contracts.B2B contracts refer to sales contracts between two professional sellers. It is often referred to as "*business to business contract*". On the other hand, business to consumer sales (B2C) contracts refer to sales contracts concluded between a professional seller and a consumer. The UAGCL does not cover B2C contracts but the expected outcome of a B2B contract under the UAGCL is to proceed to a B2C contract. In fact, the goods involved in a B2B transaction are the subject in a B2C contract. Consumers are the end-users of those goods.

Generally, the distinction B2B and B2C in sales contract is often found in civil law countries, whereas such a distinction does not exist at Common law.

Business to Business

Today, the Uniform Act is the applicable law in the OHADA Member States with regard to the B2B contract.[241] Under the Uniform Act, a B2B contract is conducted by a trader (*commerçant*).[242]

Generally, in order to determine whether a person or an entity is a trader, it is important to find out whether it carries out a particular transaction on a regular basis. Traders are considered to be those who engage in commerce as their usual professional activities.[243] Thus, traders in this sense could be anyone, a human being, a legal person including all commercial companies,

---

241 These contracts are regulated by all the Articles which fall under Book IV of the UAGCL.

242 Athanase Foko, *Le Statut du Commerçant dans l'espace OHADA*, (P.U.A., Collection Vade-Mecum, Yaoundé, 2005) p. 19–20; Jean-Marie Nyama, *Eléments de Droit des Affaires Cameroun-OHADA*, (Presse de l'UCAC, Collection Apprendre, Yaoundé 2002) p. 18–19.

243 Article 2 UAGCL. The language in this text is ambiguous to a Common law reader.

or a person governed by public law.[244] As concerns contracts of sale of goods, the Uniform Act has provided rules for natural persons and corporations who may exercise such sales contract.[245]

However, it would not be necessary here to elaborate on the broad categories of legal persons that may be involved in commercial activity under the Uniform Act on General Commercial Law.

Under the UAGCL, the seller and the buyer must be traders. In fact, the Uniform Act restricts the status of the parties that may be party to a contract of sale. The status of the traders, either a physical person[246] or a company,[247] must be acquired by registration in the Commercial Registry.[248]

The Uniform Act has listed out the different types of business transactions it intends to cover. These transactions include; the purchase of movable or immovable property for resale; banking, stock-exchange, currency exchange, brokerage, insurance, and transit transactions; contracts between traders for business purposes; the industrial exploitation of mines, quarries and any natural resource deposit and rental of movable property; manufacturing, transportation and telecommunication operations; the operations of trade middlemen such as commission, brokerage and agency, as well as middleman's operations relating to the purchase, underwriting, sale or rental of immovable property, businesses, shares in commercial companies or property development companies; a bill of exchange, a promissory note, and a warrant.[249] The list is not exhaustive.

The type of B2B contract with which we are concerned here is a contract between traders for business purposes what is here referred to as contract for sale of goods. The predominant feature of this type of contract is that it involves the selling of goods between the seller and commercial buyer. The purpose for which the goods are bought is of special relevance. This leads to the justification that the OHADA Uniform Sales law is entirely concerned

---

244 Article 1 Uniform Act. To a Common law lawyer, this notion seems strange since it has no specific legal connotation in the Common law system. A close idea to this in view to ease understanding may relate to public sector of the economy, that is public enterprises. Many public bodies are corporations in a similar sense to private companies operating in a private sector. Therefore, a public body is an organisation set up in the public interest to carry out a public service function. It may be a public enterprise of an administrative or commercial kind. They have an inherent power to protect the public interest.

245 Book IV UAGCL.

246 see Article 44 UAGCL.

247 see Article 46 UAGCL.

248 Book II UAGCL; Article 6 Uniform Act on Commercial Companies and Economic Interest Groups.

249 Articles 3–4 UAGCL.

with the reselling business of goods to non -consumers.[250] Again, undeniably, the idea connected with this issue of reselling of goods under the Uniform Act concerns expressly commercial buyers (acting as retailers or wholesalers), exercising trade for the purpose of the goods which are bought for resale and not for personal consumption.[251]

In a B2B contract under the Uniform Act, if a dispute arises that is not covered by the provisions of the Act, domestic law rules shall apply to resolve the dispute.[252] These include the commercial code, the civil code or other national sources of law in force in the OHADA Contracting States. In practice, the civil code and the commercial code are the primary reference in term of B2B and B2C contracts.[253]

Business to Consumer

The Uniform Act expressly excludes business to consumer (B2C) contracts that is, a contract between a professional trader and a consumer.[254] As aforesaid, what the Uniform Act covers is a contract between two professionals, that is, a seller and a commercial buyer, acting in their usual business activities.[255]

As a matter of distinction, the Uniform Act expressly provides that a consumer is different from a trader (*commerçant*). It follows that a consumer is a person who buys goods for personal, family or household use[256] and not for purposes of buying and selling.[257] Therefore a consumer is neither a commercial operator nor a person acting within his professional capacity. In short, the consumer is outside the provisions on contract of sale governed by the Uniform Act and consequently, B2C contracts are undoubtedly not covered by the UAGCL.[258]

Even though in the past there has been an attempt to put in place a draft OHADA Uniform Act on Consumer Law[259], it could be inferred that the law

---

250 Article 235 para.1 UAGCL.

251 Akuété Pedro Santos and Jean Yado Toé, *OHADA Droit Commercial Général*, Op. cit., p. 341.

252 Article 237 UAGCL.

253 For example, in Senegal, it is the Civil and Commercial Code of Obligations.

254 Article 235 (a) UAGCL.

255 Anne-Catherine Imhoff- Scheier, *Protection du Consommateur et Contrats Internationaux*, (Librairie de L'Université George & Cie S.A., Genève 2002) p. 76–95.

256 Article 235 (b) UAGCL.

257 Articles 1 and 3 UAGCL.

258 This is the same position under Article 2 of the CISG and the EC Directives on Unfair Contract Clause, see Official Journal, 1993 L–95/29–34, April 5, 1993.

259 Article 237 of the draft Uniform Act on Consumer Law.

governing B2C contracts in most OHADA Member countries are found in the ordinary law rules. The majority of these countries rely on Presidential decrees and ministerial orders rather than legislation to remedy the situation. Such countries include Cameroon,[260] Côte d'Ivoire[261] and Senegal.[262]

The reason for examining B2C contracts in the light of the OHADA Uniform Act on General Commercial Law, is because the usual transaction of the goods between the seller and the commercial buyer under the Act, is also by extension involves the reselling of those goods to the consumers who are the end-users of the goods. In fact, the very purpose for which the goods are bought under a sale contract is for resale with a view that of making profits. In other words, attention is given to consumers here because they buy directly from the ultimate commercial buyer, and consequently, what they can demand as quality matters to the commercial buyer. In another respect, the standard of determining resale here would be to distinguish between a retailer and a wholesaler. A retailer may normally sell to his usual customers, while a wholesaler usually has better access to different markets, for example, in different countries, and hence, to more or usual customers who may still be interested in the goods.[263]

The Legal Conception of Goods

'*Goods*' form the subject-matter of commercial sale contracts between the seller and the buyer. There is no definition of '*goods*' in the UAGCL. Nor is it possible to deduce the meaning of the term by analysing different language versions of the statute. The Uniform Act seems to embody a rather conservative concept of '*goods*', as it is considered both in legal writings and case law to apply basically to moveable tangible goods. Thus, according to most writers[264] intangible rights, such as patent rights, trademarks, copyrights, a quota of a limited liability company, as well as know-how, are not to be considered '*goods.*' The same is true for immovable property.

[260] see Cameroon, Law No. 90/031, August 10, 1990 Organising Commercial Activities in Cameroon.

[261] see Côte d'Ivoire, Article 1, Law No. 2011/012 of 6th May 2011 laying down the legal framework for Consumer Protection in Cameroon), see Article 6–3 du décret 95–29 du 30 janvier 1995.

[262] see Sénégal, Loi No. 94–63 du 22 aout 1994 sur le prix, la concurrence et le contentieux économique.

[263] Benjamin K. Leisinger, *Fundamental Breach: Considering Non-Conformity of the Goods*, (Sellier, European Law Publishers GmbH, Munchen 2007) p. 47.

[264] Akuété Pedro Santos and Jean Yado Toé, *OHADA Droit Commercial Général*, Op cit.

Under the Uniform Act, the notion of '*goods*' relates basically to movable and tangible objects. The notion of '*goods*' serves to quantify the main obligation of the seller contained in Article 250, which requires that ... the seller must deliver the '*goods*'... as required by the contract and this Uniform Act'. Therefore, to identify the ambit of the seller's conformance duty, it is relevant to identify the '*goods*' that are the object of this Uniform Act. The term '*goods*' is not defined in the Uniform Act it is the case under the CISG.[265] However, its meaning can be understood by reference to the Uniform Act's Scope and General Provisions.[266] In particular, Article 234 (a) provides that "*the provisions of this shall apply to contracts of sale goods*", whereas Articles 235 and 236 restrict the ambit of the Act, and by implication, the ambit of '*goods*'. By inference from the restrictions imposed by Article 236 UAGCL, it may be understood that the term '*goods*' is fairly not extensive, indeed, virtually not all-embracing. It clearly excludes to a greater extent non-physical items, such as electricity, negotiable instruments, company shares, which are technically '*things in action*' or incorporeal movables and so are excluded by the plain words of Article 236. Similarly, items of '*intellectual property*' such as copyright, patents and trade marks are not corporeal movables and so fall outside the definition, although of course goods may exist which embody these intellectual property rights discussed in chapter three.

The reason which may be advanced for dismissing intangible or immovable goods from the scope of the OHADA Uniform Act could be that even though these are assets available for trade, they can only be disposed of by way of trade or security and not possibly to be transferred physically to another party. The absolute interest in such types of goods may be disposed of outright or may be made the subject of security. Since by virtue of Article 250 para. 1 UAGCL, the main duty of the seller under the contract of sale is to deliver the goods to the buyer, what matters here is the physical transferability of the goods and not necessarily the transfer of a legitimate interest in the goods. The peculiar consideration here does not lie on the identification of the type of goods but rather on the physical segregation and ownership of it. Only in this situation is segregation both possible and necessary to identify the subject of the transfer obligation of the seller under the Uniform Act.

In modern commerce, a point not yet resolved by the OHADA Uniform Act on General Commercial Law, is whether computer software may constitute '*goods*' within the meaning of Article 234 para. 1. Software is normally

[265] Article 30.

[266] see Chapter1.

embedded in some physical form, such as disks, or as part of a package in which it is sold along with computer hardware, that is, computers or computer parts. Therefore, it could be considered as a tangible object capable of being transferred. This raises the question in trying to understand why such an item cannot be considered as a '*good*' under the Uniform Act. It could without any doubt be covered by the OHADA Uniform Act because such a good can be transferred to another person in a contract of sale in its physical form. Again, it is probable that a disk is physically defective due to a virus infection, for example. In this case, the seller should be liable for a physically defective car.

Under French law, goods are known as marchandises. This simply entails a collection of movable assets forming the subject-matter of a contract of sale. This is actually an element of fond de commerce. From this standpoint, there is one clear limit: this meaning will not include any form of immovable property in a contract of sale. Consequently, it can be inferred from the meaning of Article 235 para. 1 UAGCL that it limits the meaning of goods to movable property by its reference to *commerçants*. The meaning of '*sale of goods*' limits the very meaning of '*goods*'. Also, this would mean that no sale with a non-trader is of a '*good*'. The general approach that is adopted under the Uniform Act is to apply it to the *commerçant* and not to *non-commerçant*.

Purpose of the Goods

In cases where there is ambiguity on the content of the contract of sale binding the parties, the Uniform Act provides for different tools to interpret the contract accordingly.[267] In fact, according to Article 238 UAGCL, in order to determine the intent of the contracting parties, "*due consideration is to be given to all relevant circumstances*". Those relevant circumstances, other than those explicitly listed in Articles 238 and 239 UAGCL, that is, negotiations, include any practices which the parties have established themselves, known commercial conduct of the parties, or usages. Another relevant circumstance is the purpose for which the goods were purchased.[268]To give an example, if a well-known producer of foodstuffs for small children orders certain products and mentions that those products have to be "*completely harmless*", the circumstances sufficiently show that the products must be suitable for consumption by small children and that this feature is of primary importance.

---

[267] Articles 238–239 UAGCL.

[268] This method of interpretation is called 'in favor negoti'. The idea behind that interpretation is that the parties wanted a valid contract.

Consequently, on the basis of the above, the purpose for which the goods are bought is of special relevance in interpreting the contract of sale and when establishing whether there has been a breach of the contract under the OHADA Uniform Act. When a party is a commercial buyer under the UAGCL, the purpose for which the goods are usually bought is resale. This is evident by the fact that the Act does not govern consumer sales in the first place and also covers the commercial relationship only between professional business men: sellers and commercial buyers and not consumer buyers. It follows therefore that the seller will be liable for breaching Article 255 UAGCL simply because the commercial buyer is substantially deprived of what he is entitled to expect under the contract. Hence, in the case of a reseller, the goods must be fit for resale as this is what a commercial buyer under the Uniform Act expects under the contract. In cases where such resale is not possible, for example due to the fact that the goods are damaged, not packaged in a manner appropriate for resale, not labelled in a way mandatory for such kinds of goods in the intended market, or do not comply with applicable standards or other relevant public law regulations, there is a substantial deprivation of the expectation under the contract.[269]

Classification of Goods

The English Sale of Goods Act classifies goods into existing or future goods.[270] This classification is also acknowledged in the Civil Code. Moreover, there is another important classification which cuts across this one. This is the Common law distinction between specific and unascertained goods.[271]

Existing Goods

As a general rule of contract law, for an agreement to sell to be valid, the goods sold must exist. Existing goods may be either specific or unascertained. The main idea here is that the goods forming the subject-matter of the contract must be present and visible during the period of the formation of the contract. Existing or specific goods are goods identified and agreed upon at the time a contract of sale is made.[272] These are goods owned or in the seller's possession

---

[269] Donald Harris and Denis Tallon, Op. cit., pp. 45–46.

[270] see SGA 1979 s 5(1).

[271] This distinction is of greatest importance in connection with the passing of the property and risk in the contract of sale.

[272] see SGA 1893 s 62 (1).

before or at the execution of the contract.[273] Similarly, as per the civil code, the goods, subject- matter of the transaction, must exist at the time of the execution of the contract.[274]Again, the presumption rests on the fact that for such a dealing to amount to a contract, the goods must be physically present under the seller's keeping and control.

Even though the Uniform Act does not clearly define what is a '*good(s)*' under a contract of sale it covers, it would be understood to mean tangible goods necessary to conduct the business of sale of goods.[275]

The Uniform Act thus follows this position; it has already expressly identified the type of goods in a contract of sale it intends to cover [276] and by also excluding others which will not form a subject-matter of a sales contract.[277] This is another clear indication by inference of Article of 250 of the Uniform Act which considers the transfer obligation of the seller in a contract of sale of goods-meaning the existence of goods in their physical forms to the buyer together during the formation of the contract.[278] Equally, this warrants the seller not only to deliver the goods but to be sure of the conformity of the quality of the goods during the formation of the contract to the contract description. This goes to explain that the essential feature of a contract of sale under the Uniform Act by that goods must exist so that in case of any defect the seller should incur liability as laid down in the provisions relating to the seller's duty of conformity in the Uniform Act. Again, the seller's liability for defective goods should in principle depend upon the physical characteristics of the goods, which demands that the goods should be identifiable and be in the possession of the seller during the transfer obligation of the seller.

Future Goods

Generally, '*future goods*' include goods not yet in existence and goods in existence but not yet in the seller's possession. It is prudent to say that future goods are not existing goods nor specific goods. Goods to be manufactured are a typical example of future goods or any goods that can only be acquired by the buyer after the contract of sale has been executed.[279] In accordance with the Sale of Goods Act, these goods are existing or future goods and therefore

[273] see SGA 1893 s 5 (1).
[274] Akuété Pedro Santos and Jean YadoToé, *OHADA Droit Commercial Général*, Op. cit., p. 342.
[275] Ibid, p. 344.
[276] Article 234 para. 1 UAGCL.
[277] Article 236 UAGCL.
[278] Article 234.
[279] SGA 1893 s 5 (1).

can be the subject of a sales contract.[280]What may constitute future goods may be when a manufacturer agrees to build a specified piece of furniture, equipment or machine for sale to a customer.

Similarly, under the OHADA Uniform Act, these kinds of goods can form the subject-matter of sales contract especially when the goods must have been made available to the buyer to take delivery. One of the fundamental obligations of the seller is to hand over the goods to the buyer.[281] In reality, the buyer can only perform his payment obligation when the goods have been delivered to him in their physical state. Consequently, under the Uniform Act, it is possible for parties to enter into such an agreement for future goods. This position therefore follows the Common Law knowledge of specific and unascertained Goods.

Specific and Unascertained Goods

Specific goods or determined goods are goods identified and agreed on at the time a contract of sale is made, for example, a specific car.[282] Unascertained goods are those goods that, at the date of the contract, are not specific goods. An unascertained or generic goods, though not defined by the SGA has been referred to by scholars as goods to be manufactured which are necessarily future goods,[283] purely generic goods (10 kilos of rice) or an unidentified part of a specified whole (4 bottles of beer in a tray of 12 bottles of different beer).

However, a distinction should be drawn between existing and future goods. Existing goods may be either specific or unascertained; while future goods are nearly always unascertained and specific goods are almost always existing goods. For example, a contract to sell a fungible item possessed in bulk by a seller in his store room will involve goods that are both existing and unascertained.[284]

The Uniform Act does not make references to ascertained goods, which are nowhere defined. By inference, however, like in most legal systems, it is a fundamental requirement in the sales contract that unascertained goods must be ascertained or ascertainable upon performance of the contract. As a matter of interpretation under Civil law, the "*goods*" must either be determined or

---

280 SGA 1893 s 5 (1).

281 Article 262 et seq. of the Uniform Act. (Article 267 is more illustrative).

282 SGA 1979 s 61(1).

283 Roy Goode, *Commercial Law*, Op. cit., p. 210.

284 Michael Bridge, *The Sale of Goods*, Op. cit., p. 41

subject to be determined.[285] Hence, it must be specific stating, for instance, its specified name and if relevant with the quality, quantity or weight. But, if the contracting party fails to determine the quantity or quality of the goods, the civil code authorises a delivery of an average quality or quantity of the goods determined. The goods so identified are treated under the civil code as specific goods.[286]

Goods that are not Subject to a Contract of Sale

Generally, UAGCL have expressly excluded all goods being immovable or intangible.[287] In addition, the UAGCL makes express exclusion of sales to consumers,[288] sales after seizures, sales by order of the court, sales by auction,[289] sales of transferable securities, negotiable instruments, currency or foreign exchange[290] and transfer of debt as well as contracts in which a major part of the obligations of the party that delivers the goods shall be the supply of services as constituting contract of sale.[291]

The sale of vessel, aircraft, and ships, though within the definition of movable and tangible goods, remain subject to special rules applied to immovable goods.[292] Under the CISG, they have expressly been excluded.[293] However, the UAGCL treats these goods as intangible and immovable goods and excludes them as '*goods*' forming the subject- matter of a sale contract.[294]

Though the issue is rather less important, it may still be important for various reasons to distinguish a sale of goods contract from related contracts involving the transfer of goods.

In accordance with the UAGCL, intangible and immovable goods are excluded from sales contract. Put differently, these are goods that cannot be the subject matter of sales.[295]

---

[285] see Cameroon, Article 1129 CC; Côte d'Ivoire, Article 1129 CC; France, Article 1129 CC.
[286] see Cameroon, Article 1126 CC; Côte d'Ivoire1126; France, Article 1126 CC.
[287] Akuété Pedro Santos and Jean Yado Toé, *OHADA Droit Commercial Général*, Op. cit., p. 346.
[288] Article 235 (a) UAGCL.
[289] Article 236 (b) UAGCL.
[290] Article 236 (c) UAGCL.
[291] Article 235 (b) UAGCL.
[292] Akuété Pedro Santos and Jean Yado Toé, Op. cit., p. 345.
[293] see Article 2 (e) CISG.
[294] see Article 236 (e) UAGCL; Akuété Pedro Santos and Jean YadoToé, Op. cit., p. 345.
[295] see Articles 235–236 UAGCL; Articles 1–2 CISG.

Intangible Goods (stocks, shares, investment securities etc...)

Intangible goods as opposed to tangible goods are incorporate and immovable goods. Intangible goods are unascertained and not physically determinable.[296] To the UAGCL, intangible or incorporate goods are totally excluded from sales and thus stocks, shares, investment securities, currencies, foreign exchange and the transfer of debt are not considered by the UAGCL as subject matter of a sales contract.[297]

Intangible goods in law are personal rights which are often legally acquired. In the Civil Code, intangible goods may be right to acquire credit, or any intellectual property right.[298] As a general rule, they cannot be the subject matter in sale of goods contract.[299] Civil law helps us here in interpreting the UAGCL.

Similarly, under the SGA, the definition clearly excludes non-physical goods, such as company shares, which are technically "*things in action*" or incorporate movable and so are excluded by the plain words of the definition.[300] Similarly, items of "*intellectual property*" such as copyright, patents and trademarks are not "*personal chattels*" or corporeal movable, and therefore, fall outside the definition.[301] Obviously, there are goods that may exist and which embody these intellectual property rights.[302] The exclusion at Common law here is clearly more extensive than that under the Uniform Act. This comes in to fill in the gap in interpreting the UAGCL.

Also, there has been exclusion of anything that can only be claimed or enforced by action rather than by taking physical possession thereof.[303] In short, anything not physically identifiable, whether partly or wholly, falls directly outside the scope of the SGA. Thus chattels real, choses in action and money are not goods in accordance with the Sale of Goods Act.[304] However, the restriction on money can be lifted when the money becomes an antiquity.[305]

---

[296] Philippe Malaurie, Laurent Avnes & Phillippes Stoffel-Munck, *Les Obligations*, (3rd édition, Défrenois,Paris 2008) p. 115.

[297] see Article 236 (c) UAGCL; Article 2 (d) CISG.

[298] see Cameroon, Article 1689 CC; Côte d'Ivoire, Article 1689 CC; France, Article 1689 CC.

[299] Philippe Malaurie, Laurent Avnes & Phillippes Stoffel-Munck, Op. cit., p. 115.

[300] see SGA 1893 s 62 (1).

[301] P. S. Atiyah et al., Op. cit., p. 77.

[302] By contrast, for the purposes of the Law of Property Act 1925, "property" is defined so as to include intellectual property.

[303] Igweike K.I., Op. cit., p. 35.

[304] see SGA 1893 s 62 (1).

[305] E.E. Uvieghara, *Sales of Goods (and Hire Purchase) Law in Nigeria*, (Mathouse Press Ltd., ibadan 1996) pp. 4–5.

This is similar to the position of the UAGCL in its Article 236 (C) and (d).

Sale of Immovable

In line with the general principle of domestic law, scholars' interpretation of the UAGCL has established the general rule that immovable goods are excluded as subject matter in a sale of goods transaction.[306] The very notion of '*goods*' under the UAGCL as already explained excludes anything outside commerce that is, goods, not being the subject matter in a sale contract.[307] However, sale of immovable goods in domestic law is subject to a special type of contract.[308] Even though not expressly excluded from the sale contract under the UAGCL, immovable cannot be goods, in a sale contract.[309] The UAGCL therefore impliedly makes it clear that provisions relating to sale contracts govern only sale of movable and corporate goods.[310]

Electricity and Gas

Generally, electricity and gas are goods outside commerce in domestic law.[311] Moreover they are neither moveable nor tangible goods. Therefore, they cannot be treated as goods, subject-matter of a sales contract. In the UAGCL as it is the case under the CISG, electricity has expressly been excluded and the reason is that the contract for the supply of electricity often contains special conditions for which the CISG rules are unsuitable.[312] But it is pointed out that the sale of gas, oil or other energy sources are subject to a special condition of sale as regulated by the different statutes of domestic laws of each country.

As a contrast, it was held in the case of *Singer Co. Link Simulation Systems Div v. Baltimore Gas and Electricity Company*,[313] that electricity in an electricity company's distribution system was not a '*good within the meaning of Section 2-105 of the American Uniform Commercial Code (UCC). However, electricity is a 'good*' for the purposes of product liability because the term '*product*'

[306] see Articles 235–236 UAGCL; Articles 1–2 CISG.
[307] see Article 234 para. 1 UAGCL.
[308] Akuété Pedro Santos and Jean Yado Toé, Op. cit., p.346, 347.
[309] see Article 236 (C) UAGCL; Article 2 CISG.
[310] Akuété Pedro Santos & Jean Yado Toé, Op. cit., p. 347.
[311] see Cameroon, Article 1598 CC; Côte d'Ivoire, Article 1598 CC; France, Article 1598 CC.
[312] see Article 236 (f) UAGCL; Article 2 (f) CISG.
[313] 558 A 2d 419. Also, for an example of American example for liability for electricity, see *Ransome v. Winconsin Electric Power Co.* 275 NW 2d 641 (1979).

is defined by Article 2 of the Directive 99/34/EC on Liability for Defective Products as '*...includes electricity*'. This is a little wider than the definition of '*goods*' in Article 234 para. 1 UAGCL in that it includes things attached to or comprised in another product. Presumably, this means that there could be liability under the Directive for damage done by defective electrical failures of the electricity distribution system. This area may be said to have been excluded by the UAGCL because it is presumably within the province of product liability law.

As concerns gas, the UAGCL is silent. Arguably, it does not fall within the scope of the contract of sale of goods because it is considered as an immovable object. But as a matter of fact, gas could be regarded as '*goods*' under the UAGCL when it is in a fixed form loaded in a bottle, capable of being weighed and transported. In this case, the seller may incur any liability for the warranty of the quality, weight, packaging and labelling of the gas.

Companies

The sale of companies, a business generally known as "*fonds de commerce*" constitutes goods under the UAGCL.[314] Therefore, a business can be a subject matter of a sales contract. According to the UAGCL, the sale of a business are subject to the general rules of sales as well as specific provisions governing the doing of commercial activities.[315]

In some Common law countries, in line with the Statute of Frauds,[316] it has been held that shares in a stock company are not goods, wares or merchandise.[317] As an example, the Ghanaian Court of Appeal made it clear in the case of *Halaby v. Wireldu*[318] that, as per the SGA,[319] the sale of a business does not amount to a sales contract. The court in this case took the position that selling a business is selling more than mere goods. The judges in this case were unanimous that the sale of a business entails the sale of the goodwill and that of the whole business organisation.

The above decision should help us to understand that the concept of "*fonds de commerce*" which is a distinctive feature of French Commercial law. This embraces the various assets of a business, that is, assets in use, directed to the

314 see Articles 147 and 148 UAGCL.

315 see Article 147 UAGCL. This is the author's translation.

316 Statute of Fraud 1677 s 17.

317 *Humble v. Mitchell* [1839] 113 ER 392.

318 [1973] 2 GLR 249

319 Ghana SGA 1962.

common goal of serving the customers of the business. The clientele are thus fundamental to the fonds. However, the *fonds de commerce* is not simply a convenient collective term to describe the property of a business, in the way that '*assets*', for example, is in English. Made up of moveable assets, the f*onds de commerce* is itself regarded as a species of movable property. However, although many of its components may be tangible assets, it is itself treated as intangible property. The disposition of fonds will generally be considered to be a sale (*acte commercial*) and subject to special rules as it is the case under the UAGCL.

So, a Common law lawyer should understand that a sale of fonds under the UAGCL is a sale which falls under the meaning of its Articles 147 and 234. Arguably, the Civil law interpretation helps to eliminate any ambiguity, thus avoiding resort to *droit commun*.

Conclusion

Different systems of laws as it is the case with the Uniform Act on General Commercial Law have similar provisions on the formation of a contract of sale based on capacity, mutual assent, and consideration. Other rules such as, mistake and misrepresentation as it is the case under Common Law, are however, more credited as they are basically known by inference to ordinary contract law rules.

Moreover, the UAGCL has clearly identified the issue of consideration as primordial to the conclusion of a valid contract. Again, the rules relating to offer and acceptance are much more in line with the Civil law rather than Common law, and in many respects are much more closely attuned to commercial requirements.

It is clear that the UAGCL will not apply to immovable property, sale to consumers and e-commerce and it is doubtful whether it will apply to software licence agreements, sales of custom-made software and sales of electronic software. There are significant difficulties involved in determining the place of business or the place of conclusion of the contract of the parties, for the purposes of determining the applicability of the UAGCL. And the application of many of the provisions of the UAGCL to electronic contracts is problematic. It can therefore be concluded that the UAGCL is not well suited to regulate of electronic sale contracts.

It would, of course, be possible to amend the UAGCL so that it specifically addresses the problems associated with cross-border e-commerce transactions. This could be extended to the sales of immovable goods which are of very high value. Rather, the OHADA draftsmen should focus on establishing a stable legal and regulatory framework for e-commerce. In other words, they should put in place a specific Uniform Act on e-commerce. E-commerce is clearly a major issue in international trade. As more and more transactions are conducted electronically between parties in all the countries of the world, the need for clear, certain and easily applicable rules for international e-commerce contracts becomes more and more pressing. If not, it means that the significance of the OHADA treaty as a tool for the regulation of cross-border sale contracts is diminishing.

3

THE SELLER'S MATERIAL DUTY OF CONFORMITY

Introduction

In contracts of sale of goods governed by the Uniform Act, the duties of the seller are principally governed by the notion of '*conformity*'. This duty is expansive, imposing an absolute liability for defects that exist when risk passes to the seller, regardless of the fault.[320] The duties of parties to a contract of sale of goods are very important under commercial transactions. This is because parties most often show concern to what needs to be done and how it has to be done so as to achieve each other's interests in the transaction. It is not an over- statement to say that, the obligations of parties is the core of a contract of sale. Since the other requirements notably the contract formation and the terms of a contract shall have no significance if contractual parties fail to honour their respective obligations. So, the subsistence of a contract of sale largely depends on the full respect of duties by the parties concerned.

The Uniform Act, like its Common Law and the CISG counterparts, provides three obligations namely: delivery, conformity and guarantee as the seller's duties. Before the coming into force of OHADA, the seller had two principal obligations to wit, delivery of the goods and that the goods delivered are free from any encumbrances.

For the purpose of interpretation of "*conformity of goods*" in a sale contract, it is fundamental to know some particularities of domestic laws as compared

[320] Kristian Maley, 'The Limits to the Conformity of Goods in the United Nations Convention on Contacts for the International Sale of Goods (CISG)', (2009) 12 *International Trade & Business Law Review*, pp. 83–126, p. 83.

to international instruments in order to avoid a misleading interpretation.[321] For instance, rules under the UAGCL differ considerably from those of Common law and make more subtle distinctions between the different kinds of defects. Under the Civil Code[322] as well as under the UAGCL,[323] a hidden defect shall be distinguished from an apparent defect; in the SGA, conditions shall be distinguished from warranties.[324]

Common Law (warranties, conditions, innonimate terms)

Traditionally, the terms of a contract at Common law may be either a "*condition*" or "*warranty*".[325] A contractual term is any provision forming part of a contract of sale of goods. Each term gives rise to a contractual obligation, breach of which can give rise to litigation. Not all terms are stated expressly and some terms carry less legal weight as they are peripheral to the objectives of the contract.

The position of the law to enforce bargains freely is rational, to the extent to which the parties make their own law as to the terms of their agreement. It is unnecessary to look to the statutory rules as regulators of their conduct, and they will probably find the results more satisfactory than if such rules were thrust upon them.[326]

On the other hand, the law cannot always stand back and leave the parties with such an absolute discretion. In the first place, it takes two parties to make a bargain, and if the intention and undertakings of one party when making the contract do not coincide with those of the other, the court has to apply an objective test and ask what a reasonable person would have assumed was intended.

Secondly, the express terms of a contract are often confined to the barest essentials, that is the article purchased and the price, and the parties do not trouble to spell out further undertaking for example as to the quality of the goods or their fitness for the buyer's purpose.

So, where the court is not able to deduce the intention of the parties from their express declaration or language and other circumstances for

[321] Ingeborg Schwenzer, Commentary on the UN Convention on the International Sale of Goods (CISG), Op. cit., p. 570.

[322] Cameroon, Article 1641 CC; Côte d'Ivoire, Article 1641 CC.

[323] Article 231 UAGCL.

[324] SGA 1893 ss 14–15.

[325] P. S. Atiyah et al., *The Sale of Goods*, Op. cit., p. 87.

[326] Roy Goode, *Commercial Law*, Op. cit., p.72.

which negotiations were concluded, it may apply rules of law to impart into the contract certain implied terms, for instance, that the goods shall be of satisfactory quality. Such terms, designated contractual, are in truth prescribed by the law as gap-fillers on the basis of what the law considers ought properly to be implied into contracts of sale of goods in the absence of any other contrary agreement.

Condition

The terms of a contract are generally classified into conditions and warranties[327] which are either express or implied in the contract. A condition[328] is a major term of the contract breach of which is considered to go to the root of the contract so as to entitle the innocent party to treat the contract as discharged. On the other hand, the SGA, 1893 has not defined the term condition. But section 11(3) defines it indirectly as it stipulates that:

Whether a stipulation in a contract of sale is a condition a breach of which may give rise to a right to treat the contract as repudiated or a warranty, a breach of which may give rise to a claim for damages but not to a right to reject the goods and treat the contract as repudiated, depends in each case on the construction of the contract and a stipulation may be a condition though called a warranty in the contract.

It is clear from the above definitions that a condition is imperative as compared to a warranty because in the former, the contract is not only repudiatedbut discharged while in the latter, the contract will still be a going concern.

Statute may also declare a term or nature of a term to be a condition or warranty; for example the Sale of Goods Act, 1979, section 15A[329], provides that terms as to title, description, quality and sample (as described in the Act) are conditions save in certain defined circumstances.

Whether a term of a contract is a condition or a warranty depends in each case on the construction of the contract.[330] The SGA thus recognises that, a breach of a condition gives rise to the avoidance of the contract. In any event, it also entitles the innocent party to claim damages for loss sustained by the

---

[327] Not to be confused with a product warranty, this is always referred to as a 'guarantee' in law.

[328] see Roy Goode, *Commercial Law*, Op. cit., p. 279.

[329] As added by the Sale of Goods Act, 1994, section 4(1).

[330] *Suisse Atlantique Société D'Armement Maritime SA v. Rotterdam scheKolen Centrale* [1967] 1 AC 361.

breach.[331]

Considered as an obligation under the contract, a "*condition*" appears to have greater importance than a "*warranty*". Most often, it is so important that it goes to the root of the contract. Thus, it may be so essential that its non-performance may be considered as a substantial failure to perform the contract at all.[332]

Warranty

With regard to the term warranty, it is defined by the SGA as an agreement with reference to goods which is the subject of a contract of sales, but collateral to the main purpose of the contract.[333] Different to the position of a condition, a warranty must be performed as well. But it is not as vital as a condition. The breach of a warranty may give rise to a claim for damages but not the right to reject the goods and to treat the contract as repudiated.[334] However, Section 62 gives a complete definition of a warranty as it provides:

An agreement with reference to goods which are the subject matter of the contract, but collateral to the main purpose of such contract, the breach of which gives rise to a claim for damages but not to a right to reject the goods and treat the contract as repudiated.

Innonimate Terms

An intermediate or innominate term may be defined as a term of the contract which may or may not entitle the innocent party to treat himself as discharged, depending on the nature and consequences of the breach.

The Uniform Act does not expressly define the terms conditions and warranties. But Article 282 UAGCL indirectly defines the term condition in respect to its legal effect as:

The buyer may petition the competent court to terminate the contract:

(i) *where failure by the seller to comply with any of his obligations... constitutes an essential breach of the contract, or*

(ii) *In case of default in delivery, where the seller does not deliver the goods*

[331] SGA 1893, s11 (1) (b).
[332] SGA 1893, s11 (1) (b).
[333] SGA 1893, s 62.
[334] SGA 1893, s 11.

within the additional time limit that had been granted him...

Whether a term constitutes a condition, warranty or an intermediate term is definitely determined partially by the intention of the parties to the contract.[335] In the absence of an express intention, the law infers an intention or is guided by statute or judicial precedent as to the effect of a particular provision or type of provision.[336] A typical example may be found in international sales contracts, where terms that relate to the timing of the performance of obligations are, in the absence of evidence to a contrary intention, regarded as conditions.

Conditions implied by the Uniform Act

Implied conditions and warranties are not stated by the parties during negotiation or written in a contractual document but, nevertheless form part of a provision of the contract. Implied terms are classified under terms implied in fact and by law. These are terms which are implied into every contract of sale. These terms are implied by law into contracts to give them a minimum of business efficacy,[337] doubtless in accordance with the paramount intention of the parties to create a workable contractual agreement.[338] Some contracts of sale are very detailed; the parties have dealt with all or most eventualities. Whereas in others, the only thing that the parties must have dealt with is the goods to be sold and the price to be paid, the provisions of the above laws are designed by and large to fill in the gaps by implied terms and other rules so as to guarantee effective transactions of the parties.

These conditions are encapsulated into the concept of conformity in the Uniform Act, namely, quantity, quality, description, packaging, particular purpose and sample or model.[339] Basically, Article 255 states that:

The seller shall deliver the goods according to the quantity, quality, specification, and packaging provided for in the contract. Where the contract is silent, the seller shall deliver goods in conformity with the purposes for which goods of that nature are generally used, and the goods must match the

[335] P. S. Atiyahet al., *The Sale of Goods*, Op. cit., pp. 89–90.

[336] Ibid., pp. 93–94.

[337] The Moorcock, (1889) 14 PD 64; *Lister v. Romford Ice Co. Ltd.*, [1957] AC 555.

[338] Cf. Lord Tomlin in *Hillas & Co. Ltd. v. Arcos*, [1932] ALL ER 494, 499: 'The problem for a court of construction must always be so to balance matters that, without violation of essential principle, the dealings of men may so far as possible be treated as effective, and that the law may not incur the reproach of being the destroyer of bargains.'

[339] Paul-Gérard Pougoué, Jean Claude James, Yvette Rachel Kalieu, et al., in *Ecyclopedie du Droit OHADA*, Op. cit., p. 55; See sections 12–15 of the SGA, 1893, and Articles 35–44 of the CISG.

sample or model which was presented to the buyer by the seller. The seller also must deliver the goods that are packaged according to the usual method of packaging goods of the same nature or failing which, in a manner to ensure their conservation, and protection.[340]

The above implied conditions deserve careful treatment because of the protection which they now offer the buyer of goods who is almost invariably in a weaker position than the seller. These terms provide buyers with a healthier measure of protection against defective and sub-standard goods. This implies that if any of the parties breach any of the above provisions, such a breach shall be treated as a breach of condition and warranty. The terms (conditions and warranties) of a contract of sale of goods can be express or implied. These provisions have in fact moved the Common Law principle from caveat emptor to caveat venditor.[341]

The Notion and Nature of Conformity under the UAGCL

The UAGCL's notion of conformity is almost identical to that of the CISG.[342] No definition has been provided for this concept under the Uniform Act. In fact, conformity is a term with a variable content. The Uniform Act and the CISG have not given a definition to the term "*conformité*". In English Law, conformity is a noun derived from the verb to conform meaning "*agreeing with*".[343] From this, it becomes clear that the goods should agree with the terms of the contract for them to be in conformity (merchantable). In other words, the concept of conformity involves the difference that exists between the object agreed in the contract in conformity with that delivered.[344]

The term '*conformity*' is perceived in a double sense material and functional.[345] In the UAGCL, for the goods to conform, material conformity should be satisfied alongside with the functional conformity of the goods. This is the new approach adopted by the UAGCL as opposed to its former provision on this subject. Consequently, the seller has as obligation to deliver

340 This is the author's translation.

341 Walton H. Hamilton, The Ancient Maxim Caveat Emptor, (1931) 40 (8) *Yale Law Journal*, pp. 1133–1187.

342 Ibid., p. 291; Article 35 CISG.

343 Collin P.H., *Dictionary of Law*, (3rd edition, Peter Collin Publishing, 2000) p. 77.

344 Charles Mba-Owono, *Non-conformité et vices cachés dans la vente commerciale en droit Uniforme Africain*, Op. cit., p. 108.

345 see Kuate Tameghe S., *La vente Commercial dans l'Acte Uniform OHADA portant sur le Droit Commercial Général*, (Mémoire de D.E.A, Faculté des Sciences Juridiques et Politiques, Université de Dschang, 1999) p. 54.

the goods in conformity to the contract stipulation.[346]

Similar to the former French position applied in the OHADA States, goods conform to the contract when the material and functional (impropriété de la chose and vice caché)[347] parts of the goods are satisfatory, unless otherwise provided in the contract.[348] While the material conformity relates to the quality, quantity, specification and packaging of the goods,[349] the functional conformity relates to the fitness of the goods to the usual purpose or purposes for which goods of the same nature are used or to such particular purpose, expressly or impliedly made known by the buyer to the seller.[350] Material conformity therefore consists of four elements derived from the contract, quantity, quality, description, and packaging.

Arguably, the notion of conformity falls within the meaning of the subjective understanding of a defect.[351] In principle, examination of goods may be performed both during production and at the time the goods are put on sale. In both cases the purpose of examination is to establish whether the goods conform to the regulations or contractual provisions in order to uncover any defects in the goods.

Meaning of "Defectiveness"

What "*quality*" and "*defect*" exactly are, has often been a question of great confusion, especially in connection with express representation of goods.[352] Considering the legal implications of the seller's duty of conformity, the Uniform Act makes the seller liable for lack of conformity to deliver quality goods. Hence, the question of the relationship between these two concepts need to be understood. This basic concept has been modified under the UAGCL in several respects, imposing on the buyer the duty of giving notice of

---

[346] Charles Mba-Owono, Op. cit., p. 110 ; Kamwe Mouaffo Marie C., *L'obligation de Conformité dans la Vente Commerciale en OHADA*, Op. cit., pp. 6–8.

[347] Under French law, the element of hidden defect is dealt under sale law. This is actually in effect the purport of the text. see Paul-Gérard Pougoué, Jean Claude James, Yvette Rachel Kalieu, et al., in *Eycyclopedie du Droit OHADA*, Op. cit., p. 55; Francis Fourment, 'Défauts caches de la chose vendue que reste-t-il de l'action en garantie des vices caches?', (1997) 3 *Revue Trimestrielle de Droit Commercial et de Droit Economique*, pp. 416–419; Jacques Ghestin, *Conformité et Garanties dans la Vente* (produits mobiliers), (L.G.D.J., Paris 1993).

[348] Akuété Pedro Santos & Jean Yado Toé, Op. cit., pp. 392–393.

[349] Article255 para. 1 UAGCL.

[350] Charles Mba-Owono, Op. cit., pp. 110–116.

[351] Akuété Pedro Santos & Jean Yado Toé, Op. cit., p. 392–393; Ingeborg Schwenzer, *Commentary on the UN Convention on the International Sale of Goods* (CISG), Op. cit., p. 569.

[352] Ernst Rabel, Op. cit., p. 282.

the defects. Under French law, for the purpose of implied or legal guarantee, the defects must be unknown to the buyer, hidden defects (vice cachés). This is the content of Article 1641 of the Civil Code tending to require gravity of the vice when it merely diminishes the use, and involving redhibition as well as price reduction.

As section 3 (1) of the British Consumer Protection Act 1987 has it, there is a defect in a product "*if the safety of the product is not such as persons generally are entitled to expect; and for those purposes "safety"*, in relation to a product, shall include safety with respect to products comprised in that product and safety in the context of risks of damage to property, as well as in the context of risks of death or personal injury". Safety is defined as a relative notion, and this detracts considerably from the alleged strict liability basis scheme. In determining what persons generally are entitled to expect in relation to a product:

> *all the circumstances shall be taken into account, including- (a) the manner in which, and the purpose for which, the product has been marketed, its get-up, the use of any mark in relation to the product and any instructions for, or warning with respect to, doing or refraining from doing anything with or in relation to the product; (b) what might reasonably be expected to be done with or in relation to the product; (c) the time when the product was supplied by its producer to another; and nothing in this section shall require a defect to be inferred from the fact alone that safety of a product which is supplied after that time is greater than the safety of the product in question.*[353]

It is implicit in the foregoing that in determining the issue of defectiveness, approaches such as the cost-benefit analysis and the consumer expectation test will be relevant. Cost-benefit computations and the notion of reasonableness (for example, in determining what people are entitled to expect in section 3(2) (b) are factors used in deciding whether the defendant's conduct is negligent or fraudulent or not. It has to be said that the expression such as persons generally are entitled to expect", instead of "*a person*", covers, other users, and bystanders.[354] The interest of the individual does not sufficiently matter here but the public utility of the product. Safety is thus a factor in determining

[353] Section 3 (2) of the British Consumer Protection Act, 1987.

[354] This view has been better expressed at Common Law under the concept of neighbour principle as was propounded by Lord Esher M.R. in the case of *Heaven v. Pender* (1883) O.B. at page 503. In that case Atkin L.J. posed the question "*who then is my neighbor?*" and replied "*persons who are so closely and directly affected by acts, that I ought reasonably to have them in mind as being so affected when I am directing my mind to acts or omissions which are called in question*".

defectiveness, and in making that the quality, quantity, labelling, packaging and design of the product "*adequate*" or "*effective*"accompanied the product in question, are all relevant factors. This may be laudable, especially from the seller or manufacturer's perspective, in ascertaining the quality of the goods they offer in the markets.

In line with this reasoning, the Cameroonian case of *Egbe Maureen Arrey v. ELF Oil Cameroon,*[355] illustrates the above assertion. The facts are as follow:

> *The plaintiff a girl of 16, bought kerosene one morning from the ELF filing station owned by the ELF Oil Cameroon and managed by the first defendant—Ruth Eyong, in Kumba (Common law jurisdiction). When she poured the kerosene into her tanker and ignited the lamp there was an explosion that burnt the plaintiff to the second degree. Aggrieved, she sued. It was held, inter alia, that the provisions of Decree No. 77/528 of 23rd December 1977 regulating the storage and distribution of petroleum products in Cameroon, the defendant was liable for the tort of negligence. By virtue of section 14(2),all petroleum companies, of which ELF is one, must see to the regular supply of all their petrol stations. Again, by section 15 of the said Decree petroleum distribution Companies shall be bound to give Managers of petrol stations and their personnel sufficient training on the properties of the products they handle and on the safety measures to take. Section 17 stipulates that storage and distribution Companies shall be responsible for the quality of the products delivered for sale provided such responsibility shall devolve upon Managers if their negligence is established. By section 18 Managers must be present during the off-loading of products to see to it that safety measures are observed and carry out the control of the quality of the products.*[356]

The Uniform Act is also concerned with the issue of quality goods in regulating a contract of sale of goods between a seller and a commercial buyer. Particularly, as defined in the UAGCL, the material and the functional aspects of the goods determine the conformity of those goods.[357] In accordance with

---

355 Suit No. HCK/11/94 of 7th February, 1997 in the High Court of Meme Division, Kumba, Cameroon. This case is culled from Cameroon Common Law Report-1 CCLR (Quarterly Law), Liberty Publications, Part 6, (2000), pp. 21–56.

356 A Ministerial Order signed by the Minister of Mines, Water Resources and Energy enforcing the Prime Minister's Decree No. 95/135/PM of 3rd March, 1995 governing the control of petroleum products in Cameroon has added more bite to the existing 1977 Decree. It gives priority to the protection of the customer's interest and places the buyer in a better position to claim compensation for damage caused by any poor quality petroleum product purchased.

357 Article 255 para. 1 UAGCL.

their respective provisions,[358] the seller is required to deliver the goods in conformity to the quantity, quality, specification and packaging as provided by the contract.[359] Hence, the conformity of the goods is first and foremost condition on the "*material*" specification of the goods in the contract.[360]This is similar to the concept of subjective defect as known under the United Nations Convention on Contracts for the International Sale of Goods 1980 (CISG).[361]

Quantity

Under the UAGCL, unless otherwise agreed, the seller must deliver the goods to the buyer in the exact quantity stipulated in the contract of sale. Failure of the seller to comply with this obligation amounts to a breach of contract.[362] It may sometimes occur that the seller delivers a quantity below or beyond the one requested. In this case, the buyer is entitled to the remedy available that is to allow him either to take delivery or to refuse delivery of the excessive or reduced quantity.[363] One way or the other, if the buyer accepts delivery, the seller is entitled to the payment at the contract price.[364] It should be noted that the exactness of quantity requirement is not emphasized in Article 255 of the UAGCL. Basically, this is guided by the contract stipulation of the parties.

The above is similar to contracts relating to the marketing of agricultural produce in Cameroon because they affect a large number of people (cash crop cultivators) and also because of their multiplier effect on the economy. The disappearance of the National Produce Marketing Board whose chief aim was to serve as a buyer and export seller of cocoa and coffee from farmers and also to fix and maintain prices through a fund for stabilizing prices has led to unfairness in business. Currently, licensed buying agents and co-operatives operate in this business and contract with farmers most of the time who for the most part carry out unfair practices as against farmers.[365] Before the

[358] Article 255 para.1 UAGCL.

[359] Ibid.

[360] Ingeborg Schwenzer, Commentary on the UN Convention on the International Sale of Goods (CISG), Op. cit., p. 571.

[361] Article 35 CISG.

[362] Article 255 para. 1 UAGCL; Article 35 (1) CISG.

[363] Article 262 UAGCL; Article 52 (2) CISG.

[364] Ibid.

[365] Many licensed agents today set up sham companies designed to defraud ignorant farmers. In *Ndefru v. George Fonkwo and Others*, Appeal No. BCA/7/76 of March 4th 1977, Bamenda, the appellant's company was described by the judge as founded on "*actual dishonesty*", designed to take advantage of farmers.

harvesting season, buyers enter into contracts with producers for the supply of specific quantities of the produce with a stipulation that if the producer does not supply that quantity, he will be subject to the payment of a fine. In the case of *Muyuka Co-operative Ltd. v. Otto Enow,*[366] the Buea High Court held that such a term was a penalty and was invalid. This decision is surely right (much depending on the weather), as it would be unfair to impose a fine on a producer who does not produce the amount stipulated in the contract. A second widespread malpractice consists in wrongly grading the quality of the produce by buyers. Because many farmers are uncertain about the buyer's good faith, they accept lower prices for ungraded produce.[367]

The response to the question whether the goods conform to the contract is determined by their description in the contract. The majority of Common law countries in Africa have taken a similar approach as can be seen in a number of cases.[368] Thus, if the seller delivers less than the contractual quantity of the goods required, the buyer has the option either to accept the goods and pay for them at the contract rate or reject them.[369] Where the quantity is above what was contracted for, the buyer may decide either to accept the goods as provided by the contract and reject the additional goods or he may accept the whole quantity and pay for the additional goods at the contract rate; otherwise he may totally reject the whole delivery.[370] Where the goods delivered are mixed with goods of a different description than that included in the contract, the buyer may either accept only the goods stated in the contract and reject the rest or rejects the whole delivery.[371] Statutory provisions related to quantity of the goods are subject to any usage of trade, special agreement, or course of dealing between the contracting parties.[372] In Africa, Common law jurisdictions follow the position of English courts, *mutandis mutandis*, from statutes to case law. In *Acros Ltd v. EA Ronaasen & Son,*[373] the buyer ordered ½

---

[366] Suit No. HCSW/3/76, High Court Buea (1976), (unreported).

[367] see *Patrick Ateghang v. Ntamadam C.P.M.S. Ltd.* Suit No. HCB/13/76 of February 2nd 1977, Bamenda High Court, (unreported).

[368] *Vigers Brothers v. Anderson Brothers* (1901) 1 K.B. 608; *Robert Monroe & Co Ltd. v. Meyer* (1930) 2.K.B 312; *Pinnock Bros. v. Lewis & Peat Ltd.* (1923) 1 K.B 690; These cases are used acrosscourts in Africa of common jurisdiction in determining the issue related to sale by description.

[369] SGA 1893 s 30 (1).The leading case observes here is *Shipton v. Casson* (1876) 5B. & C 378 at 382–3.

[370] SGA 1893 s 30 (2).

[371] SGA 1893s 30 (3). This position was respectively observed in the following cases applied as precedents in courts in Africa: *Hart v. Mills* (1846) 15 M. & W. 85; *Levy v. Green* (1857) 8 E. & B. 575 at 587.

[372] SGA 1893 s 30 (4).

[373] [1933] AC 470, 479–80.

inch thick timber staves as clearly indicated in the contract but got delivered a consignment with 9/16 inch thick staves. In the House of Lord, Lord Atkin pointed out that half an inch does not mean about an inch. Based on this fact, it was held that the contract terms on quantity were to be strictly followed.

In the Tanzanian case of *Wimble, Sons & co. v. Lilico & Sons*[374], the seller agreed to deliver a cotton cake containing 40% protein and 30 % oil but, instead, delivered a cotton cake containing 32.28% protein and 7.78 % oil. In the same line, a contract for the supply of medium sized onions was turned to have at delivery 6–7% of the goods found undersized as decided in *Rapall v. K.L. Take Ltd.*[375] Thus, as a failure from the seller to deliver the right quantity of the goods entitles the buyer to reject the goods on the ground of incorrect quantity,[376] the above cases were held to have breached the statutory requirement of a sale by description.[377]

Quality

Disputes involving the delivery of non-conforming goods may turn on any number of points covered by the provision describing the seller's obligation under the UAGCL. Among these, two particularly important and complex sets of issues deserve further analysis both because they are resolved differently by different laws, and because they go to the heart of the conformity problem.[378] These are the questions of how to define the quality standard to which goods are to adhere, and what constitutes effective notice of nonconformity.

According to the Sale of Goods Act, the term "*quality*" refers to the state and condition of the goods.[379] At common law, there has sometimes been confusion between identification and quality. But in practice, it appears difficult to apply that distinction as similar facts resulting from the breach of quality[380] can also result in the breach of description or identity.[381] These provisions are exclusive at some points.[382] As a matter of fact, it may appear

[374] [1922] 38 T.L.R. 296.

[375] [1958] 2 Lloyds, Rep. 469.

[376] A.G. Guest, *Benjamin's Sale of Goods*, (7th edition, Sweet & Maxwell, London 2006) p. 432.

[377] SGA 1893 s 13.

[378] Adam M. Giuliano, Non-conformity in the Sale of Goods between the United States and China: The New Chinese Contract Law, the Uniform Commercial Code, and the Convention on Contracts for the International Sale of Goods, (2006) 18 Florida *Journal of International Law*, 331, p. 7.

[379] SGA 1893 s 62.

[380] As per the breach of the implied condition as to the quality or fitness; SGA 1893 s 14.

[381] As per the breach of sale by description; SGA 1893 s 13.

[382] A. G. G Guest, *Benjamin's Sale of Goods*, Op. cit., p. 545.

that a statement of quality regarding the goods form the descriptive part of the goods and vice versa.[383]

In *Toépfer v. Continental Grain Co*,[384] the word "*hard*" leading to the quality in the contract based on the "*Hard Amber Durum Wheat*" for the purpose of the finality of a certificate as to quality was, without doubt, also meant to describe the goods. Sometimes, the goods can be of such a poor quality that its description will rather amount to identify the goods than the quality of those goods. However, the quality of the goods per se can be determined differently. Under the SGA, there is no implied warranty or condition that goods supplied under the contract shall be of merchantable quality. So, the famous doctrine of *caveat emptor* (let the buyer beware) remains the guiding principle under certain circumstances where the provision of the Act applied.[385]As a principle of legal relationship between buyer and seller, *caveat emptor* is today a pretty sick horse. It is not so much the buyer as it is the manufacturer and the seller who must beware, on penalty of fine, or imprisonment.

Under the UAGCL, the notions of '*'quality*' and '*'specification*" have also been a question as to the limit of one to the other.[386]The issue has generally been raised under Civil law. Hence, the notions of "*quality*" and "*specification*"[387] have been defined by French case law[388] and scholars[389] as different, but complementary. The reason is that the extent of the seller's duty depends largely upon the meaning to be attached to the description of the goods. The view is that the OHADA Uniform Act does not provide any statutory meaning to the term '*quality*' which has little substantive content. This tends to be meaningless in practice. It does not only suffice for the buyer to be entitled to goods which conform to quality. What is the buyer entitled to expect under the contract? As an answer to this, the buyer is entitled to expect goods of satisfactory quality, that is, goods suitable for reasonable usage. This reasonable use will certainly be for commercial re-saleability and not for personal consumption. This is the purport of Article 255 para. 2 of the UAGCL. The present provision provides that the quality of the goods includes their state and condition and that among other things which are aspects of the

---

[383] As per the argument advanced in the leading case of *Ashington Piggeries Ltd v. Chrisptopher Hill Ltd.*

[384] [1974] 1 Llyod'd Rep. 11.

[385] SGA 1893 s 14..

[386] Akuété Pedro Santos & Jean Yado Toe, OHADA Droit Commercial Général, op cit,. p. 394.

[387] Article 255 UAGCL.

[388] Civ., 4 déc. 1871., D.P., 1873, 5, 201.

[389] Gerard Cornu, *Vocabulaire Juridique*, (8 édition, Presses Universitaires de France, 1987) p. 756 ; Akuété Pedro Santos & Jean Yado Toé, Op. cit., p. 394.

quality of goods for the purpose for which goods of the kind in question are commonly used. Clearly, fitness for all purposes is an important, indeed, an essential-element in the concept of conformity and remains important under the current provision of the Uniform Act.

> *The question arises whether the new provision of the Uniform Act clears up one major ambiguity which had previously been mentioned. Many goods are used for the variety of purposes, and the goods supplied under the contract may be fit for some of these purposes while unfit for others. The solution to this simply lies on the particular specification contained in a contract of sale provided by the buyer to the seller. This specification may among other things relate to the particular purpose the buyer wanted the goods for (in which case he could sue under Article 255 para. 1 UAGCL) as the goods are not of only merchantable but not satisfactory quality as well.*

The UAGCL provides that, in the absence of agreement by the parties to the contrary, goods must be "*fit for the purposes for which goods of the same description would ordinarily be used.*"[390] This standard "*does not require that the goods be perfect or flawless, unless perfection is required for the goods to fulfill their ordinary purpose.*" On the other hand, what the standard positively requires regarding the minimum acceptable quality level remains unresolved. At least three standards have received support both from various courts and in academic literature; the standards are merchantable, average, and reasonable quality.[391] The first two standards depend upon standards and practices external to the parties, while the third standard relates in part to party expectations.[392]

Therefore, the phrase '*conformity*' as used under the OHADA Uniform Act on General Commercial Law must be re-phrased to suit modern commerce and to avoid a litany of unnecessary cases to flood our law courts.[393] This is so because reference to conformity does not adequately convey the concept of acceptable quality of the goods. A particular attention should be given to the point under the UAGCL rather that making it cumbersome for one

---

390 Article 255 para. 2 UAGCL.

391 Adam M. Giuliano, *Nonconformity in the Sale of Goods between the United States and China: The New Chinese Contract Law, the Uniform Commercial Code, and the Convention on Contracts for the International Sale of Goods*, Op. cit., p. 7

392 P. S. Atiyah, *The Sale of Goods*, Op. cit., p.162.

393 see the case of *Brasseries du Cameroun v. Ambe John*, Appeal No. BCA/8/93 24th March 1994, (unreported), in *Juridis Périodique*, (1997) No. 29–40 (A commentary by Ewang Sone Andy on the topic: 'Brewed Drinks unfit for Human Consumption can Warrant an Action for Product Liability'.

to clearly understand the seller's duty under the phrase "*conformity*". This is merely an umbrella term which embodies lots of issues to be deciphered by one's ingenuity. Regard should be paid to the change of this nomenclature introduced in England by the Sale and Supply of Goods Act 1994.[394] Goods are considered to be of satisfactory quality "*if they meet the standard that a reasonable person would regard as satisfactory, taking account of any description of the goods, the price (if relevant) and all the other relevant circumstances*". This suggests that description goes to the essence of what it is that the seller has contracted to sell, so that whether goods are of satisfactory quality almost inevitably depends on the description under which they are sold.[395]

In the opinion of P. S. Atiyah and others,[396] "*all vague statements or definitions of the standard of quality required by the law, it may be suggested, are somewhat vacuous in practice*". This suggests that these either concepts of satisfactory quality or conformity, should be replaced with concepts of reasonableness which have substantial flexibility. Most such standards give little guidance as to what kind of defects or damage will render goods not to conform (unsatisfactory under the SGA), and is unhelpful in the practical application of the law. All rely heavily upon the test of reasonableness: would a reasonable buyer, if he knew the condition of the goods, accept them under the contract? Would a reasonable buyer expect goods of that condition to be delivered under that sort of contract? Tests which depend so heavily upon standard of reasonableness tend to be somewhat circular in practice. In fact, the buyer is entitled to expect goods of quality and reasonable for that use. The "*reasonable*" use is the sort of the use which a reasonable buyer would intend.

If the quality of the goods has been accurately determined in the contract, the seller must comply with the detail criteria as strictly stated in the agreement and deliver the goods in conformity with the contract. Thus, goods delivered with a quality higher or lower than the contract stipulation will not satisfy the requirement of conformity. By way of explanation, if the buyer requires Senegalese black wood to make a dugout, but received Kenyan black wood for a dugout, there will be defect on the quality of the goods. The notion of quality is therefore not restricted to the physical characteristics of the goods. It rather relates to some other aspects of quality which as a matter of importance concerns the fitness for the purpose(s) for which the commercial buyer under the UAGCL intends to use them.

---

394 Atiyah et al., *The Sale of Goods*, Op. cit., p. 162; See Sections 14 (2) & 15 (2).

395 Roy Goode, *Commercial Law*, Op. cit., pp. 304–305.

396 Ibid., p. 174.

To illustrate this point, in *Andrews Brothers (Bournemouth), Ltd. v. Singer & Co.*[397] a clause exempted all implied warranties and all liabilities. The court held that the clause did not apply to an express term describing the article in the contract and therefore, it did not exempt the seller from liability for delivering an article of a different description. Also, in *Henry Kendall & Sons v. William Lillico& Sons*,[398] there was a clause excluding liability for "*latent defects*" of goods. The House of Lords held that the expression "*latent defects*" only covered liability for the quality of the goods and did not exclude liability for breach of Section 14 (1) of the Sale of Goods Act 1893, that is, fitness for purpose.

Moreover, in addition to the quality of the goods, the usage intended for the goods shall also be satisfied otherwise, as conformity will not have been met. If the contract makes it clear that the Senegalese black wood is meant to build a dugout, if the wood, with the exact quality criteria as required has been provided, but turns out not to be able to make a dugout, there will be defect on conformity. Otherwise if the contract does not specify a precise usage, the ordinary usage of goods of the same kind must be satisfied.[399]

As a general rule under the UAGCL, conformity on the quality of the goods will be met if and only if their usage criterion is also satisfied.[400] It follows therefore that as a consequence of the non-conformity of the material or functional quality or of both, there is a breach of contract.[401] Moreover, if essential, such a breach may give rise to a fundamental breach,[402] enabling the buyer to avoid the contract[403] or to claim for substitute delivery.[404]

While uniformity does not exist regarding the applicable standard, the scope of this ambiguity is smaller than it appears. In most cases, the question of fitness for an ordinary purpose represents a factual question; in a given dispute, each of the possible quality standards might lead to the same conclusion. In the breach, the best guide to the appropriate quality level should be the parties' expectations.[405]For example, it has been argued that:

397 (1934) 1 K.B. 17.

398 1911 A.C. 394.

399 Akuété Pedro Santos & Jean Yado Toé, *OHADA Droit Commercial Général*, Op. cit., p. 394–395.

400 Article 255 para. 2 UAGCL; As per the position in Cameroon, Article 1641 CC; Côte d'Ivoire, Article 1641 CC; France, Article 1641 CC.

401 Article 281 UAGCL; Article 45 CISG.

402 Article 281 UAGCL.

403 Article 283–284 UAGCL.

404 Article 283 UAGCL.

405 Adam M. Giuliano, Op. cit, p. 7.

> *the role of Article 255 para. 2 UAGCL is to aid in construing the agreement of the parties. The question is this: What was the parties' understanding of the contract provision describing the goods? More precisely (in the language of Article 255 para.2 UAGCL), what was their understanding of the 'purposes for which goods of the same description would ordinarily be used'? Since the problem concerns fitness for the 'ordinary' use of goods described in the contract, serious misunderstandings should be infrequent.*

The view that the parties' agreement cabins the quality standard under Article 255 para. 2 UAGCL gains support both from the Article's text, which references the goods' "*description.*" This is in line with the Secretariat Commentary to the draft CISG. The Secretariat Commentary balances such party expectations with a kind of reasonableness level commensurate with the ordinary use of the good, stating that "*the standard of quality which is implied from the contract must be ascertained in the light of the normal expectations of persons buying goods of this contract description.*"

Aspects of Quality

It is worth at this point to examine some characteristics of quality in relation to the goods sold by the seller with a view to ascertain the extent of the seller's liability. Should the seller be expected to always sell goods of first or best quality? What does the buyer expect of the quality of the goods?

Liability for Commercial Seller's for Used-Goods

One still remains baffled about whether strict liability should apply to commercial sellers of used products. The expectation of the quality of these types of goods is usually not the same as those newly sold. From the text of the Uniform Act, liability will be imposed on "*regular*" used-goods sellers. Several field trips by this researcher reveal that used -product markets are common in the major cities of Cameroon in particular and in some African Countries.[406] These goods vary from cars, household equipments to consumer goods. It is an everyday practice now to find a line-up of stores in the towns of Douala and Yaoundé operating in this trade. Observation from this experience reveals that consumers prefer and expect diminished quality and safety from used goods. This is because of the cheap prices of these goods and their accessibility.

[406] Specifically in some major markets in Abidjan-Côte d'Ivoire and Accra-Ghana, where research was conducted by the author.

Another justification for this is the public habits and beliefs in certain virtues of these goods which have stood their test of time. Such a picture is typical in Cameroon where from socio-economic and psychological perspectives, the purchasing public still hold tight to the buying of some goods of old reputable trade mark or taste. For example, certain brand of goods such as, shoes like "*pierre cadin*" from France, "*clarks*" from England are still believed to be durable even sold as a used goods.

It is staggering to note that the magnitude of this problem of used-goods may be better appreciated by bearing in mind the potential problem of product dumping from countries with stricter safety laws.[407] It is not inconceivable for unscrupulous foreign manufacturers to target the markets of developing countries with products that fail to meet the safety requirements in terms of their period of expiration or damaged in their packing of their home countries by charging low prices for these products in the importing country. Banned or used-goods are dumped in developing countries through a number of ways. This is effected either simply through changing the product's name or slightly altering the chemical formula or subtracting an inert part of the good. Sometimes the parts of the banned product are then exported separately to the country, where a recombining facility is set up for assembly. It could be said that most of the components of these products are used to build up a "*new*" structure. These unscrupulous businessmen would close down their plants at home and establish more lucrative business in third world countries, where they can freely manipulate with products of low quality and sell those whose shelf-lives have expired in their home countries.

Used-product sellers serve an essential role in fostering an efficient economy. They help businesses and government's recycle, which reduces the cost and environmental impact of the manufacture of new products. By broadening the reasonable standard of care of used-product sellers, courts should recognise these legitimate social benefits of a used-product market.[408] However, expanded absolute liability should force used-product sellers to act as virtual insurers for any kind of latent defect.[409] This justification should also rest on the fact that it should be maintained because of breach of the duty of conformity as well as misrepresentation in accordance with rules under the

---

[407] Samgena D. Galega, *Strict Liability for Defective Products in Cameron? Some Illuminating Lessons from Abroad*, Op. cit., p. 253.

[408] J. Paul Peter & Jerry C. Olson, *Consumer Behavior and Marketing Strategy*, (2nd edition, Homewood 1998) pp. 496–510.

[409] Antonio J. Senagore, The Benefits of Limiting Strict Liability for Used-Product Sellers, (2010) 30 *Northern Illinois University Law Review*, pp. 1–34, p. 3.

Uniform Act. Regard should not be given to the new or old state of the goods but much attention should be paid to the economic value incurred by the commercial buyer and the personal injury to the consumer. By imposing this liability on the used-product sellers, it will force manufacturers or suppliers of goods to discard these types of businessmen from their business line because they are unable to guarantee the safety and quality of those goods, which may tend to drive similar products of the same brand from the market. Thus, such a measure would make manufacturers to stand behind the goods they sell in the marketplace. As a mate of public policy, to properly price all goods according to their true social and economic costs, liability must apply to all sellers of defective goods. Otherwise, one defective product seller would cost relatively less, thereby encouraging consumers to buy the cheaper, more dangerous products. A used- product seller is no different from a new-product seller, and therefore, is liable for the sale of defective goods. Only the imposition of liability on sellers' of used-goods can effectively deter the spread of defective goods.

Consequently, making a market incentive to sell quality used-products would increase the likelihood that consumers will buy quality used-products from retail or wholesale buyers who may stand as proxy for product quality.[410] A seller interested in providing its customers with a product whose performance will fully meet both the needs of the latter might be able to establish a system of quality control that would eliminate the risk that deficient products would be delivered to customers. An alternative approach would be to use less stringent quality control practices and compensate buyers for defects in products when buyers discern those defects and complain about them.[411]

Consider the current market in which goods are sold honestly or dishonestly; quality may be represented, or it may be misrepresented. The commercial buyer's problem, of course, is to identify quality. The presence of sellers in the local markets who are willing to offer inferior goods tends to drive the market of some specific brand of goods out of existence—as is the case of bad automobiles or building construction materials. In *Scholastic Nsaiboti v. Felix Ezeafor*, [412] the appellant bought a second—hand car from the respondent car dealer who made oral representations to the effect that the car was one year old and in good working condition. The oral representation

[410] Ibid., p. 12.

[411] Arthur Best & Alan R. Andreasen, Consumer Response to Unsatisfactory Purchase: A Survey of Perceiving Defects, Voicing Complaints, and Obtaining Redress, (1977) 11 *Law & Society*, pp. 701–742, p. 703.

[412] Appeal No. BCA/6/73 of March 1974, Bamenda Court of Appeal (unreported).

proved to be untrue since the car was indeed older than that and was utterly defective. The contract, however, contained a term that excluded liability for any defect in the car and for any implied express warranty. The Bamenda Court of Appeal (in the English speaking region of Cameroon), in upholding the High Court's decision in favour of the respondent had this to say: "*Restricted though the doctrine of 'caveat emptor' might be in its application to contracts of sale, its application in the buying of a second-hand car is in my opinion most fitting since there is very little by way of guarantee that the seller could give as to fitness*"—per Rupert Thomas J., President of the Court.

If the above case shows the courts in dealing with the problem of the sale of second-hand cars, the case of *Michael Ebwe v. Hubert Euverte*[413] accentuates this point. On the 13th of May 1974, at about 10 a.m., the plaintiff entered into a written contract with the defendant for the sale of a second-hand car. The contractual document stipulated that the buyer has been given the opportunity of examining the car and that any liability whatsoever was excluded. The plaintiff signed the contractual document allegedly without reading it. On the same day the sale took place, at about 5 p.m., the car's engine stalled and the car was, on later examination, proved to be considerably defective. The plaintiff tried to get a refund of the contract price from the defendant on the grounds that the car was worthless, whereupon he brought this action. The Buea High Court held that the terms of the contract were clear and wholly unambiguous and that in the absence of fraud, they were binding on the parties.

It is this possibility that represents the major costs of dishonesty - for dishonest dealings tend to drive honest business dealings of some goods out of the market. There may be potential buyers of good quality products and there may be potential sellers of such products in the appropriate price range; however, the presence of dishonest sellers who wish to pawn bad wares as good wares tends to drive out the legitimate business, causing scarcity. The cost of dishonesty, therefore, lies not only in the amount by which the buyer is cheated; the cost also must include the loss incurred from reducing the size of the legitimate business of certain goods out of the market.

It is now a common practice in most countries that before goods are sold nationally or internationally, they should meet the minimum ethical and quality requirements. This could be inspected by the contracting parties as they deem it necessary for this to be conducted by a third party.

---

413 Suit No. HCSW/24, 1974, Buea High Court (unreported).

Ethical values

Ethical value is an emerging applied subject. It is still currently debated as it is applied to all aspects of business conduct and getting much more relevant to the conduct of individuals, the manufacturing of goods and the quality standard of goods. In general, ethical values appear to contribute to the development of legal systems in which contracts are enforced fairly, and bribery and corruption are less prevalent, enabling business entities to have equal access to legal process and equal protection under the law.

At the international level for instance, private initiatives such as the principles laid down in the United Nations Global Compact covering issues such as human rights, labour, environment and anti-corruption aim to assist its member countries to comply with the international standards required on these issues.

Although these are not yet much debated to prevent corruption, promote fair dealing and ensure a standard ethical quality. In Africa, ethical values are known and recognised in international and national sales contracts as one of the solutions to the defective goods as from the manufacturing process.

An ethical value contractual clause can be express or implied in the contract of sale. When implied, they may be inferred from trade and usages. Whether expressly or impliedly in a contract of sale, they become part of the contract and may be enforced, or their violation sanctioned, in the same way as with any other term. However, the parties agree on their express stipulation.[414]

In Cameroon, for instance, most organised professions and some trade associations have codes of practice which set out ethical behaviour for members in their dealings with their clientele.[415] For instance, the company in charge of distributing energy[416] makes available to the public an e-mail address for anyone who wants to make a complaint and report any violations of their Code of Business Conduct and Ethics. A clause ensuring ethical code and conduct is prior inserted in the contract signed by customers, before they benefit from the services of the company. This is done in favour of its customers.

In line with the above example, it should be pointed out that in most, if not all contracts of sale of goods, including both domestic or international

[414] Peter H. Schlectreim, Non-Material Damages—Recovery under the CISG?, (2007) Reproduced with permission of 19 *Pace International Law Review*, p. 89–102, point III (3). see <http://www.cisg.law.pace.edu/cisg/biblio/schlechtriem15.html>.

[415] These would include the code of ethics of manufacturers' associations, association of advertising practitioners, etc.

[416] This para-statal company is known as AES-SONEL.

contracts, the quality of goods is not restricted to its physical appearance; it also has to comply with any other requirements which are prescribed by the law or subject to trade usages.[417] Therefore, if the origin of the goods prescribes an ethical value standard at production, the standard will definitely constitute a quality of the goods. As a result, the requirement of quality will not be met if the goods produced do not meet with the ethical standard as required.

It is not easy to determine the non-conformity of goods based on the ethical value.[418] Such difficulty is due to the hidden character of its nature and also to the fact that it does not physically influence the physical feature of the goods. If the party in breach does not in good faith disclose or cure the defect, an expert may sometimes be required to determine the breach.

Unless the parties have agreed otherwise, failure from the seller to deliver the goods in conformity with the ethical standards amounts to a breach of contract. In particular, this is so when the seller is required to deliver goods that are fit for the purpose for which goods of that nature are commonly used or when a special request on an ethic (such as health and environmental considerations) was made known to the seller.[419] The buyer's remedy will be rights of redress[420] and claim for damages.[421]

Good Manufacturing Practice (GMP)

"*Good Manufacturing Practice*" (GMP) is a well-known policy whose purpose is to ensure appropriate manufacturing process that would impact on the quality of the products. Good Manufacturing Practice is a series of policies that are binding on the contracting business parties, (if agreed) requiring food producers, manufacturers, pharmaceutical companies[422] and packagers of drugs to ensure that their products are safe, pure and totally effective. These measures are meant to ensure a level of quality approach to manufacturers of goods in order to protect consumers from contracting for non-effective and dangerous goods. In summary, Good Manufacturing Practice plays a paramount role of quality assurance that ensure that products are consistently produced and controlled with respect to the quality standards appropriate for their intended use and their legal requirements or simply as required by

[417] Article 238–239 UAGCL.
[418] Article 255 para. 1 UAGCL.
[419] Article 255 para. 2 UAGCL.
[420] Article 282–283 UAGCL.
[421] Article 292–293 UAGCL.
[422] Definition of GMP by the World Health Organisation and as per GMP institute found at <http//www.gmp1st.com/index.htm> (Last accessed on 24/10/09).

the marketing board or in some countries by the government department in charge of regulating trade and commerce.

Sometimes, GMP is referred to as CGMP meaning "*Current Good Manufacturing Practice*". This is a mere call to producers, packagers or manufacturers to update their machineries, systems or equipment in order to comply with the new technology, capacity and /or legal requirement in their business. Generally, GMP's guidelines provide regulation on products such as foods, drugs, blood, and medical devices. Accordingly, countries do update their cGMP regulations for local companies to act in accordance with the legislation. In medicine, for instance, the Medicines Control Council (MCC) is a statutory body that was established in terms of the medicines and related substances control to oversee the regulation of medicines in South Africa.[423] The role of the MCC is to ensure that all medicines that are sold and used in South Africa are safe, therapeutically effective and consistently meet acceptable standards of quality. A series of other cGMP are enforced in South Africa[424] and across the region[425] to ensure the effectiveness of the quality of the goods. Particularly in Cameroon, the "*Standard and Quality Agency (ANOR)*" and the "*Service de la Normalisation*" in the Ministry of Trade and Commerce have the mandate to ensure the quality of products in meeting required standards.[426]At the continental level, the "*African Organisation for Standardisation*" also acts as a watchdog in ensuring quality goods and services in its member States. In Nigeria, the National Agency for Food and Drug Administration and Control (NAFDAC),[427] has the burden to regulate, control and process the quality standards for Foods, Drugs, Cosmetics, Medical

---

[423] South Africa, Known as MCC; Act 101 of 1965.

[424] (South Africa), Regulations relating to the fortification of Foodstuffs, under the Foodstuffs, Cosmetics and Disinfectants Act 1972, Act No. 54; Regulations Governing Microbiological Standards for Foodstuff and related Matters, promulgated under the notice No. R. 692 of 16th May 1997 and amended recently under the notice No. R. 490 of 8th June 2001; Regulations Relating to Milk and Dairy Products, promulgated under the notice No. R. 1555 of 21st November 1997 and amended under the notice No. R. 489 of 8th June 2001; Regulations under the Food, Drugs and Disinfectants Act (Act No. 13 of 1929).

[425] Kenya, Pharmacy and Poisons Act 1972; Kenya, Tanzania; Uganda, Fish and Fishery Products (AFIPEK 2000) for handling and processing fish and fishery products in Kenya; (Sénégal), Arrêté Ministériel No. 2004–099 du 14 janvier portant application des bonnes pratiques de fabrication des médicaments, Loi No. 54–418 du 15 Avril 1954 portant code de la santé Publique dans les Territoires d'Outre Mer.

[426] This Ministry was created by Decree No. 88/204 of 5th February 1988, re-organising the Ministry of Commerce. This full text of this Ministerial Decree is found in Juridis Périodique, No. 5, 1991, p. 13. These structures were created with the objective of protecting consumers and ensuring the technical supervision of the quality and quantity of goods through inspection.

[427] Decree No. 15 of 1993 as amended by Decree No. 20 of 1999.

Devices, Chemicals, Detergents and packaged water imported, manufactured locally and distributed in Nigeria.

Even though not prescribed by the UAGCL, such a business practice or measure is relevant in enhancing the warranty of quality of goods which flood the markets. This goes a long way to improve on the quality of goods which the end- users would obtain from commercial buyers.A respect of such a measure is left to the wishes of the parties in a contract of sale or could be implied from the trade usage of specific goods in a given branch of business. This is the very meaning of Articles 237 and 239 of the UAGCL.

Description

In the leading Ashingston Piggeries case,[428] Lord Diplock pointed out that:

> *The "description" by which unascertained goods are sold is, in my view, confined to those words in the contract which were intended by the parties to identify the kind of goods which were to be supplied... Objectively, on the issue of sale by description and in line with the contractual requirements, the word description is to be understood as the identity of the goods in question.*[429]

The test used by Lord Diplock was to determine whether the goods will be rejected because they are different in kind than those agreed upon. It follows that the determining factor in sale by description is "*identification*".[430] Therefore, it is only on rare occasion that sale other than sale by description get to come into existence.[431] Particularly, certain sale contracts of specific goods may not be sale by description when the statement on the goods is immaterial to the identity of the goods or where without statement the buyer buys the goods as they are. But under the SGA, specific goods require to be identified.[432]

Also, identification through description has been extended to unascertained goods and future goods. From these, it can be inferred in practice across the region that even buying in a self- service shop may be sale by description, provided the goods are either described on the shelf or they are labelled as

---

[428] [1972] AC at 503–4.

[429] A. G. Guest, Benjamin's Sale of Goods, Op. cit., p. 541.

[430] Sale by Description lies in SGA 1893 s 13.

[431] A.G. Guest, *Benjamin's Sale of Goods*, Op. cit., p. 541.

[432] SGA 1893 s 62.

relating to their contract.[433] But it should be pointed out that it is not because the sale by description has taken place that all statements in relation to the goods are necessarily descriptive.

In *Harrison v. Knowles and Foster*[434]the court considered a "*mere representation*" the statements about the deadweight capacity of two ships. Thus, the statement has to be descriptive enough and not only qualitative or any other statement that can be used to avoid liability. However, it was held in *Varley v. Whipp*[435]that there is sale by description even when the purchaser has not seen the goods but relies on the description provided.[436]

As explained above, under the UAGCL, the seller's contractual duty is to deliver quality goods in consonance to the specification made by the buyer. In fact, quality and specification are complementary under the Uniform Act. But in particular, there are instances where contractual agreements on sale determine with accuracy technical specifications expected on the goods; or when the parties define the label of a good to be manufactured following the exact ingredients or products to be used. Most often, the seller is required to deliver the goods identical to a sample made available to the buyer.

In case there is a failure to comply with the description of the goods (exact technical specification, model or sample) the result will be non-conformity of the goods.[437] Non-conformity as such sometimes leads to a delivery of goods totally different from those agreed upon. An example may be the delivery of bean instead of green beans.

Furthermore, if the required specifications or description of the goods have been met, the goods must also conform to the required usage determined on the contract. If it was not determined in the contract, the goods must satisfy the common usage of goods of the same kind. Thus, non-conformity of this requirement amounts to a breach[438] and the remedies available to the buyer are similar to those under non-conformity as to quality of the goods.[439]

Implied warranties of quality in connection with sales or contract for the sale of goods by description must usually be proved by evidence of facts which

433 A. G. Guest, Benjamin's Sale of Goods, Op. cit., p. 541; Franck L. Mechem, Implied and Oral warranties and the Parol Evidence Rule, (1928) 12 (3) *Minnesota Law Review*, pp. 209–224, p. 215.

434 [1918] 1.K.B 608.

435 [1900] 1 K.B. 513 at 516

436 Samuel Williston, Liability for Honest Misrepresentation, (1911) 24(6) *Harvard Law Review*, pp. 417–439, p. 435–437; George Gleason Bogert, Express Warranties in Sales of Goods, (1923–1924), 33 *Yale Law Journal* 14, pp. 14–32, p. 19.

437 Article 255 para. 1 UAGCL.

438 Ibid.

439 Articles 282, 288, 283 UAGCL.

are extrinsic to the contract. Again, when the sale or contract of sale is oral, any evidence necessary to show the presence of those elements is ordinarily admissible. At least, it is never excluded because it is parol evidence. The case of *Joseph Neba Abongwa v. Ngang Cletus Achu*[440] is illustrative:

The parties to this suit who are business men all reside in Bamenda. On the 8th day of August 1996, the respondent expressed an intention to hire the appellant's two compressor tubes. Verbally, the parties agreed that the respondent would first test the tubes and if efficient, the parties would enter into a formal hiring contract. The respondent detained the tubes for 511 days and despite entreaties by the appellant, the respondent failed to return the tubes. The appellant sued the respondent at the Mezam High Court, for breach of contract and conversion. His claim for breach of contract was dismissed but nothing was said of conversion. The court however awarded the appellant the sum of 250.000 francs as general damages for negligence. Being grossly dissatisfied, the appellant appealed to the North West Court of Appeal and succeeded. It was held that there was also an existence of a contract between the parties; a contract comprises every description of an agreement, obligation of legal tie that is, some engagement which the parties contemplate shall have a legal binding effect whereby one party binds himself or becomes bound expressly or impliedly to another to pay a sum of money or to obligation and agreement. The learned trial judge observed that there was inference as to the fact that the parties had actually agreed to enter into a legal obligation containing certain stipulations.

Packaging

Considering the huge amount and nature of goods being transported for sale, packaging is essential. Its purpose is not only to protect the product but also to present it to the buyer in an attractive manner for commercial use. However, it is important to point out that packaging requirements are closely connected with delivery of the goods so that any packaging defects may become quality defects of the goods, particularly when the goods are sold in the so-called "*original packaging*" without which they would not be put on sale. In the latter case, the packaging is "*incorporated*" into the goods and is considered to be an integral part of the very goods to be delivered.

---

[440] Appeal No. BCA/58/98–99 of 12th October 2000 in the North West Court of Appeal, Bamenda, Cameroon. This case is culled from Cameroon Common Law Report-1 CCLR (Quarterly Law), Liberty Publications, (2001) Part 7, pp. 107–112.

Packaging is defined as all containers or other products used for the containment of goods, for facilitating their transport or their presentation to the public.[441] Packaging is an important contractual duty under the Uniform Act. It applies to sales and entails secondary packaging destined for commerce and by extension to household. The UAGCL thereby channels all liability on the seller directly concerned with the packaged product. The scope of the UAGCL is limited here because it concerns sellers and commercial buyers;[442] —persons responsible for putting the said packaged products in the market for the first time, are under the duty to ensure the disposal of the packaging of their products with the view to their marketing. Essentially, this duty is mostly important to the commercial buyer because he has an obligation to resell the products to the end- user in the conditions in which he bought them. This plays an essential role as the end-user expects to receive quality packaged goods directly from the commercial buyer because it is the end- user who separates finally the packaging from the product in order to use or consume the said products.

Packaging, just like quality and quantity of the goods constitutes in the UAGCL a fundamental element in the conformity definition of the goods.[443] Therefore, if the parties' contract determined the safety and packaging type, the seller must conform to them. If the contract is silent on this requirement, the parties must refer to trade and usage in the context of their contractual agreement.[444] This is true of goods in general, the use and quality of the packaging may also be regulated and the seller is bound to observe those regulations, as the products in question cannot otherwise be put on sale. In this regard, standards and usages may also exist and the seller (or the buyer, depending on who is to provide the packaging according to the contract), is bound to observe those standards and usages. Non-conformity on the packaging amounts to a breach of contract.[445] This was illustrated in the case of *Société MADELACH c/ Société FEREX*,[446] where the Court of Appeal in Douala pronounced the cancellation of a contract of sale between the two companies due to a lack of conformity of delivery of goods in a packaging

---

441 Caroline London and Michael Llamas, Packaging Laws in France and Germany (1994) 6 (1) *Journal of Environmental Law*, p. 1–3; Catherine Elliot & Frances Quinn, *Contract Law*, (4th edition, Longman, 2003) p. 360; as per the Sale of Goods Act's definition on goods; see SGA 1893 s 62 (1).

442 As oppose to manufacturers.

443 Akuété Pedros & Jean Yado Toé, *OHADA Droit Commercial Général*, Op. cit., p. 395.

444 Article 238 para. 2 UAGCL.

445 Article 255 para. 1 UAGCL.

446 Cour d'Appel du Littoral, ArretNo. 88/C du 15 Mai 1995

of 100 kg instead of 50 kg as requested by the plaintiff. In international sale contract, parties to the contract are also must respect rules on packaging in conformity with the environmental regulations in the buyer's country or place of location.

This has been the concern within the CEMAC[447] contracting states regulating the export-trade of goods within the sub-region.[448]As part of its common commercial policy, and in order to ensure equal treatment in all member States for goods exported within the CEMAC region, thereby enabling all goods in circulation within the community to benefit equally from the free movement provisions, the CEMAC Treaty provided for the introduction of the common custom tariff. This measure is to the effect that all products imported within the Community must be adequately packaged and certified with a label on the packaged marked with the CEMAC initials.[449] This certification which permits circulation must carry the following information: address of the supplier, the country of origin of the production of the product, the name of the producer, and information regarding the product (weight, etc). The operation is governed by the CEMAC regulations.[450]Under the common custom tariff, goods are classified according to a common nomenclature, and are subject to common Community rules as to value, packaging and origin.[451]

Again, the question of packaging is dealt with more strictly under the UAGCL when it involves cross-border sales, owing to long journeys. In respect of defect in the packaging, the seller and the buyer[452] may be liable; even though this may also be the responsibility of the forwarding agent of the carrier. Packaging is a component of quality. Unless otherwise agreed by the contracting parties, the packaging must be of a quality permitting safe transportation of the goods to their destination. An important role is played

[447] This French acroynm stands for "*Communauté Economique et Monétaire de l'Afrique Centrale*". In English as "*Economic and Monetary Community of Central Africa*".

[448] Edouard Gnimpieba Tonnang, Le Nouveau Régime Juridique des Exportations entre les Etats d'Afrique Centrale : Entre Reformes Laborieuses et Influences Européennes, (2006) 857, *Penant*, pp. 433–483, p. 443–445.

[449] It is commonly written in French as: FABRIQUE AU (pays d'origine) VENTE EN CEMAC.

[450] Article 9 de l'annexe a l'acte No. 7/93–UDEAC–566–SE1 du 21 Juin 1993 portant révision du TEC et fixant les modalités d'application du TPG en UDEAC; Règlement No. 17/99/ UEAC–CM–639 portant règlement des pratiques commerciales anticoncurrentielles, 1999; Règlement No. 4/99/ UEAC–CM–639 portant règlement des pratiques étatiques affectant le commerce entre Etats membres, 1999.

[451] Until recent, it is now a governmental practice to find alcoholic drinks such as wine to be affixed a labeling with the CEMAC initials on each bottle to be sold within Cameroon. This is a measure to certify the quality and origin of this product. This is carried out at the Douala seaport supervised by customer officials.

[452] Article 269 UAGCL

here by the seller under the UAGCL in that he is bound to deliver goods in conformity to the order.[453] In fact, the goods shall conform to the contract if packaged in the manner usual for such goods to be transported.[454]

In certain trade branches, especially in connection with transportation of the goods by sea, the usual means of packaging is containerisation, that is, packaging of the goods in containers. Such means of packaging ease the movement of goods from ship to truck or rail and, hence, substantially reduced so -called "port costs and loading time.[455] If such usage with regard to packaging by the seller can be established, the goods have to be packed in containers in order to comply with Article 255 UAGCL. It is a general practice in export-import trade in Cameroon that it is the duty of a packer[456] or importer[457] of a relevant package to ensure that when a group of packages is marked with the same nominal quantity they conform to the average system. A packer or importer of packages must also ensure that the container included in the package is marked with a statement of quantity, either of weight or volume, or with his name and address or a mark which enables his name and address to be readily ascertained by an inspector (custom officer).

Again, unless special provisions on packaging are contained in the contract, the seller is required to forward the goods as packaged in his country, taking into account possible trans-shipment under proper and usual handling of the goods in order to prevent damage to or deterioration of the goods before they reach their destination as stated in the contract or otherwise.[458] However, the prevalent idea is that sale of the goods not conforming to the packaging by the seller does not prevent the buyer from having recourse to the remedies recognised in cases of lack of conformity of packaging.[459] The buyer may refuse delivery, request for replacement of the goods (may be by demanding a re-packaging of the goods), and payment of damages.[460]

---

453 Article 250 UAGCL.

454 This is the purport of Article 255 UAGCL.

455 Benjamin K. Leisiger, *Fundamental Breach Considering Non-Conformity of the Goods*, Op. cit., p. 23.

456 'Packer' means, in relation to a package, the person who placed in the container includedin the package the goods included in it.

457 Importer' means, in relation to a package, the person by whom or on whose behalf the package is entered for customs purposes on importation.

458 Article 252 UAGCL. On a procedural level, an important Prime Ministerial Decree was passed in 2008 to lay down the modalities for the packaging for importation, sale and distribution of retail and wholesale veterinary drugs in Cameroon: Decret No. 2008/2009/PM du 5 Decembre 2008 fixant les conditions de fabrication, de conditionnement, d'importation, de vente de distribution en gros et au detail des medicaments veterinaires.

459 This could be deduced from the wordings of Article 272 UAGCL.

460 Articles 288 and 292 UAGCL.

At common law, the seller is under the obligation to deliver the goods in a "*deliverable state*"; to some authors, "*deliverable state*" refers to packaging.[461] Hence, to the SGA, goods are in a deliverable state when they are in such a way that the buyer would, under the contract, be bound to take delivery of them.[462] The term "*deliverable state*" was further defined in the case of *Underwood Ltd v. Burgh Castle Brick & Cement Syndicate*[463]where Banks LJ stated that deliverable state "*... depends on the actual state of the goods at the date of the contract in which they are to be delivered...*" in accordance with the terms of the contract.[464] In other words, the packaging of the goods shall therefore be in conformity with the contract as agreed upon.

Conclusion

The concept of conformity in the OHADA Uniform Act on General Commercial Law is an umbrella term which encompasses lots of factors which the commercial buyer may expect. As the seller's material duty of conformity is concerned, it is common for the quality or description of the goods to incorporate some elements that are not part of the physical characteristics of the goods, and such requirements such as Good Manufacturing Practices and ethical values should not be seen as novel. The prime consideration in determining the seller's material obligation of conformity under the Uniform Act is the intention of the parties. The text of the Uniform Act emphasises the need to uphold the intention of the parties, including with reference to any trade usages. The notion of ethical and GMP practices will often form part of these trade usages. Article 255 of the Act is structured to create rules of interpretation rather than that of binding force.

---

461 Ewoud Hondius, Sales (PELS), (Study Group on a European Civil Code Principles of European Law, 2008, p.199; Atiyah et al., *The Sale of Goods*, Op. cit., p. 324.

462 SGA 1893 s 62 (4).

463 [1928] 1 K.B. 343.

464 Igweike K.I., *Sales of Goods, Nigerian Commercial Law*, Op. cit., p. 107.

4

THE SELLER'S FUNCTIONAL DUTY OF CONFORMITY

Introduction

The seller's functional duty of conformity relates to the purpose for which the goods are bought under a sale of goods contract. Contracts of sale of goods are by far the most common type of contracts and often concern goods of a utilitarian nature, with a clearly defined purpose. People enter into agreements every day to buy goods for diverse reasons. The most obvious, of course, is to enjoy and acquire their ownership and use them for different purposes. But in commercial transactions, traders, not being consumers, are not interested in the goods as such, but rather only in the profit that can be made, or the loss that can be avoided, by reselling them

Most, if not all, contracts, whether they involve goods, real property or services, are necessarily economic activities. This is a fortiori true of the types of contracts which are the subject of this thesis: contract of sale of manufactured goods purchased for resale. Importantly, the utility of this type of goods for the commercial buyer may be influenced by a broad range of factors. The buyer may choose particular goods based on their brand or reputation. The environmental and social practices involved in their manufacture may also be significant. Moreover, consumer tastes and preferences matter to the commercial buyer, as the brand of goods in the markets may rise and fall.

In order to make sense of the web of facts in which these complex transactions occur, it is appropriate that a thesis of this kind examines the fitness of the goods to the usual purpose or purposes for which goods of the same description would ordinarily be used; or are fit for any specific purpose,[465] expressly or impliedly made known by the buyer to the seller.[466]

One way the seller may satisfy the functional conformity,[467] is for him to be able to guarantee that there are no hidden defects on the goods.[468] However, it should be pointed out that a hidden defect, as provided in the Uniform Act, does not only relate to the non-conformity but also to the usage as well.[469] By way of explanation, the goods should conform to the general usage of such goods or the particular usage for which the buyer expressly intended the goods for. It is implicit from this standpoint that the implied duties of the seller, codified in Article 255 UAGCL, is no less than the seller's implied promise that the goods sold in a contract of sale will work. It is a warranty that arises as an operation of law, as opposed to an affirmative promise from the seller, and simply codifies the parties' expectations of what the goods are for and what they will accomplish for the buyer.[470] In this way, the implied condition of "*conformity*" in the Uniform Act gives teeth to the bargain and provides the buyer with one method for forcing the seller to behave properly. As the seller is a merchant, the buyer's expectation is to benefit from the promise that the goods will fulfill the basic function of their ordinary purpose.

It follows that unlike the Civil Code, the notion of conformity is broader as it combines both the obligation of conformity of the goods and that of hidden defect,[471] whereby the expected particular usage of the goods in question is required.[472]

This position makes the UAGCL unique, that is, intermediary between the French Civil code and the CISG's position.[473] Moreover, the seller's guarantee as per the UAGCL is another seller's duty, which does not only cover claims of non-conformity from the buyer against the seller but also the sub-buyer against the manufacturer or an intermediary seller, in order to cover a hidden defect affecting the goods sold, as from the time they were

465 Article 255 para. 1 and 2 UAGCL.

466 Charles Mba-Owono, *Non-Conformité et Vice Cachés dans la Vente Commerciale en Droit Uniformé Africain*, Op. cit., p. 110–116.

467 Article 255 para. (1) and (2) UAGCL.

468 Mevoungou Nsana Roger, *Les Obligations du Vendeur de Marchandises dans l'Acte Uniforme OHADA*, Op. cit., pp. 8–12.

469 Meaning that there is no conformity when the defect affects the usage of the goods.

470 Franklin E. Crawford, Fit for its Ordinary Purpose? Tobacco, Fast Food, and the Implied Warranty of Merchantability, (2002) 63 *Ohio State Law Journal*, 1165, p. 2.

471 Cameroon, Article 1641 CC; Côte d'Ivoire, Article 1641 CC; France, Article 1641 CC.

472 Phillippe Malaurie et al., *Les Contrats Spéciaux*, (3 édition, Defrénois, Paris 2007) p. 228

473 Akuété Pedro Santos & Jean Yado Toé, *OHADA Droit Commercial Général*, Op. cit., p. 395.

manufactured.[474] Each of the seller's functional duty of conformity will be examined in detail.

Fitness for ordinary use

Lord Diplock's statements in the case of *Ashington Piggeries v. Christopher Hill Ltd.*,[475] defines fitness of goods for ordinary use as goods of a kind, those verbally identified by a description that is wide enough to include goods which are intended for use for the particular purpose for which the buyer requires the goods, which are the subject matter of the contract.

In various countries having adopted the SGA,[476] particularly on the question of the fitness for ordinary use, the Act states that, where the buyer, expressly or by implication, makes known to the seller the purpose for which the goods are required, so as to show that the buyer relies on the seller's skill or judgment, and the goods are of a description which it is in the course of the seller's business to supply, there is an implied condition that the goods shall reasonably be fit for that purpose. Thereon, it is immaterial whether or not the seller is a manufacturer of the goods.[477] This position has been complemented by case law interpretations in practice.

Under the UAGCL, the delivery of goods in a sale contract does not satisfy the requirement of conformity unless and until they are fit for the purpose and purposes for which goods of the same description would normally be used.[478] Therefore, this raises the problem of measuring how the fitness of the ordinary use is met. Accordingly, it is advanced that an objective test should be used to determine the ordinary use. Thus, whether or not the goods are fit for the purpose and purposes for which goods of such description are ordinarily used, must be determined in light with what a reasonable person in the same trade as the parties to the contract would best do.[479]

However, if any precise purpose was brought to the knowledge of the seller[480] at the time of the conclusion of the contract, goods which do not

[474] Article 260 para. 1 UAGCL. This duty shall be examined in the subsequent chapter.

[475] Op. cit.

[476] Cameroon, Botswana, Ghana, Kenya, Malawi, Mozambique, Namibia, Nigeria, Tanzania, Uganda, Zimbabwe, Zambia,

[477] George Gleason Bogert, *Express Warranties in Sales of Goods*, Op. cit., p. 17;14 (1) SGA 1893 s 14 (1).

[478] Article 255 para. 2 UAGCL.

[479] Articles 238 para. 1 & 239 UAGCL.

[480] Article 255 para. 2 UAGCL.

serve the precise purpose will be considered as being not in conformity with contract even if the ordinary purposes do exist.[481] Generally, for the purpose of convenience, courts are required to first attempt to determine whether any indication as to the usage[482] of the goods was brought to the seller's attention before seeking a reasonable man position as to what amounts to the ordinary use[483].

Fitness for Particular Purpose

The UAGCL clearly states that goods under the contract of sale are fit for the specific or particular purpose provided the seller knew of this at the time of the conclusion of the contract.[484] The aim is to protect any buyer who acquires goods by informing the seller on the particular purpose and purposes on which the goods will be used for. In reality, it appears that the requirement for goods fit for ordinary use overlaps with that on the fitness for a particular purpose. Nevertheless, two elements constitute their distinction: first, the requirement for the fitness for particular purpose must only be used where the buyer makes known to the seller the specific or particular purpose for which he intends to use the goods. It follows therefore that accuracy the particular information of the goods, will aid the seller to satisfy the buyer's need.

The second aspect concerns reliance. As a professional businessman, the seller is an expert in the field of the goods contracted by the buyer, and latter usually relies on the seller's skill to provide him with the exact goods requested.

In accordance with the SGA, whenever the buyer, expressly or by impliedly, makes known to the seller the particular purpose for which the goods are required, there is an implied condition that the goods shall be reasonably fit for such purpose. As a matter of fact, the buyer relies on the seller's skill or judgment, and the goods are of a description which it is in the course of the seller's business to supply (regardless of whether he is the manufacturer or not). However, there is no implied condition as to its fitness for any particular purpose over the sale of a specific article under its patent or other trade name.[485]

---

481 Article 255 para. 2 UAGCL.
482 Article 238 para. 2 UAGCL.
483 Article 238 para. 1 UAGCL.
484 Article 255 para. 2 UAGCL.
485 SGA 1893 s 14 (1).

A distinction has to be made between fitness for a particular purpose as opposed to general purpose. Firstly, within the meaning of the provision, "*particular purpose*" shall be understood to be "*specific purpose*";[486] notwithstanding that the purpose may be a general one, for instance, a cloth to wear. In *Mac Gill v. Tailbot*[487] a car collector made known to the car seller that he wanted a Rolls Royce car that was reasonably fit for the purpose of economic restoration. It was held that the purpose for which the car was to be used in this case was communicated.

But, in *Manchester Liners v. Rea Ltd.*,[488] it was held that no express disclosure is necessary if the seller is aware of the particular purpose for which the goods are required. He might be aware due to his knowledge of past transactions or by the implied nature of the goods. It follows that the disclosure of the particular purpose of the goods can be made either expressly or in circumstance that let the buyer beware that he relies on the seller's skill and judgement.[489]

In *Ijomo v. Mid Motors Nigeria Ltd.*,[490] there was no breach of contract as to the implied condition on quality or fitness of the goods.[491] Thus, Lagos High Court established that there was no evidence at all as to whether the buyer informed the seller of the purpose for which the cars were bought. The reliance on the seller can therefore either be express[492] or implied and such reliance must have induced the buyer to enter into contract. The reliance is not subjective but rather objective as it is generally a matter of inference because what matters is what a reasonable man in the position of a seller would have realised, by relying or not on the purpose of the goods made known to him. Lastly, with regard to the fitness for particular purpose, it is being considered by case law that it is a relative issue that does not depend either on the objective or the subjective contemplation between the parties but rather on factual and material circumstances of each case.

In *Onutu v. Adeleke and Another*,[493] the Kaduna High court held that because the car was broken five days after the day it was purchased while driven on the road, the requirement of fitness of the particular purpose of the car as stated in the contract of sale was not satisfied. The buyer in contracting

486 *Kendall v. Lillico* (1969) 2 AC 31, 123 as per Lord Wilberforce.

487 2002 GWD 12–382 (Sherriff G. J. Evans).

488 [1922] 2 A.C.74 .

489 Igweike K.I., Sales of Goods, *Nigerian Commercial Law*, Op. cit., p. 54–55.

490 CCHCJ /9/ 754 p. 1326.

491 SGA 1893 s 14 (1).

492 For instance the particular purpose is mentioned in the contract as in the case of *Manchester Liners v. Rea Ltd.*, Op. cit.

493 [1975] N.L.R. 130.

with the seller asked for a new car but the seller sold him a second-hand car. It is not reasonable for a new car to be broken after five days of being driven. It is important to note that there is no implied condition that the goods shall fit absolutely to the particular purpose expressly nor impliedly determined. If, for instance, an unusual consequence occurs producing an unexpected accidental injury, as a result of an undisclosed information regarding a defect in the good by the buyer which was not known to the seller, the latter will not be held liable in the circumstances as it was decided in the case of *Griffiths v. Peter Conway Ltd.*[494]

Sale by Sample

Sale by sample is most often employed in respect of the sale of generic goods. Instead of describing the subject-matter of the contract, the contracting parties may determine that quality should be identical to that of sample. This type of sale is particularly common in cases of sale through agencies, travelling salesmen who bring small quantities of articles that can give the prospective buyer a complete picture of the quality and other properties of the goods.[495]

Under the UAGCL, like it is the case under Common law, it must be emphasised that where a description of the quality of the goods is given, the sample will be considered to have been used for identification of the goods or determination of their quality and properties. In other words, if the goods delivered do not conform to the sample, the Uniform Act will regard this act on the part of the seller as lack of conformity. What is essential is whether the sample has been used as a term of the contract or not. The goods do not conform with the contract unless they possess the qualities of goods which the seller has held out to the buyer as a sample or model.[496] Thus, from the provisions of the UAGCL, it can be understood that in a contract of sale, the sample is the exclusive standard of quality of the goods and, in such a case, any variation from the sample entitles the buyer to repudiate the contract. There is insistence on the full conformity of the goods to the sample (if so contracted).

Unfortunately, the Uniform Act is silent on cases where the sample or model is shown during negotiations but there is no reliable proof in the contract thereof nor can it be proved with certainty in some other way that

---

494 [1939] 1 All ER 685; same decision in *Ingham v. Ernes* (1955) 2 Q.B. 366.

495 Stoljar Samuel J., *Conditions, Warranties and Description of Quality in Sale of Goods*, Op. cit., p. 443–446.

496 Article 255 UAGCL.

the parties intended the quality of the goods to conform to the sample in every respect. The UAGCL does not contain any provision on sale by sample used unconditionally in respect of full conformity. However, much regard should be given to the intent and conduct of the parties during the bargaining phase. Nevertheless, from the spirit of the law, the sample is an appropriate method of determining quality and property in the goods by the buyer under the Act in consideration of the very purpose of goods which the commercial buyer desires to use in his business. Therefore, the seller shall be held liable for non-conformity if the goods delivered do not correspond to the sample.

Another important consideration that arises is whether sale by sample entitles the buyer to make a case against the seller for inherent vice if the goods delivered correspond to the sample. Under the UAGCL, this kind of a problem does not prevent the buyer from having recourse to the remedies available for cases of inherent vice.[497] Furthermore, the Uniform Act imposes on the seller the duty to provide guarantee for the goods.[498] Presumably, this is whether the sale is by sample or not. This protects the buyer because goods sold by sample must necessarily be suitable for resale. Accordingly, regardless of the fact that the sample had a latent defect, there is a presumption that the goods must be of merchantable quality.

In Common law jurisdictions, sale by sample is governed by the SGA.[499] There is a contract for sale by sample when there is an express or implied term to that effect in the contract. In respect of sale by sample, English law provides "*an implied condition that the goods be free from any defect rendering them unmerchantable which would not be apparent on reasonable examination of the sample*".[500] Thus, if any sample is made as part of the contract of sale, it creates an essential condition of the contract, that is, an express warranty that the goods shall correspond to the sample.[501]In short, whether there exists a contract of sale by sample is a question of law and not a question of fact. In other words, the fact that a seller provides to the buyer an item for inspection does not, *ipso factor*, amount to sale by sample, unless there is evidence of a clear intention of the parties to contract as such.[502] Similarly, in case of a contract in writing, there must be written evidence that the parties intended to be contracted as such. It follows that parol evidence when contract is in

---

497 Articles 256–259 UAGCL.

498 Article 260 para. 1 UAGCL.

499 SGA 1893 s 15.

500 see Section 15(2) (6) SGA

501 see also similarly the American Uniform Commercial Code (Section 2-313).

502 P. S. Atiyah et al., *The Sale of Goods*, Op. cit., p. 212–213.

writing will be inadmissible in determining whether or not there was a sale by sample.[503] Therefore, for an effective sale by sample, the parties must either expressly or by implication make it clear as was stated in the case of *Ernest Friedrischdorf and Co v. Fuja.*[504]

However, the exception in the latter point may occur in circumstances where the contract of sale is backed up by custom or usage of trade. Here, it is immaterial whether the contract itself makes reference of the sample.[505] Once it has been legally established that there is a sale by sample, the statute (SGA) provides a series of implied terms that must be considered. First, there is an implied condition that the goods shall correspond with the sample in quality.[506] In other words, the bulk and the sample shall match each other. In *Warwick v. Mackenzie Co Ltd.*,[507] the court pointed out that for a sale by sample to be made, the parties must have contracted with reference to a sample and with a common understanding that the sample constitutes the description of the goods to be purchased.

Sometimes the contract determines the limit of the description in a sale by sample. For instance, if the contract states that the bulk shall correspond in type and quality to the sample, whatever fault and value the bulk might have will in no way effect a breach of the contract of sale.[508] It might appear that the sample does not dictate for it itself but rather that, the contract defines the criteria of the bulk. Second, it is an implied term that the buyer shall have a reasonable opportunity of comparing the sample with the bulk.[509] Reasonable inspection by the buyer of both the bulk and the sample should reveal any defect. If this opportunity is offered, the buyer is usually bound as was the case in *Lorymer v. Smith.*[510] Third, there is an implied term that goods shall be free from any defect rendering them unmerchantable, which would not be apparent on reasonable examination of the sample.[511] The case implied term was laid down in the case of *Godley v. Perry*,[512] where the breach of conformity of the sale by sample was clearly established.[513] In this case, a child, after a

[503] *Ginner v. King* (1890) 7 TLR 140.
[504] [1967] LLR 115.
[505] *Seyers v. Jones* [1848] 154 ER 426.
[506] SGA 1893 s 15 (2) (a).
[507] [1921] 2 W.N.R.
[508] *Champanthac & Co Ltd v. Waller & Co Ltd.* (1979) 1K.B 254 at. 260.
[509] SGA 1893 s 15 (2) (b).
[510] (1822) 1 B & C 1.
[511] SGA 1893 ss 15 (2) (c).
[512] [1887] 12 App. Cas. 284, at. 297.
[513] SGA 1893 s 15 (2) (c).

careful look at the sample, went ahead and purchased the plastic toy catapult which he examined by pulling back its elastic. The elastic cut and injured him on the eye. Such a defect would not therefore have been apparent by a mere examination of the good.

Usual Packaging

Unless and until the goods are packaged in accordance with the contract, there is non-conformity of the goods.[514] This seller's obligation is therefore emphasised in the same provision which requires that, in the absence of a contrary stipulation between the parties, the goods must be packaged or contained in the usual method of packaging goods of the same nature, or in a manner to ensure their conservation and protection.[515]

Because conformity of the goods to the sample and the passing of risk occur at the same time, any damage occurring after that point will be borne by the buyer. If the goods get damaged while in transit therefore and such damage is due to inadequate packaging by the seller, such a situation will be treated as non-conformity already existing during the passing of the risk.[516] This is so because the transfer of title to goods shifts the risk of loss. The seller will therefore be liable for breach of non-conformity.[517]

The test for usual packaging is that of a reasonable man, in the same trade or transactions, in addition to any relevant trade usages.[518] But generally, as to the question regarding what package is adequate for the goods, the answer will depend on the nature, descriptions and/or conditions of the goods in every contract of sale.

Generally, after seeing the sample of the bulk, the buyer is expecting to receive goods identical to the sample he had inspected. In other words, the goods have to correspond with the description or the sample. Thereof, the packaging must also be accurate. The SGA at this instance makes it clear that where there is a contract for sale by description, there is an implied condition that the goods shall correspond with the description. In case of both sale by sample and by description, it is not sufficient that the bulk corresponds with

514 Article 255 para. 2 UAGCL.

515 Ibid., UAGCL; See also the publication of Centre du Commerce International sur La Promotion de L'Emballage pour L'Exportation, Volume I : Guide des mesures institutionnelles a aprendre et de l'assistance technique, Genève, 1975.

516 Articles 256 (upon delivery); 275 (taking delivery shifts title) and 277 para.1 UAGCL.

517 Article 255 UAGCL.

518 Articles 238 para. 2 and 239, UAGCL.

the sample if the goods do not also correspond with the description.[519] In practice, if a cloth is provided as a sample and is described on the label as 100% cotton, then it should be exactly that. This was the issue in Privy Council case of *Boshali v. Allied Commercial Exported Ltd*[520]which involved a sale by sample and sale by description. Similarly, when buying meat, if it is described as fresh meat, then it should not have previously been frozen.

Weight and Measures

The seller's duty to deliver goods of conformity in relation to the quantity can be estimated in terms of weight and measures. Weight is important information for the commercial buyer in evaluating the quantity of certain goods. It is also needed in the export-import trade which requires goods to bear this information dictated by customs regulations. The Uniform Act has not clearly stipulated this but it can be inferred there from that weight and the measures of goods are considerable extrinsic characteristics of a product which form part of a seller's duty of conformance to deliver goods of the right quantity. Weight and Measurement control in Cameroon provide an illustration of the desire to control unconscionability in contracts. This is all the more necessary because, as pointed out earlier, the supply of most goods does not bare the accurate information as promised by some sellers. The Cameroonian legislature, like those of other African countries has therefore, from very early years, sought to control predatory weights and measuring; of which consumers are exposed to. Nevertheless, relevant legislations were passed in this light to correct such malpractices.[521] There is also support from the administration under the Ministry of Trade and Commerce who usually cause inspection to be made of, or of any part of, local weights and measures arrangements by agents authorised on the behalf of the Ministry. These officers have as mandate to examine any equipment and give report of results of their inspection to the Heads of each Regional Delegations of Trade

519 SGA 1893 s 13.

520 [1961] All N.L.R. 946; this case was about 'Quality AS 1,000 grey cloth'.

521 Law No. 2004/002) of 21 April governing legal metrology in Cameroon. Décret No. 85/1290 du 26 Septembre 1985 réglementant la catégories d'instruments de mesure dits : 'instrument de pesage' ; Décret No. 85/1293 du 26 Septembre 1985 réglementant la catégorie d'instruments de mesure dits : 'Recipiants-Mesure' ; Décret No. 85–1405 du 10 Octobre 1985 fixant les modalités de contrôles des instruments de mesure; Décret No. 90/1475 du 09 Novembre modifiant et complétant certaines dispositions du Décret No. 85/1405 du 10 Octobre 1985 fixant les modalités du contrôle des instruments de mesure ; Annexe au décret No. 92/005/ PM du 06 Janvier 1992 fixant taux des taxes de vérification primitive et périodique.

and Commerce.

Measures have been made establishing a system of quantity control known as the "*average system*" applicable to the packaging of goods sold by weight and volume.[522] Package goods are divided into two groups: Class A packages, being packages containing goods of a specified description, made up in a predetermined constant quantity within a specified upper and lower limit; and class B packages, being packages of any other description which are determined for sale and normally sold by weight or volume or volume in packages made up in a predetermined constant quantity.

Examination of Goods by the Parties to the Contract

Under the UAGCL effective notification of non-conformity depends on two requirements; the content of the notice and the timing of such notice. These two elements represent an extremely important concern because the failure of either one can preclude a buyer from claiming against the effects of non-conformity, even when non-conformity exists.[523] Overall, the Uniform Act imposes relatively stricter requirements upon buyer who examines the goods with a view to ascertaining its state and functionality.

As for the sale of goods (to which compulsory regulations do not apply), the Uniform Act makes provision for the buyer to examine the goods. This seems to be a right. In other words, this is a domain where the contracting parties are free to make their own contractual provision regarding the inspection of the goods, if they wish to. As a rule, however, the buyer usually inspects the goods before accepting them so that, in the event that they do not conform to the contract specification, he may give notice of it to the seller. Thus, the law has put the buyer in a position in which he cannot avail himself of his rights unless the inspection has been carried out in the first place. This is understandable as safety in trade is ensured by such means.

Among the many questions and problems arising in connection with the examination of the goods, the following seem to occur most often: should the inspection of the quality of the goods come first or should the buyer first effect

[522] see Décret No. 2005/1928/PM du 03 Juin 2005 fixant les caractéristiques métrologiques des produits préemballés ou assimiles et les modalités de leur contrôles; Annexe au Décret No. 2005/1928/PM du 03 Juin 2005 fixant les caractéristiques métrologiques des produits préemballés ou assimiles ; Arrêté No. 00017/MINCOMMERCE du 03 Juillet 2006 fixantles caractéristiques propres aux citernes destinées au transport routier et ferroviaire des produits liquides.

[523] Article 257 UAGCL.

payment? Is it more convenient for the buyer to inspect the goods at the time of dispatch or on arrival? Can the buyer rely on the seller's quality certificate, as provided by some laws? What happens when '*random tests*' prove that the goods conform to the quality required and later on it is established that the goods do not conform to the contract? However, regardless of these and a range of other problems encountered by the parties, the courts and arbitrators, it should be stressed that quality inspection has been given an extraordinary important place recently, particularly in view of technical and technological development, and also because it is constantly developing toward specialised activities without which modern trade cannot even be imagined.

Examination by the Seller

The *raison d'être* for the application of Article 255 UAGCL is that a buyer ought to be able to rely on what the parties have agreed. Therefore, the starting point is an assumption by the buyer that the seller will make good any defects if there is any discrepancy between the contract specification and the goods inspected. The presumptive rule in Article 255 UAGCL therefore is that it is the seller who must first show that the parties have agreed that the goods shall have a quality different from that stated in the agreement; in other words, the fact that the buyer knew of or could not have been unaware of the defect, and those parts of the agreement which conflict with this cannot be relied on by the buyer. In any event, Article 255 of the Uniform Act protects the buyer. The buyer is entitled to expect that the goods will conform to the agreement, in practice the written agreement, and that any variance from what should apply under the agreement and under Article 255 para. 1 will be made good by the seller prior to delivering the goods to the buyer. This applies regardless of whether the buyer knows of a defect, if it is agreed that the seller shall deliver the goods without defects.[524]At this point, the parties must be assumed to have expressed their intention in their written agreement in relation to the requirements for the goods in question. By interpretation, Article 255 para. 1 of the Uniform Act seems to restrict application of the *caveat emptor* principle.

Control of quality may also be conducted by the seller, in which case its quality certificate is attached to other documents (which is significant in respect of certain goods since quality may be considerably affected during

---

[524] René Franz Henschel, *Conformity of Goods in International Sales Governed by CISG Article 35: Caveat Venditor, Caveat Emptor and Contract Law as Background Law and as a Comparing Set of Rules*, Op. cit., p. 10.

transportation by reason of environmental considerations and other circumstances). This method of inspection is provided by some governmental or international bodies. The certificate of inspection is the only proof of what it is bound to furnish under the contract. There is, however, another view to the effect that the other party is always entitled to a further inspection.

Examination by the Buyer

As mentioned in the introduction of this chapter, inspection by the buyer is not binding upon him for if he fails to inspect the goods he will incur no sanctions. Therefore, this matter is dealt with by some laws, such as those of the Anglo-Saxon countries, not as being an obligation of the buyer but rather a right.

Under the UAGCL,[525] it is the duty of the buyer obligation to examine the goods or have them examined. Therefore, the law grants an opportunity to the buyer to inspect the goods and report immediately to the seller whether or not they correspond to the contractual description as agreed upon with the seller.[526] The reason behind this exercise may be that, this is duty is stipulated not only in the interest of the seller but also in that of the buyer himself. This duty may be justified first by the need to obtain a clear situation, for by sending the goods to the buyer the seller is put in an uncertain position which cannot last forever. He must know the fate of the goods.

Although the law does not provide any sanction for the buyer if he fails to perform this duty or fails to report any defect on the goods, he nevertheless loses all his right of action to non conformity of the goods to the contract of sale.[527] Moreover, the buyer losses the same right of action if he fails to notify any defect within a time frame from the time he noticed or ought to have noticed it the defect.[528] That is, depending on the circumstances, the examination of the goods shall be carried out immediately a after he takes delivery to enable the parties determine whether or not the goods are in accordance with the contractual description.[529]

The examination of the goods may be done either by the buyer himself or a third party appointed by him. But he remains the sole person responsible for

---

525 Article 258 UAGCL.

526 Akuété Pedro Santos & Jean Yado Toé, *OHADA Droit Commercial Général*, Op. cit., p. 405.

527 Ibid.

528 Ibid.

529 Articles 258–259 UAGCL.

the performance of that duty even if it is carried out by some other person.[530] Like the CISG, the UAGCL is very clear on this point when it provides that the buyer must examine the goods.[531] However, if an examination is carelessly carried out by a third party duly appointed by him and who does not discover the defect, the buyer is responsible under the contract even though he can institute an action against the appointed examiner.

The basic rule is that examination of the goods is always carried out at the place of delivery, unless the places of delivery and destination are one and the same place. However, the places differ the question that comes up is which of the two should have priority. All depends, of course, on the intention of the parties to the contract and on what they have agreed upon in this regard. For the buyer, however, the place of dispatch may have a number of disadvantages. No matter what the condition of the goods is at the time of loading, it is important for the buyer that they reach him in good condition. It is important for him and therefore to insist that the place of inspection should be at the destination. The presence of the buyer or his representative during inspection at the place of dispatch may incur considerable expense[532], and for this reason, except when this is in the buyer's interest, the latter would rather have the goods inspected at the place of destination.

In some instances, contractual agreements spell out the method to be used to examine the goods.[533] For some industrial engines, for instance, the methods of examining the goods are usually prescribed in the notice guide (hand book). However, where there is no express stipulation on the examination process, the law requires the buyer to rely on common practice, custom and usages for the examination of the goods in question. If neither of the two alternatives is plausible, then a reasonable approach should be used to have the goods thoroughly inspected. What amounts to "*reasonable*" approach depends on the fact of each case. It does not necessarily mean that the method to be used should be the most sophisticated or costly. What matters is that the buyer should take all necessary steps to have the goods inspected.

As a general rule at Common law,, when the buyer or a third party acting on his behalf examines the goods, such examination is that of the buyer. If carried out, the implied condition as to the defect which such examination

---

530 Article 258 UAGCL.

531 Ibid.

532 The reason for this may be that only financially strong buyers will agree to inspection at the place of dispatch. See Jacques Ghestin, *Conformité et Garanties dans la Vente* (produits mobiliers), Op. cit., pp. 263–272.

533 Case of commodities contracts.

ought to have revealed will not be applied.[534]

The examination shall be an objective one, as opposed to the subjective test and any attempt to examine the goods in anyway will merely jeopardise the buyer's right to benefit from the implied condition as to the defect of the goods if they are defective. In other words, a lazy buyer who does not care to examine the goods is more protected than one who did examine only casually.[535]

In the West African Court of Appeal decision's in *Khalil and Dibo v. Mastronikolis*[536] there was no evidence that the oil was not of merchantable quality when the agent of the buyer examined the outside of the drums of the oil and took the sample. The leading Common law authority in this case, most often referred to by courts (of Common law jurisdiction) in Arica is the case of *Thornett and Febr v. Beers and Sons.*[537] With a fact of the case similar to the *Khalil and Dibo's* case, *Bary, J. in Thornett and Febr's* case held that there was no implied condition to be observed as the buyer was given opportunity to examine the goods, which he did. The buyer in this case, carried out examination of the outside of some barrels of glue; he did not go through a thorough examination though he had been given opportunity and facilities to do so. Taking into account case law and statutory position, it appears that what matters is not the mere opportunity given for examination but the proper examination itself.

However, Common law and statutory positions have not in these circumstances explained what exactly amounts to examination, when there is examination and what it entails. Even as concerns the sale by sample, the buyer should be given a reasonable opportunity to compare the bulk with the sample.[538] It may be inferred from trade practice that comparison may imply examination of the goods. In the SGA, this is a mere restatement of buyer's right to examine the goods supplied before acceptance.[539] In the case of *Lorymer v. Smith,*[540] it was held that the buyer of the consignment of wheat by sample has the inalienable right to inspect the whole in bulk at any proper and convenient time and that in case the seller refuses to show it, the buyer may rescind the whole contract. In other words, common law makes it clear that, once the buyer inspects and compares the sample, he cannot complain

534 P. S. Atiyah et al., *The Sale of Goods*, Op. cit., p .182.

535 Ibid., pp.171–172.

536 [1949] 12 WACA 462.

537 [1919] 1 K.B 486.

538 SGA 1893 s 15 (2) (b).

539 SGA 1893 s 34.

540 1822] 1B & C 1.

later of any defect in the bulk which a reasonable examination ought to have revealed.[541]

However, what amounts to reasonable examination was determined in the case of *Godley v. Perry*.[542] It was held that practical examination of the goods does not constitute reasonable examination. In this case, when the child bought a toy catapult after seeing a sample on the window, the examination was carried out pulling back its elastic. Later on, in using the toy, the plastic got cut and injured the child on his eye. It was held that the seller was in breach of a contract of sale[543] as the defect that caused harm to the child was not apparent and his inspection as a buyer was all that a reasonable purchaser could have done. But whenever the buyer examines the goods and does in fact discovers the defect, but decides to take the goods all the same, if the defect in the sample turns the goods unmerchantable, whether or not the buyer has knowledge of that fact, he has no ground to complaint at all.[544]

Method of Examination

The Uniform Act is silent as to the methods of examining the goods by the buyer. Methods of examination are determined either by the contract or in accordance with the laws and customs of the place where the inspection is carried out. What is legally relevant in connection with the method of examination is that any method of inspection is allowed (as per the intention of the parties) which will enable ascertainment of the quality of goods. The fact that one method of inspection is stipulated in the contract and another applied is of no importance. As a matter of fact, there are various methods of quality inspection and among them the most frequent are expert examination, comparison with the sample or by the condition in which the goods are sold.

Examination by Sample

The type of examination required also depends on the circumstances of each case and the kind of goods in question: thus agricultural products would usually be inspected by comparison with the sample whilst the control of automobiles and machinery necessitates a very complex expert analysis

541 *Moody v. Gregson* [1868] LR Ex 49.
542 Supra.
543 SGA 1893 s 17 (2) .
544 Igweike K.I., Sales of Goods, *Nigerian Commercial Law*, Op. cit., pp. 82–83.

(comparison with specifications, technical conditions, etc.)

When generic goods are sold examination by sample is normally sufficient—and also required within a very short time after delivery: the buyer is deemed to have been able to find out the defects on delivery if they are easily discoverable. The inspection may be total or partial, and which of the two will be undertaken does not depend on the will of the parties but on the kind of the goods in question. A full control of bulbs, for example, would mean destruction of the product. However, there are products which necessitate a complete inspection (particularly when their use and application are connected with human safety).

Hence, it is understandable why the Uniform Act regulating the question of quality of goods provide that the seller shall deliver goods of the same quality as the sample.[545]Consequently, it is a duty of the buyer to ascertain the quality and character of the goods delivered in comparison with the sample which was presented to him by the buyer during the formation of the contract.

The SGA gives the buyer the right to examine the goods at delivery if they have not previously been examined. The buyer is not deemed to have accepted them unless and until he has a reasonable opportunity of examining them for the purpose of ascertaining whether they are in conformity with the contract.[546]

In most cases, where the buyer is entitled to reject the goods due to the non-conformity or when the contract is subject to some condition express or implied as to quality[547] or otherwise with the contract of sale, as the case particularly with contract for sale by sample[548] or by description,[549] the position is similar; the buyer is given the reasonable opportunity to examine the goods otherwise he is not deemed to have accepted the them.

Still under the SGA, there is an implied condition that the buyer shall have a reasonable opportunity of comparing the bulk with the sample.[550] Under a contract for sale by description, whether the seller of these goods is a manufacturer or not, there is an implied condition that the goods shall be of good quality; provided that if the buyer has examined the goods, there is no implied condition as regards defects which such examination

---

[545] Article 255 para. 2 UAGCL.

[546] SGA 1893 s 34.

[547] A breach of warrantee does not give rise to the rejection of the goods.

[548] SGA 1893 s 15 (2) (c).

[549] SGA 1893 s 14 (2).

[550] SGA 1893, s 13 (1).

ought to have revealed.[551]

Examination as to the Condition in which the Goods are Sold

It is not certain that an opportunity to inspect goods conditioned in certain form such as packaging, frozen goods, or can foods will reveal true facts about the goods. The question is thus a double one: is a seller or retailer who sells food products in the ordinary tin can or other sealed container responsible for injury caused to his customers either from some foreign article in the can or from unwholesomeness of the food; and second, is the seller who sells the food products in bulk, which are defective in some way for which the retailer cannot reasonably be held at fault liable for injuries resulting to his customers from the defect?[552] It is therefore understandable why the Uniform Act regulating the quality of goods provides that the seller shall be liable to deliver the goods "*in the usual manner*" the goods are packaged.[553] This suggests that the buyer is liable to inspect the goods in conformity with the usual method in which such goods are packaged. In this condition, the warranty will have to be implied although the buyer has made complete examination of the product on the basis of the seller's ability to judge and having knowledge of the goods which he has been dealing for long. This may be justified by the fact it is sometimes not possible for the buyer to detect inherent latent defects of goods which are sealed or packaged since the buyer has just the immediate opportunity to appreciate the goods from their appearance.

There is a strong line of authority in favour of holding the seller who is dealer in such products in a sealed container liable for from injuries resulting from the unwholesomeness of the food or some foreign substance in the can. Suffice it to say at this point that a retailer should not be exempted from liability based on the tort of negligence.

There are a number of problems which are closely connected with the problem now under consideration- that is, the liability of the seller-the dealer of such packaged products. The fundamental reason for the extreme liability with respect to sales of such products (especially sales of food) is the necessity for the protection of public health and safety. The OHADA laws on conformity should be extended to such articles where there is substantial degree of injury not particularly personal but detrimental to the buyer's

[551] SGA 1893 s 16 (2).

[552] Robert C. Brown, *The Liability of Retail Dedalers for Defective Food Products*, Op. cit.

[553] Article 255 para. 2 UAGCL.

business in that economic loss may be incurred. Yet the OHADA Uniform Act does not seem to have gone far. Certainly, it has not imposed rigid liability for personal injury because the whole provisions on warranty under the Uniform Act are actionable under contract law. It appears to fall under the domain of consumer law since the Uniform Act on General Commercial Law does not cover goods for personal consumption or use.[554] The same argument, however, may be made in regard to any implied warranty, not only for food, but of other articles where the seller could not discover the defect. There is strong reason for holding the seller liable for selling defective can food than in any other kind of sale.[555]

It may then be conceded that the argument in favour of exempting the dealer under such circumstances from liability is not entirely foreclosed by the terms of the UAGCL; but it seems clear that the Act neither does nor was intended to make any special provision for this situation, and that under the general rules laid down by the Uniform Act, a warranty of fitness for the purpose and merchantability may be applied. It seems rather obvious that in this situation, the present rule is and ought to be *caveat venditor*—let the seller beware.

Inspection by the Seller

Although in practice the goods are usually inspected by the buyer, there are situations where the examination made by the seller will be the only inspection. This will be the case when the contracting parties so agree, that is, if such inspection is "*in the interest of both contracting parties*". It is often impractical (or expensive) for the buyer to attend the inspection at the time of loading, and in such cases the parties may agree that the seller himself shall inspect the goods. In the case of sales at a distance at the time of delivery of the goods to the carrier, the seller is obliged to inspect the goods before forwarding them to the buyer along with the necessary supporting documents as to their quality.[556]

Inspection by Third Parties

As mentioned above, the inspection may be carried out by the parties (usually the buyer) and many problems may arise in this connection, the most

[554] Article 235 (a) UAGCL.

[555] see Rollin M. Pekins, Unwholesome Food as a Source of Liability, (1919–1920) 5 *Iowa L. Bull.* 6, pp. 86–111.

[556] Article 250 UAGCL.

important of which is when an allegation is made that the party who inspected the goods has not been impartial. On the other hand, with trade at a distance it may be far too expensive for the buyer to send his representative to the place of inspection of the goods, for which reason (and often due to insufficient expertise) the buyer (and sometimes the seller, as well) enter with into a separate contract with a "*third party*" who is to inspect the goods and send the report on the findings. This is the purport of Article 270 of the UAGCL. The "*third party*" may be an individual or (more commonly) a private organisation specialised in providing this type of service.

Time for examination

As to the time of the examination, of the goods, there is a generally accepted view that it should be done "*immediately*", "*without delay*", "*as soon as (conveniently) possible*". It should be stressed here that in interpreting these expressions attention should be paid to the circumstances of each case and that the time be limited to what is normal in the trade in that particular kind of goods. These are of course factual questions and a significant role played here by the commercial customs of each branch of trade.

The UAGCL suggests no more than a short period within which the examination of the goods should be carried out, if necessary, as quickly as possible.[557] Unlike in the former UAGCL, there now exist a prescribed time period for the buyer to conduct examination of the goods as governed by the amended UAGCL. The time preceding this process determines the end of the inspection and it is immaterial whether or not the goods conform to the terms of the contract. Henceforth, the question to be answered is when in fact the inspection or examination starts and ends.

The UAGCL provides that the examination of the goods starts upon delivery or one month following delivery,[558] or sometimes depending on the circumstances, the time may be different from the delivery time particularly when the goods are in transit or when they are redirected, deviated or re-dispatched.[559]

The examination of the goods at delivery may sometimes be delayed when the contract requires the transportation of the goods. This certainly occurs

557 Articles 258, 259 and 270 para. 1 UAGCL. The predecessor of this was Article 227 (1)of the old version of the UAGCL.

558 Articles 256 and 258, UAGCL.

559 Article 270 para. 2 UAGCL.

in many international contracts of sale of goods where the goods have to be handed over to a carrier. This position is dealt with under the UAGCL when it provides that the examination will take place once the goods reach destination.[560] Also, unlike the general rule, the time of examination of the goods will be when they reach their new destination. In this case, the UAGCL allows for a period of one year for the buyer to report any latent defect from the time the defect is discovered. This solution applies when the goods have been re-dispatched, deviated or redirected by the buyer without him having the chance them. However, this solution will not only apply if the buyer, at the time of the conclusion of the contract, knew or ought to have known of the possibility of such deviation or re-dispatching.[561] In practice, a buyer operating as a middleman or a buyer who intends to sell is presumed to be aware of either the redirection or deviation. In this case, practice sometimes requires such a buyer to inform the seller beforehand.

Notice Requirement

As to the content of a notice of non-conformity, under the CISG such notice must be sufficiently specific regarding the "*nature of the lack of conformity*" in order for the buyer to meet up with his business needs. Sufficiency in this respect is determined by the purpose of the notice in mind. As one commentator has suggested, [questions] as to what the notice should be answered with regard to the functions served by the notice ... [and] the principal functions [under the CISG] are to give the seller an opportunity to obtain and preserve evidence of the condition of the goods and to cure the deficiency.[562]

The UAGCL provides two instances where the buyer should give notice to the seller for any lack of conformity of the goods being delivered: the buyer must give notice of a lack of conformity discovered one month after the day of delivery.[563] Failure to observe these requirements, the buyer will be deprived of his right to claim redress of the non-conformity. Secondly, the buyer must give notice of any hidden defect of conformity within one year from the moment when this was discovered or ought to be known.[564] To this effect, notice is therefore necessary in order to exercise all remedies available to the buyer

[560] Article 270 para. 2 UAGCL.
[561] Article 259 UAGCL.
[562] John O.Honnold, *Uniform Law for International Sales*, Op. cit., p. 277–278.
[563] Article 257 UAGCL.
[564] Article 259 UAGCL; under the CISG, the time frame is (2 years) Article 39 CISG.

under the Uniform Act.[565]

There is no requirement as to a specific form of notice under the Uniform Act. Notice need not be written;[566] it may be given by word of mouth, for example by telephone. This problem in the latter case is of course evidence. Pursuant to Article 240 UAGCL, the buyer can prove it simply by all possible means.

Time Limits (Prescription) for Giving Notice

The question of time limit to the buyer's action must be clearly distinguished from the one addressed in Article 259 UAGCL, where the cut-off period of one year to give notice of non-conformity is provided. The period to give notice runs from the moment the buyer either discovered or ought to have discovered the lack of conformity.[567]

Before he examines the goods, someone may inform the buyer of the lack of conformity. In this case, the time of giving notice begins to run at the moment the buyer acquired this knowledge. It is therefore immaterial whether or not he had examined the goods.

Prescription concerns legal actions and bars a claim even if the buyer did give notice. Conversely, a longer time limit for an action does not influence the cut-off period of Article 259 UAGCL. In theory, the buyer would still be able to lay his claim, but he cannot rely on a lack of conformity if he has not given notice within one year of delivery. Parties may derogate to the latter rule by stipulating a different period of guarantee.

It is important to the seller that notice is not only timely, but also sufficiently specific as to the goods concerned and the nature of the defect. It has been stated by a writer that even if the buyer has bought a single item of a certain kind from the seller, he must give notice referring not only to the type of goods, but also to the specific item in question (serial number, date of delivery), in order for the seller to identify with precision the allegedly defective goods without having to read all sales documents or to gather information.[568]

[565] Articles 282, 283 and 284 UAGCL.

[566] The word 'written' shall mean any communication using a written medium, including the telegram, telex, telefax or e-mail .

[567] Article 258 UAGCL.

[568] Anna Veneziano, *Non-Conformity of Goods in International Sales; A Survey of Current Caselaw on CISG*, Op. cit., p. 52.

As in the CISG, the period of time in the UAGCL related to the report on the notice of conformity[569] is independent but additional to the period of the examination of the goods.[570] In other words, nothing prevents the buyer from examining the goods in spite of the cut-off period of one year. Although the two durations may appear similar, the clear distinction between them lies on the fact that the buyer will lose his right to rely on the lack of conformity, unless the one time period has expired.[571] The buyer up to that period has the right to continue with the examination of the goods, which may reveal some immediate true facts of the goods before a period of one year. It follows therefore that in determining what amount to "*one year*" as the duration for giving notice will depend on the facts of each case. Most often regard is made as to whether the goods are seasonal or perishable, or whether the goods require an additional expert opinion. Hence, depending on each particular case, the time to give notice is defined.[572]

As a general rule, the "*1 year*" time limit to give notice runs from the moment the goods are handed over to the buyer.[573] Thereafter, the time limit elapses and the buyer loses all rights to rely on the lack of conformity. It is irrelevant and immaterial whether or not the buyer could not have knowledge of it or it was impossible to discover the lack of conformity.[574] The seller is therefore free from any lack of conformity claim after the time limit has elapsed. However, one year time limit remains a default rule. The UAGCL makes it clear that parties are free to determine their time limit for notice.[575] It therefore appears that parties can either exclude or modify this limitation period but the seller still has the obligation to perform his duties as contained in Article 255 regarding the quality of the goods.

Once the buyer fails to observe the notice requirement as provided by the law, he immediately losses all rights to rely on the lack of conformity.[576] It follows that the buyer losses all available remedies[577] he would have been entitled to if he had performed the requirement of notice.[578] In short, he will be solely responsible if the goods happen to be defective.

[569] Ibid, UAGCL; Article 39(1) CISG.
[570] Article 257 UAGCL; Article 38 CISG.
[571] Articles 258–259 UAGCL.
[572] Ingebord Schwenzer, Op. cit., p. 630.
[573] Article 259 UAGCL.
[574] Ingebord Schwenzer, Op. cit., p. 637.
[575] Article 259 UAGCL.
[576] Articles 282, 283 and 284 UAGCL.
[577] Articles 282–284 UAGCL.
[578] Articles 258 & 259 UAGCL.

From the reading of some provisions of the Uniform Act, parties may derogate by agreement from the examination and notice requirements. The case makes it clear that the opportunity of drafting a more complete set of terms on lack of conformity is to be taken into account. One solution might be to distinguish between apparent and hidden defects, providing for a longer period of time under the Uniform Act which is one year period.[579] This leaves the courts the task of interpreting when a lack of conformity is easy to discover. Another option is to leave out any reference to the nature of the non- conformity and provide for a short term starting together with a maximum period guarantee starting from delivery: which is one month under the Uniform Act.[580]

Finally, Articles 258 and 259 of the Uniform Act may be derogated also by usage under Article 238 para. 2 UAGCL. When parties have agreed on a contractual time for notice, however, the applicability of usage is excluded.

Conclusion

The seller's act in exercising his material duty of conformity is not enough. The seller is also expected to deliver goods which will satisfactorily serve the purpose for which commercial buyers intend to use them. As the seller's duty of conformity is expansive, imposing an absolute liability, it is critical for the buyer to clearly articulate the purpose(s) for which he intends to use the goods which is considered as the seller's functional duty of conformity. This is especially important for manufactured goods, where the quality of the goods is relevant for its saleability by the commercial buyer in view to meet up with consumer expectations. The utility of the goods for re-sale matters for the commercial buyer in the first place. That is why the seller under the UAGCL is under the duty to deliver goods for the required purpose.

The seller's expected obligation to deliver goods satisfying the requirements of the contract would hardly in practice be that. The seller in most cases is not always to be blamed for all lack of conformity. The buyer also has the responsibility to ensure conformity. Thus, since doing business is at the heart of the mind of the commercial buyer, he has been given the opportunity by the OHADA Uniform Act on General Commercial Law to examine the existence of any defect in the goods supplied to him by the seller. This inadequacy takes

579 259 UAGCL.

580 Article 258 UAGCL.

the form of latent or hidden defects which may be inherent in the goods. This situation seems to show how the principle of *caveat venditor* confronts with the principle of *caveat emptor*. Arguably, this task seems to be difficult with the increment of sophisticated goods being manufactured today. The bare eyes of a buyer cannot detect some deficiency existing in some kinds of goods. Some technical methods need to be employed by the buyer. Time allocation has also been specified for the buyer to report any such lack of conformity to the seller for a possible remedy. The buyer's right to examine the goods could be said to be a contribution in ascertaining the quality of goods in the markets. The commercial buyer cares because his customers are his interest in the re-selling business he operates.

5

SELLER'S DUTY TO GUARANTEE AGAINST THIRD PARTY RIGHTS

Introduction

By definition, a contract of sale is a contract by which the seller agrees to transfer to the buyer such title as he has to the absolute legal interest in the goods, for a money consideration called the price. It follows from this definition that as a fundamental point the whole object of a sale is to transfer property from one person to another. Transfer of property over goods is the essence of a contract of sale. Legally, it is the transfer of title which distinguishes sale of goods contract from other transactions. In practical application therefore, a seller is required under a contract of sale to transfer the best title in the goods, so that if someone has a title superior so that received by the buyer, the seller is in breach of contract.

This explains the fact that the seller's obligation to deliver goods which are free from any rights of a third party is embodied in his duty to guarantee which is an extended duty of the seller in the OHADA Uniform Act on General Commercial Law. By definition, the Black's Law Dictionary[581] considers guarantee to be "*the assurance that a contract or legal act will be duly carried out*". It equally implies warranty, but preference goes to the former as far as this work is concerned. In practice, it is often for example, in the context of consumer warranties or other assurances of quality or performance. Thus, Article 260 of the Uniform Act stipulates that:

the seller shall deliver the goods with the assurance that no third party has a

[581] Bryan A. Garner et al., *Black's Law Dictionary*, Op. cit., p. 772.

> *right or claim to them, unless the buyer accepts to collect the goods under such conditions.*[582]

Accordingly, Article 1641 of the French Civil Code states that: "*The seller is held to guarantee against hidden defects in the thing sold which render it unsuitable to the use for which it is intended, or which so diminish such use that the buyer would have purchased it, or would have given only a lesser price for it, had he known of them*".[583]

In England, by section 12(1) of the Sale of Good states that ds Act, 1893 there is an implied condition that the seller has a right to sell the goods and in case of an agreement to sell, that he will have such a right at the time when property in the goods is to pass to the buyer. Hence, the seller must pass a good title[584] failing which he will be in breach of the contract of sale because he does not have the right or power to transfer the title in the goods to the buyer. There need not be any other interference with the buyer's possession of the goods; the mere absence of a right to sell is sufficient to cause the breach of the implied term. This was the view of *Scrutton L.J., in Niblett v. Confectioners' Materials Co. Ltd.*[585] as he said: "If the seller can be stopped from selling by process of the law, then he does not have the right to sell." This was the same position in the case of *Karlshamns Oljefabriker v. Eastport Navigation Corp.*[586]

The consequences of such a breach is that there is a total failure of consideration on the part of the seller which entitles the buyer to repudiate the contract. The *locus classicus* is the case of *Rowland v. Divall*[587] where Lord Atkin observed that "*The buyer has not received any part of that which he contracted to receive, namely, the property and the right to possession and that being so, there has been a total failure of consideration*". The buyer had not received any part of that which contracted to receive, namely the property and the right to possess due to a defective title.

It has to be pointed out that the Law Commission suggested that the buyer in these circumstances should be entitled to recover no more than his actual loss taking into consideration any benefit he may have derived from the goods

582 Article 230 of the old Uniform Act is the forerunner to Article 260, which still maintains the wordings.

583 Author's translation.

584 see also section 2 of the Supply of Goods Act 1982.

585 [1921] 3 K.B. 387.

586 (The Elafi) [1986] 1 All ER 208.

587 Op. cit., See also *Butterworth v. Kingsway Ltd.*, [1954] 1 W.L.R. 1286.

when they remained in his possession.[588]

From a reading of Article 275 UAGCL, it is clear that the main purpose and effect of the seller's duty to deliver is to require the seller to transfer the property or title to the goods to the buyer. This implies that the seller should not necessarily be the owner of the goods but have a right to sell. In reference to Section 12 (1) SGA, the natural and primary meaning of the word '*right*' seems to be '*power*'; in other words, the seller must have the power to vest the general property in the goods in the buyer.

Accordingly, from the provision text of the Uniform Act, the '*power*' to confer a title and the duty to deliver the goods to the buyer go together. This is the purport of the seller's duty to deliver goods concurrently with the relevant documents relating to the goods to the buyer.[589] As a matter of commercial practice, documents of certain types of goods like a bill of lading represents the actual title to the real owner of the goods in matters of sale. Thus, the seller has the duty to vest the documents relating to goods to the buyer through a carrier when it involves sales at distance,[590] or at the place indicated in the contract.[591] This finds importance to the fact that, the passing of title to the commercial buyer under the Uniform Act is vital for the running of its business. As a Common law principle expressed in the Latin phrase, *nemo dat quod non habet*, (no one can sell what he does not have), the seller would be in breach of a contact of sale where he is not able to pass a good title to the commercial buyer. But there are exceptional cases in which the seller may find difficulties in conferring good title on the buyer.[592]

Similar to the CISG,[593] the Uniform Act ensures the buyer's protection of eviction by the third party. Guarantees are a standard part of most commercial transactions, with both buyers and sellers choosing to make and demand these guarantees. The seller's guarantees in particular are a common feature of commercial contracts because they are often in the interest of both the buyer and the seller. One of the main ways they serve both interests is by solving an adverse selection problem, commonly referred to as the "*lemons problems*". For buyers, a seller's guarantee lends credibility to a product and reduces risks related to a possible product defect. As a result, sellers will often want to include these guarantees in their contracts in order to signal to the buyer that

588 Article 255 of the Uniform Act states that: the seller shall deliver the goods according to the quantity, quality, specification, and packaging provided for in the contract.

589 Articles 250 & 252 UAGCL.

590 Article 252 UAGCL.

591 Article 254 UAGCL.

592 In cases of seizure of the goods by a sheriff or custom authorities.

593 Article 41 CISG.

their product is not a bad one, thus reducing the effect of bad products as well as helping sellers complete a deal that might be difficult to close otherwise.[594]

Despite the legal and practical importance of this rule, the language used by the Act in this connection is far from clear. The Uniform Act uses the terms '*right*' or '*claim*' but does not provide any meanings for them which may afford the protection of buyers vis-a-vis third parties' interest over the goods in a contract of sale.

In England, there is a similar provision which corresponds to the above seller's obligation contained in Article 260 (1) of the Uniform Act. Section 12 of the Sale of Goods Act 1979 implies three terms into the contract of sale: first, a condition that the seller has a right to sell the goods;[595] second, a warranty that the goods are free from undisclosed encumbrances;[596] and third, a warranty that the buyer should enjoy quiet possession of the goods.[597] These various sections raise numerous questions, each of which requires separate consideration.

The prevailing position at common law suggests that the chances for the use of the provision related to third party property right are so remote that the application of this area of the law remains unknown.[598] This is based on the fact that the practical operation of that part of Section 12 (1) (b) dealing with freedom from encumbrances is limited because the law does not generally recognise real encumbrances over chattels by a person not in possession. For instance, if the third party is in possession of the goods, the seller will simply be unable to deliver what he does not physically have.[599] Even when he is not in possession, it is only rarely that the goods can have encumbrances binding on the buyer, bona fide purchaser of the goods.

Unlike the Uniform Act, the implied terms mentioned above can never be excluded or limited by any contract term and the first of them is so absolutely fundamental that a breach may involve a total failure by the seller to perform the contract.[600]

Similarly, unlike the Uniform Act, the Civil Code's provisions relating to the buyer's protection of eviction is broader as it includes the warranty on

---

594 Kabir Mason, *Paradox of Presumptions: Seller Warranties and Reliance Waivers in Commercial Contracts*, Op. cit., p. 2–3.

595 Section 12 (1).

596 Section 12 (2a).

597 Section (2) (b).

598 Atiyah et al., *The Sale of Goods*, Op. cit., p. 121.

599 Ibid, p.121.

600 Michael Bridge, *The Sale of Goods*, Op. cit., p. 357; Roy Goode, *Commercial Law*, Op. cit., p. 283.

personal property right[601] and third party property rights.[602]As opposed to movable property, personal property right is not covered by the Uniform Act. Rather, immovable property seems to be the most appropriate when dealing with issues touching on personal property rights.[603] The UAGCL followed the CISG on this point.

The CISG does not deal with the warranty on personal property rights but it has nevertheless been extended to right and claim related to industrial and other intellectual property rights.[604] The Uniform Act's provision extends to any goods, subject to pledge, secure legal guarantee or attached to a third party rights when they have been acquired by the seller.[605] These goods should not be subject to the pledging of stock.[606]

Third Party Rights

A third party right should be understood to mean any form of deprivation or disturbance on the right acquired by the buyer over the goods or any disturbance by a third party to the use or exploitation or disposal of the goods acquired by the buyer. In any of these situations, it is practically assumed that the third party has exercised his right as the true owner over the goods.[607]

To avoid such a situation, the seller must observe the principle that the goods must be delivered to the buyer free from any right of a third party.[608] In other words, a seller cannot transfer to the buyer a third party property right on the goods at the time of the contract.[609] The main idea is that the seller is required to transfer the best title or absolute legal interest in the goods to the

601 Cameroon, Article 1628 CC; Côte d'Ivoire, Article 1628 CC; France, Article 1628.In the French Law (qui doit garantir ne peut évincer) i.e. whoever should guarantee cannot deprive. Guarantee on Personal property right is aimed to stop the seller to get possession of the goods by tricky means. It includes all claims related to legal rights (competition) and any other non legal rights caused by the seller. The seller is therefore under the duty not to frustrate the buyer's right on the peaceful possession of the goods sold.

602 Cameroon, Article 1625–40 CC; Côte d'Ivoire, Article 1625–40 CC; France, Article 1625–40 CC.

603 Akuété Pedro Santos & Jean Yado Toé, *OHADA Droit Commercial Général*, Op. cit., p. 398.

604 Article 42 CISG.

605 Editions FFA Ernst & Young International, Les études pratiques de Ernst & Young en Afrique, (1st edition, Editions FFA Ernst & Young International, 2006) p. 607.

606 Article 100 Uniform Act Organisig Securities..

607 AkuétéPedro Santos & Jean Yado Toé, Op. cit., pp. 397–401; Peter Schlechtriem and Ingebord Schwenzer, Op. cit., p. 483–485.

608 Article 230 UAGCL; Article 41 CISG.

609 Article 284 para.2 UAGCL.

buyer. Unless the buyer knew of any third party rights over the goods, the seller is in breach on his obligation to guarantee to the buy that there will not be any eviction over the goods. It should be pointed out that, it is totally immaterial whether or not the seller knew of the third party rights over the goods.[610]

The Seller's Right to Sell the Goods

As a general rule, a seller is obliged to deliver goods to the buyer which are free from any rights of a third party. This suggests that in the first place, the seller should have the capacity to pass over ownership to the buyer as conditioned by his right to sell the goods in question. The seller must not necessarily be the owner of the goods[611] but he must hold a right to sell the goods at the time property is to pass to the buyer.

A good illustration is the case of *Niblett v. Confectioners' Materials Co Ltd*:[612]

> *The defendants sold to the plaintiffs 1,000 cases of condensed milk in tins bearing the label 'Nissly Brand'. Nestle and Anglo-Swiss Condensed milk Co Ltd then threatened proceedings for infringement of their trade mark and exacted an undertaking from the defendants not to dispose of condensed milk with the label 'Nissly'. In order to secure the release of the purchased Goods from the Customs the plaintiffs were forced to remove the offending labels and sell the condensed milk unlabelled for the best price they could get. It was held that the plaintiffs were entitled to damages for breach of the implied condition*[613] *as to the defendants' right to sell. The obligation of the defendants was not merely to pass a good title but also to ensure that the goods did not infringe the trade mark of a third party so as to enable that party to interfere with the sale.*[614]

The words '*right to sell*', though normally equated with title, have both a wider and narrower importance.[615] There must not necessarily be the existence of the goods under the seller's keeping at the time of concluding the contract. A breach will not be considered where the seller contracts to sell goods he

---

610 Akuété Pedro Santos & Jean Yado Toé, Op. cit., p. 399.

611 There is no breach if the goods are sold by an agent with authority to sell the goods.

612 [1921] 3 KB 387

613 It was equally considered by Atkin L.J. that the warranty of quiet possession was also infringed and that the defendants were in breach of the implied condition of merchantable quality.

614 see the facts of this case from Roy Goode, *Commercial Law*, Op. cit., pp. 284–285.

615 Ibid, p. 284.

does not own at the time of the contract, provided he does have a right to sell at the time property is to pass.

The fundamental requirement here is to qualify the seller's right to sell and also the third party's right(s) over the goods. As concerns the seller's right to sell, the seller must not necessarily be in the possession of the goods and be able to transfer property to the buyer. To avoid any third party's claim, the seller must be the right holder of some patent, trade mark or other proprietary interest over the goods. Any possibility for the third party to have access to the goods on such reasons will amount to a defect in title and the seller will be liable for this. The essence here is for the seller to be able to transfer to the buyer a title overriding that of the true owner.

Freedom from Encumbrances

The literal meaning of the word '*encumbrance*' means "*something that prevents you from moving normally or doing what you want*".[616] In other words, it denotes some defects, impediments which may hinder a person from using or disposing of a thing. Though this is a well-known implied term at common law, headed '*freedom from encumbrances*',[617] the Uniform Act seems not to have boldly highlighted this concept but from a cursory reading of its Article 260 para. 2, the obligation of the seller to warranty to the buyer that the goods bought are free and will remain free from any charge or encumbrance not disclosed or known to the buyer before the contract was concluded is clear.

Such encumbrances may impair the marketability of the goods as well the title over the goods. The warranty is therefore broken by the mere existence of an undisclosed encumbrance.

In the first place, an encumbrance will impair the marketability of the goods when it particularly relates to the quality of the goods which will amount to defects in quality, because liability for defects in quality is already excluded under Article 256 of the Uniform Act if the buyer's lack of knowledge is due to negligence on his part to report in reporting the defects to the seller on time. On the other hand, the one-year time limit stipulated under the Uniform Act only applies to defects in the goods, but not to defects in title.[618]

Also, public law restrictions relating to characteristics of the goods, such as their failure to comply with domestic rules for the protection of consumers,

[616] *Macmillan English Dictionary*, Op. cit., p. 455

[617] Section 12 (2) (b) of the Sale of Goods Act, 1893.

[618] Article 259 (1) of the Uniform Act.

public health, or environment, do not constitute a defect in title, but could instead give rise to liability for defects in quality under Article 255 para. 1 of the Uniform Act.

Secondly, the encumbrance may also impair the seller's title over the goods, because liability for a defect in title is excluded only if the buyer agrees to accept the goods subject to defects in title.[619] In other words, it is immaterial whether the buyer had knowledge of the seller's want of title. The crucial question should be whether the intention of the parties is that the buyer shall take delivery of the goods subject to or free from the encumbrance in question.[620] It is noteworthy that encumbrances over the seller's title over the goods are generally possessory (lien and pledges) relating to immovable property.[621] However, the OHADA Uniform Act is mostly concerned with this issue when it concerns movable property under a contract of sale and particularly when the seller has a right to sell as discussed above.

Moreover, public law encumbrances may also be considered to amount to a defect in title for the purposes of the provision of Article 260 of the Uniform Act. In cases where taxes and custom duties encumbering the goods may constitute a defect in title, as may public law measures resulting there from, to the extent that the contract provides that those costs are to be borne by the seller. Liability for a defect in title may also occur if the goods are seized in connection with a third party's right,[622] such as a seizure of stolen goods, security interest, [623]and challenge of a right to dispose of goods under OHADA Insolvency laws and its simplified recovery procedures.

The Right to Quiet Possession

Article 260 para. 2 of the Uniform Act implies into a contract of sale a warranty that the buyer will enjoy quiet possession of the goods. [624] Under the Uniform Act, the warranty of quiet possession can be associated with the seller's guaranty against a third party's right or claim under as enshrined in its

619 Article 260 para. 1 UAGCL.

620 Roy Goode, Op. cit., p. 289.

621 Robert Bradgate, *Commercial Law*, (3rd ed., Oxford University Press, New York 2005) p. 363.

622 Provided the third party's right does not exist or the third party does not exert any direct claim against the buyer.

623 see Article 41 et seq. of the Uniform Act on *Simplified Recovery Procedures and Enforcement Measures*.

624 This is the similar position under French Civil Code–Article 1626 which stipulates that the seller is obliged to warranty the buyer the quiet possession of the goods: 'la possession paisible de la chose vendue'.

Article 260 para. 1.[625] Despite the fact that the seller will be required to have the right of disposal by the time the property would vest in the buyer, the warranty of quiet possession is a continuous warranty on the part of the seller. This warranty applies even after the sale has been effected by the seller, and if the buyer's possession is disturbed by the seller himself,[626] and the seller is in breach even though at the time of sale he had a good title over the goods.

It follows therefore that that the seller will be liable if the buyer's possession is disturbed by a wrongful act of the seller or any person claiming through him a right, or by a lawful act of any other person, including a true, dispossessed owner of the goods.[627]

Under the Uniform Act, the provisions of Article 260 work in favour of the buyer against a wrongful disturbance of his quiet possession by the seller himself. Where the disturbance of the buyer's possession is by a third party, the buyer may be entitled to treat this disturbance as the responsibility of the seller if, as a result of any acts or defaults of the seller, some third party with the seller is in contractual relations asserts an encumbrance or lien on the goods. Any interference with the buyer's possession will amount to tortuous liability and will not extend to a mere contractual right.[628]

Exclusion of Seller's Liability

Knowledge of the Buyer

From a reading of Article 260 para.1 of the Uniform Act, the buyer loses his right of action against the seller if he accepts to collect the goods under conditions where there is a claim or a right has been exercised upon. Thus, the word '*condition*' used in this provision may be considered to entail a third party right or claim over the goods. By implication, this means the buyer has to affirmatively demonstrate that he relied on the substance of the promise made by the seller in the guaranty. From this standpoint, it is trite knowledge that without reliance, courts will find no harm to the buyer and therefore no action for damages. The standard of establishing a guarantee under the contract in the Uniform Act is based on the knowledge of the buyer of the existence of such a right or claim over the goods as expressed in article 261.

[625] At Common law, it is an implied term sanctioned by Section 12 (2) (b) of the Sale of Good Act, 1893.

[626] Article 260 para. 2 UAGCL.

[627] Robert Bradgate, Op. cit., p. 363; Kamwe Mouaffo Colette, Op. cit., pp. 23–25.

[628] P. S. Atiyah, et al., Op. cit., p. 120.

Knowledge of the guaranty is not sufficient because they must also have been reliance on the seller's promise.

From the language of the text, there is a shift toward a more contract-based approach in contrast to torts, to guaranty law in the Uniform Act. It effectively holds the presumption of enforceability. The seller's guarantee is still presumptively unenforceable until the buyer shows that the "*express guarantee*" (was) in existence during the conclusion of the contract. The practical effect of shifting the burden to the seller is to show that the guarantee was part of the bargain between the seller and the commercial buyer making the guarantee clause presumptively enforceable. Arguably, this moves the law of guaranty under the Uniform Act closer to standard contract law, which treats all contract terms as presumptively valid. However, it also shifts both risks and cost of the enforcement of the guaranty to the seller from the buyer.[629]

The knowledge of the buyer with regard to this condition that is, third party intellectual property right over goods is of relevance in determining whether the seller is liable or not. In accordance with the duties of the buyer to disclose any lack of conformity of goods under the Uniform Act,[630], the buyer must give notice to the seller of such right specifying the nature or claim of the third party within a period of time[631] after he becomes aware or ought to have been aware of such rights. Unlike the CISG where the buyer has an obligation to disclose within a '*reasonable time*',[632] the buyer under the Uniform Act has a period of one year to report or lay a complaint against the seller.

The seller's liability will be excluded where the buyer fails to report to the buyer under such a time-frame and most especially if he knew or ought to have known of the third party's of intellectual property rights over the goods.

In addition, the seller will be precluded from any liability where it is obvious that the buyer had failed to report to the seller of a foreseeable infringement of an intellectual property right in the third party's state, where the goods are to be used or resold, or to be delivered which he knew or ought to have known.

However, if the seller becomes aware of the knowledge of the buyer on a third party property rights or claims over the goods, he will not be entitled to use it as a defence if he goes ahead and deliver the goods under such condition.[633] Delivery under such condition and knowledge will amount to

---

629 Kabir Mason, Op. cit., p. 4.

630 Articles 256 and 258 UAGCL.

631 The time-frame may be immediately after the conclusion of the contract, or from the moment delivery has been performed or a month after delivery.

632 Article 41 et seq. CISG.

633 Article 43 (2) CISG.

breach of his obligation to guaranty.[634]

The issue of course of dealing and usage may also be used by the seller in support of the buyer's knowledge of the existence of such a guarantee or limiting clause. Where there has been a previous dealing between the parties, the party seeking to rely on the exclusion clause or other terms may presume that the other is aware of the terms. If therefore on any occasion the terms are not communicated to the other party, they may nonetheless apply. Course of dealing must be distinguished from trade usage. In the former, the parties may not consider themselves bound by such a term at all times while the latter, they must. It suffices that there must be a regularity of dealings between the parties for a course of dealing to be implied. In *Henry & Sons v. William Lillico & Sons*,[635] a contract for the sale of poultry feeding stuffs was made and a confirmation note was sent the next day which included exemption clauses. The parties had dealt with each other for about three years, entering into three or four contracts monthly. The House of Lords held that there was a sufficient course of dealing to warrant the incorporation of the exemption clauses.

Clauses Limiting the Seller's Guarantee

In principle, parties under a contract may agree on the clauses limiting guarantee in the contract. Exclusion clauses are in principle upheld with the principle of freedom of contract. This is in line with Article 1134 of the Civil code, which applies in the French Cameroon, states in categorical terms that: "*Agreements legally made stands as law for those who make them.*"[636] This follows that the courts have considered themselves as having the authority to nullify a contract which has been properly concluded between two or more parties.

Article 260 para.1 of the Uniform Act states that the seller is held to guarantee the buyer's against a third party right or claim over goods intended to be sold during the conclusion of the contract. This law is however not imperative and can be varied by and accepted by the parties. This has led to the possibility under the OHADA Uniform Act for the insertion by parties of limitation clauses in their sale contract. This may be initiated by the seller as Article 261 para. 1 provides that: "*Any clause limiting the guarantee shall be interpreted narrowly*". From this Article, it can be inferred that if the seller

634 Article 260 para. 1 UAGCL.

635 1968 2 All.E.R. 444 (House of Lords).

636 The author"s translation.

knows of any third party claim or right over the goods before the conclusion of the contract of sale with the buyer, then the exclusion or limitation clause will not apply. The interpretation of this article is therefore consistent with the general interpretation of exclusion or limitation clauses, that is,if there is deceit or a serious fault on the part of the person relying on the clause, the clause becomes inapplicable.[637]

This is also similar to Article 1643 of the French Civil Code which states that: "*He [the seller] is liable for hidden defects, even though he did not know of them, unless, in such a case, he had stipulated he would not be obligated for any guarantee*".[638]

However, the seller's liability will be circumvented where "*...the buyer knew and accepted the existence of that clause when the sale was concluded*".[639] In fact, knowledge of the clause by the buyer is not sufficient. To make it imperative and enforceable, the buyer must rely and accept such a term into their sale contract. The burden of proof lies on the seller to satisfy that the complete facts were known to the buyer.

However, contrary to the spirit of Article 261 para.1 UAGCL, although accepted by the buyer, guarantee clauses are always drafted by the seller who usually does so in his favour; they must therefore subject to the judge's interpretation so as to avoid abusive or controversial clauses.[640] Interpreted narrowly, this explains the general rule in ordinary law that the agreement shall be interpreted against the party who drafted it and in favour of the adhering party.[641] In fact, the notion of reasonableness of contract clauses should be given closed attention. In the case of *Kendu v. Cameroon International C. Ltd.*[642], the plaintiff paid for a deep-freezer but up to six months later he had not obtained delivery of the same. In an action for breach of contract, the defendants contended that it was the practice, which was made known to the plaintiff, that their customers had to wait for some time before obtaining delivery and that this was indeed a term of their contract with the plaintiff. The Court held that such a term must be subject to a condition of reasonableness

637 Joseph Dion Ngute, *Standardized Contracts in a Bi-Jural State: The United Republic of Cameroon*, (Ph.D. Thesis, University of Warwick, Law School 1982) pp. 160–161, (unpublished).

638 The author's translation.

639 Article 261 para.2 UAGCL.

640 Akuété Pedro Santos & Jean Yado Toé, Op. cit., pp. 400–401.

641 English law has used three tools in interpreting limitation clauses. A court may construe the clause strictly, against the party relying on it; it can decide that the party in breach has committed a fundamental breach; finally, the court may use the doctrine of privity of contract to limit the range of persons who are entitled to be covered by such a clause.

642 Suit No. HCSW/12/78, 1979, High Court, Kumba, (unreported).

and that in this case, six months was an unreasonably long time to wait for delivery.

In support to this interpretation of Article 261 para. 2 of the Uniform Act which provides the rules on guarantee and limitation clauses, the courts within the OHADA Member countries need to adopt a strict approach in applying these rules. A greater consideration need to be taken irrespective of the seller's obligation to guarantee or of whether the seller knows of any third party claim or right in the goods. So long as the seller is a professional person- manufacturer, wholesaler or even a retailer- in the business concerned, the established presumption is that such a seller has knowledge of the undisclosed third party right or claim or any hidden defect in the goods and this presumption is irrebuttable.[643] In addition to the obligation to guarantee, the seller as a professional also has the duty to protect the rights of commercial and consumer buyers. This will rather have as impact to strengthen the contractual bond of parties in their business. Again, it is in the public interest that the public at large should at all times be protected from defective goods and unpleasant legal actions. Thus, it is the place of the seller to insure against possible inconveniences in the selling of their goods. All that the limitation clause achieves in this connection is to limit the damages that would have to be paid to the buyer; it does not absolve the seller from liability altogether.

A widespread complaint made by Cameroonian consumers against sellers is that although most of them sell valuable items such as cars with guarantees, the guarantee clauses are often not respected or are construed very restrictively by the sellers. Two decisions of the Yaoundé courts in the French speaking region of the country demonstrate this point. In *Levendis Athanase c/ SHO Africauto*,[644] the appellant bought two cars from the respondents. Clause 7 of the respondents' standard sales agreement provided that the cars were sold under a guarantee for twelve months or fifteen thousand kilometres, whichever was longer. Before this guarantee had run out, various parts of the car were replaced in the respondents' garage and the respondent brought a claim before the Yaoundé Court of First Instance for the cost of the replaced parts. The Court of First Instance held that the guarantee clause did not cover such replacements but that decision was reversed by the Court of Appeal in Yaoundé which held that such a limitation of the guarantee clause was improper.

643 Joseph Dion Ngute, Op. cit., p. 162.

644 Affaire No. 25/72, 1973, Cour d'Appel, Yaoundé, (unreported).

A good many of the guarantee clauses examined provided that the guarantee covers only major defects. That was the case on *Kandem Simon c/ SHO Africauto*,[645] where the guarantee clause, similar to the one above provided that only major defects in the car were covered. Before the guarantee expired, the car developed minor faults which were repaired by the defendant and paid by the plaintiff. Thereafter, a series of faults developed in the car which, taken separately, were minor but which, taken together, were major. The plaintiff then instructed the defendants to sell the car and the latter did so for the sum of six hundred thousand CFA francs, claiming that the balance, five hundred and fourteen thousand francs, covered the cost of repairs. The Yaoundé High Court held that the defects in the car were covered by the guarantee clause and further held that in any event such a limitation of the guarantee was unfair. In the words of the Court, the defendant has acted in an "*abusive, arbitrary and unjustified*" manner. This is illustrative of the high-handedness with which dealers treat consumers.

A classic example of this high-handedness is the case of *Brasseries du Cameroun v. Mokake Elali*.[646] In 1970, an agreement was entered into between the appellant brewers and the respondent, whereby the former were to supply the latter with their drinks, which the latter sold on a commission basis. Sometime thereafter, some of the respondent's customers complained that they had bought unwholesome beer from the latter's off-licence shop. The respondent wrote to the appellants about it and the latter sent five bottles of beer as compensation which he refused to accept. In 1973, the respondent again received many complaints which were corroborated by the local health superintendent. As a result, the plaintiff began losing a lot of his customers. He then wrote to the Director of the local branch of the appellant company expressing his concern. Consequently, the appellants stopped supplying him with their products whereupon he brought an action for breach of contract. It must be pointed out that the appellants, who accounted for about seventy per cent of the country's total drink production, had entered into similar agreements with small retailers all over the country. A card is issued by the company to the retailer containing the retailer's address and a code number. The High Court judge held that the issuing of the card, along with the subsequent practice of delivering their drinks at the respondent's shop, constituted a definite agreement which the appellant had breached.[647] The

[645] Judgment No. 55 du Janvier 22, 1974,Grande Instance, Yaoundé, (unreported).

[646] Civ. Appeal No. CASWP /14/79, 1982, Buea Court of Appeal, (unreported).

[647] The High Court judge relied partly on the principle of equitable, and cited *Central London Property Trust Ltd. v. High Trees House Ltd.* 1947 1 K.B.

company appealed, contending that the issuing of the card and the subsequent course of conduct were insufficient to imply a continuing contract between the parties, and that each delivery by them constituted a separate contract of sale. The Court of Appeal in Buea (common law jurisdiction) agreed with the appellants. Thus, in spite of the fact that the company's action to ceasing supplies was an act of victimization for the plaintiff's justified complaints, and regardless of the course of conduct of the parties which was consistent for four years, the Court of Appeal held that there was no definite contract between the parties.

Hence, by deliberately eschewing definite terms from their contracts, the company can breach an agreement entered into with retailers at their pleasure with absolute impunity. The Court of Appeal decided this case purely in terms of offer and acceptance, paying no attention to the reasonableness of the agreement, and to the fact that numerous other retailers will be equally affected.

Related to the problem is that of entering into a contract of guarantee written in a language alien to a contracting party, a problem which recurs constantly in as much as there are two official languages in Cameroon; French and English. This is not only common with contracts with consumers, but even the professional commercial buyer or seller may be illiterate or not conversant with an alien language. A typical example is the current influx of Chinese pharmaceutical goods into the country which have indications only printed in Chinese. This makes the understanding of any limiting clause difficult for a Cameroonian seller or buyer. However, given the bilingual nature of Cameroon, the Law requires manufacturers or those selling new consumer goods for use in the country to provide a manual in English and French indicating the principal features of the product as well as the scope and duration of any guarantee given to the customer, including the provisions of the legal guarantee for hidden defects.[648]

On the basis of the above analysis of these pre-OHADA cases and sellers' liability, the seller under the Uniform Act can only try to water down the rigours of this strict liability rule by relying on the time during which a claim based on the legal guarantee required. The courts would be more ready to treat such clauses as limitation clauses separate from the period specified for the buyer to make a complaint predicated upon lack of conformity as stipulated in Article 259 para.1.

[648] Section 21(1) of Law No. 90/031, August 10, 1990 organising commercial activities in Cameroon.

Time of the Third Party Rights and Claims

If the third party's action is genuine meaning that he is acting by virtue of the fact that he has ownership of the buyer's goods, (an ownership acquired before the new buyer's contract of sale) then, the third party, true owner of the goods, can claim his right over that of the buyer.[649]

The third party claim should occur only after delivery to the buyer. In other words, when the legal rights are deemed to have passed. However, if the third party claim arrives before delivery, an action of specific performance for the seller to deliver the goods is open to the buyer.[650] It is important that the buyer informs the seller at the time of his knowledge about the third party claim over his right. Once informed, the seller will then take necessary measures to challenge the third party on his purported rights over the goods. For the seller to act, he should be notified on time since dispossession ceases where the purchaser has allowed a final judgment to be handed down against him without joining his seller in the proceedings, if the latter proves that there were sufficient grounds to have the action dismissed.[651]

Conclusion

The above analysis place a duty on the seller under the UAGCL to deliver goods not only free from any right, but also free from any claim of a third party. It does not depend on the existence of third party's right. Third party[652] claims are equally governed by domestic law which is the seller's state. They will, as a rule, be the result of previous events affecting the goods or the seller's previous conduct.

The seller's guarantee against third party rights or claim over the goods he supplies is a salutary duty under the OHADA Uniform Act. This is an important consideration of the sanctity of the very object of a contract, which mandates the parties to enjoy rights which accrue from their undertakings. This translates the fact that the very purpose of a contract of sale, which is the ability to transfer title, must not be impinged with any third party's claim

649 Phillippe Van De Wiele, La vente d'Immeubles, (2eme édition, DeBoeck Université 2001) p. 78–80.

650 Ibid.

651 Cameroon, Article 1140 CC; Côte d'Ivoire, Artcle 1140 CC.

652 John O. Honnold, Op. cit., aptly points out that it is necessary to 'protect the normal expectation of a buyer that he is not purchasing a law suit'.

or right over it. In this connection, the OHADA Uniform Act has impliedly given consideration to intellectual property rights which constitute an integral component of goods sold by the seller forming part of a contract of sale. The imposition of the duty of guarantee on the seller ensures business confidence credibility and reputation for goods, as well as creates a foothold in the crowded goods market. It secures investments and sustains meaningful competition for the sale of goods at the international level.

Furthermore, the Uniform Act asserts the possibility of seller and buyer to enter into a limiting clause. In this manner, the enforcement of the seller's guarantee scheme under the Uniform Act is contract-based.

6

THE PASSING OF PROPERTY AND RISK IN GOODS

Introduction

Under the UAGCL, the passing of risk is tied with the passing of property. This means that, the risk in the goods *prima facie* passes to the buyer with the property. The wide variety of ways in which goods can be damaged, destroyed, or lost after the parties have contracted for the sale of those goods create the need for a simple and workable set of legal rules allocating risk of loss between the contracting parties immediately after the property must have passed to the buyer. The complexity of modern commercial practices underscores this need. This chapter sets out to examine how the provisions of the current Uniform Act on General Commercial Law allocate the risk of loss to parties when transfer of title must have been effected. In this chapter we shall also determine the seller's liability for the passing of title to the buyer and make an attempt to identify the different instances of his liability with respect to the passing of the risk. This discussion is important to the theme of this work in that the commercial buyer is concerned with the condition of the goods involved in his reselling business that he operates. This relates especially to the non physical aspects associated to the goods sold to him by the seller. Thus, the commercial buyer's interest on the transfer of property and risk could be said to be a contribution to a greater extent in ascertaining the seller's duty of conformity as to the specifications of the contract. The rules on conformity are also essential in terms of the function of allocating commercial risks between the parties. Many buyers will complain about the conformity of the goods, allege a breach, and invoke remedies. It is essential, therefore, that there be fairly clear legal rules, particularly those applied by default, that are capable of allocating risks, thereby producing legal certainty and possibly reducing litigation.

In this vein, we shall attempt a summary interpretation of the provisions of the Uniform Act and explain the legal theories on which the current law is based. Furthermore, we shall explore how the law operates in common international sales transactions involving shipment of goods across frontiers. We therefore realise that Article 278 of the Uniform Act does not allocate the risk of loss fairly, clearly, or consistently: it does not identify the kinds of risk which may be shifted to the buyer.

Rules Governing Transfer of Title

In the UAGCL, unless otherwise agreed by the parties, the transfer of title takes place at delivery,[653] or to be more accurate, from the moment the buyer takes delivery of the goods.[654]

Title Passes Upon the Conclusion of the Contract

Under the SGA, provided the contract of sales in question is unconditional, title passes from the seller to the buyer upon conclusion of the contract.[655] As a general rule at English law, title to the goods is transferred from the seller to the buyer when they intend it to be transferred.[656] But it should be observed that there is no transfer of title in a contract of sales of unascertained goods. Transfer of title will only be possible as soon as the goods become ascertained.[657]

Under the SGA, there is an established rule that the accurate point in time when the transfer of title takes place depends on the type or category of goods. This is the reason why the SGA makes a clear distinction between specific or ascertained goods on the one hand and unascertained or future goods on the other.[658]

---

653 Akuété Pedro Santos Jean Ydo Toé, *OHADA Droit Commercial Général*, Op. cit., p. 434.

654 Article 275 UAGCL.

655 SGA 1893 s 20.

656 SGA 1893 s 17.

657 SGA 1893 s 18.

658 see Chapter Two on the type of goods already examined.

Specific Goods

In a sale of goods contract for specific or ascertained goods the contracting parties have the option, in accordance with the SGA, to insert in their contract the time they intend the title over the goods to be transferred.[659] But if for some reasons such intention is not expressly stated but rather implied in one way or the other, it may be ascertained through either the parties' conducts, the terms of the contract or the circumstances of the case.

It is in the light of the above that the "*Romalpa clause*" principle was retained at common law. The principle was established in the case of *Aluminum Industries Vaassen BV v. Romalpa Aluminum Ltd.*[660] In this case, the seller made it clear, and both parties agreed on the terms, that the title over the goods purchased will only be transferred to the buyer when he had fully paid up all what he owed under the contract, no matter the excuse. But once the buyer received the goods (a consignment of aluminium foils), he resold part of it before he went into liquidation. The seller then sought an action before the court to enforce the contract they both agreed upon in order to secure his own payment, prior to the distribution of the buyer's asset to the general creditors.

The question before the court was to determine whether the seller could recover both the unused foils supplied to *Romalpa Ltd.* which had been stored and the proceeds of sales by *Romalpa Ltd.* of some unused foils.

In deciding the matter, the Court of Appeal quashed previous decisions and ruled that the seller was entitled to both "*unused foils supplied and the proceeds of sales*" due to the fact that *Romalpa* was simply a bailee of the goods. Moreover, the court was of the opinion that there was no breach by *Romalpa* complying with the company law registration of assets. It was pointless because company law had no application in this case since the title of the unused foils had never been transferred to *Romalpa* and therefore the proceeds from the sub-sale belonged to the seller and could not therefore be the subject of a charge on the company's assets.

Sometimes, parties totally fail to give any indication of intention in their contract; for this reason, the SGA provides four basic rules for ascertaining the intention of the parties. It should be made clear that these rules only come into play where there is no express or implied declaration of the intention by the contracting parties.

659 SGA 1893 s 19 (1).

660 [1976] 2 All ER 522 Similar position delivered in *Leigh & Siclavan v. Aliakmn Shipping Co. Ltd.* [1985] 2 All ER 44.

According to the first rule, when there is an unconditional contract of sale of specific goods, in a deliverable state, the title is transferred upon the conclusion of the contract. It is immaterial whether payment is made or the buyer has taken possession of the goods. In the *Associated Press of Nig. Ltd. v. Phillips (W.A) Records Ltd.*,[661] the contracting parties agreed that a linotype should remain in the premises of the seller until such a time that the buyers could obtain the services of a competent operator. At the Lagos High court in Nigeria, it was held that the title of the machine was transferred to the buyer even though delivery could not be effected until the happening of the specified event.[662]

For the second rule, if the contract of sale of specific goods requires something to be done in order for the goods to be in a deliverable state, the transfer of title will take place upon the performance of such thing and the buyer is given notice thereof.[663] In *Acraman and Anor v. Morrice*,[664] the seller of a quantity of timber was required to sever the tops, cut off the siding, square the trunks and at his expense convey them to the buyer at the agreed destination. The seller later on became bankrupt and the buyer anxiously went ahead to where they had been lying and took upon himself to sever, cut and carry them away in order to get possession of the timber. It was held that no title was transferred to him by doing so.

By reason of the third rule, if the sales contract of specific goods in a deliverable state needs either to be measured or weighed, before ascertaining the price of the goods, for instance, the transfer will only take place until such requirement is fulfilled.[665] In *Turley v. Bates*,[666] weighing was to be done by the buyer. The court held that the transfer of title was not suspended but rather that it was, be considered made after the goods had been weighed.

Under the fourth and last rule, the transfer of title is regulated, for instance, when the goods are delivered to the buyer on approval, or on sale or a similar term. Thus, the title will be transferred to the buyer if he gives approval to the seller or does something indicating acquiescence of the transaction on the one hand or if he just retains the goods beyond the required time or a reasonable length of time. It was held in *Kirkham v. Attenborough*[667] that by

661 CCHCJ/9/72 p. 17.
662 SGA 1893 s 18.
663 SGA 1893 s 19 .
664 [1850] 19 L.J.C. p. 57.
665 SGA 1893 s 18.
666 [1863] 2 H & C 200.
667 [1897] 1 Q.B. 201.

pledging the goods which were received on sale, the buyer had performed an at which amounted to approval of the transaction.

Unascertained Goods & Future Goods

It is a general rule under the SGA that there is no transfer of title when the goods are unascertained or future goods, unless and until the goods become ascertained and agreed upon by the parties.[668] Considered declamatory at Common law, this fundamental common law position was stated by Cotton LJ in *Marubita v. Imperial Ottoman Bank*[669]. However, if the goods must be ascertained before the title is transferred from the seller to the buyer, when then do unascertained goods become ascertained?

According to the SGA, when a sales contract involves unascertained or future goods that fit the description required and goods of that description are in a deliverable state, unconditionally appropriated to the contract, either by the seller with an assent of the buyer and vice versa, the title is transferred thereupon to the buyer. The assent may be explicit or implied, and may be given either before or after the appropriation is made.

Unconditional appropriation referred to above is the usual method by which the title is transferred in a sales contract. Strictly speaking, the requirement of an unconditional appropriation means that some ascertained and identified goods must be irrevocably attached or earmarked for the particular contract in question.[670] Hence, subject to the condition of assent, the title will then be transferred from the seller to the buyer.

With regard to unascertained goods, the question to be answered is how do they become unconditionally appropriated to the contract? To be accurate, the most obvious and common means for this to happen is by delivery. By way of explanation, upon delivery of the goods to the buyer, and the goods correspond to the contract description, constitute an appropriation which, assuming it to be unconditional, and subject to the question of assent, will thereupon transfer title to the buyer, if the goods are delivered at the right place.

Generally, if the seller delivers goods to the buyer mixed with other goods, there will be no transfer of title under these circumstances because the goods are unascertained at this stage, despite what could amount to an unconditional

---

[668] SGA 1893 s 18.

[669] [1878] 3 Ex. D 164.

[670] P. S. Atiyah, et al., *The Sale of Goods*, Op. cit., p. 283.

appropriation. The case of *Healy v. Howlettand Sons*[671] is commonly used to highlight this position.

In this case, the seller (plaintiff) entered into contract to sell 20 boxes of mackerel to the buyer (defendant). He subsequently delivered 190 boxes to the railway company with the instruction to earmark 20 of the boxes for the defendant and the other boxes to be delivered to several of his customers. Unfortunately, the train was delayed and the goods got deteriorated before the defendant's boxes were earmarked or attached to the contract. It was held that the title had not passed to the defendant because it was not possible to determine which of the boxes belonged to the defendant; therefore no identified or ascertained goods had yet to be appropriated to the contract to each individual buyer.

In looking at what amounts to appropriation, it was held in *Forster v. Klyth Shipbuilding & Dry Docks Co Ltd.*,[672] that appropriation as a term is a legal act, it must be supplemented. There must also be some definite act or some definite agreements between the parties which amount to an assent. The assent may be given expressly or impliedly. In particular, to be legally binding and effective, an unconditional appropriation must receive the assent of the contracting parties in the sales contract. In some cases, an assent to an appropriation may be conferred to the contract in advance. A typical situation occurred in *Pletts v. Beattie*[673] where the buyer agreed in the contract to abide whatever appropriation the seller might make.

In addition to the appropriation by delivery which is statutorily recognised,[674] appropriation by exhaustion is also known by common law courts. It follows that unascertained goods may become ascertained through the exhaustion process.

To illustrate an appropriation by exhaustion, the case of *Wait and James v. Midland Bank*[675] is most often cited. In this case, WJ stored a cargo of wheat in a warehouse and, by separate contracts, sold various lots to different purchasers which where however not separate to the bulk. All the lots were taken away by purchaser leaving only the quantity which corresponded with what was due to MB under the contract. It was held that by process of exhaustion, those goods became ascertained and property in them passed to MB.

---

671 [1917] 1 K.B. 337.

672 [1926] Ch. D. 494.

673 [1896] 1 Q.B. 519.

674 SGA 1893 s 18 Rule 2.

675 [1926] 31 Comm. Cas. 172

Title Passes by the Handing over of Goods

Unless otherwise agreed by the parties, the position under the UAGCL is that the title is transferred from the seller to the buyer when the latter takes delivery of the goods sold.[676] However, the time of delivery of goods may vary. It may be when the buyer takes delivery of the goods or when the goods are handed over to the first carrier or when they are made available to the buyer to collect. It should be noted that the transfer of title will definitely take place in any of these instances.

In circumstances where the sale contract requires that the goods be transported and delivery is not to be made at a specific place, the transfer of title will take place upon handing over the goods to the first carrier by the seller, for the buyer.[677] Even if the buyer is not in physical possession of the goods at the moment the title is transferred, as suggested by the default rule, it has been suggested that the UAGCL intended to ensure that the goods are under the buyer's control as soon as they are handed over to the first carrier, on his behalf.[678]

In circumstances where the contract of sale is silent as concerns the specific place of delivery, and the seller makes the goods available to the buyer by either storing them in a warehouse, or at his place of business,[679] it has also been suggested that the transfer of title takes place upon the buyer taking delivery of the goods.[680] However, there is a prevailing opinion that the appropriate time the title must be considered to have been transferred is when the goods are made available for collection, rather than actual taking of the delivery.[681]

While the first position can be justified by the rules governing the transfer of title, the second position is based on the argument of fairness and equity. In other words, it may happen that the buyer fails to take delivery; in this case, the seller is bound to keep the goods[682] and grant him an additional period to comply with his obligation to take delivery.[683]

---

676 Article 275 UAGCL.

677 Article 251 UAGCL.

678 Akuété Pedros Santos & Jean Yado Toé, Op. cit., p. 435–436.

679 Article 251 UAGCL.

680 Akuété Pedros Santos & Jean Yado Toé, Op. cit., p. 436–437.

681 Ibid., p.436–437.

682 Articles 273–274 UAGCL.

683 Article 286 UAGCL.

Transfer of Title by a Non-Owner

The UAGCL is silent on the transfer of title by a non-owner but when a question arises before the court, reference is often made to the domestic Civil Code. This was, for instance, the attitude of the Common Court of Justice and Arbitration (CCJA) in *Société Générale de Financement par Crédit-bail c/ Monsieur Hassana Dramera*[684] when it approved the procedure used by lower courts of Abidjan in Cote d'Ivoire. In common law countries, the buyer can generally acquire no better title than the seller had (*nemo dat quod non habet*).[685]In civil law countries a buyer acting in good faith can acquire property (*en fait de meubles la possession vaut titre*).[686]Generally, the aim of the rule related to the transfer of title by non-owner is to protect the proprietary rights over the goods.

At Common law, the Latin maxim "*Nemo plus iurisadalium transferre potest quam ipso habet has been dignified by the use of the Latin in the tag "Nemo Dat Quod Non Habet*" or put shortly Nemo dat.[687] The rule laid down in this maxim was stated by Lord Denning in *Bishopsgate Motor Finance Corpn v Transport Brakes Ltd.*,[688] where he said "*no one can give a better title than he himself has*". Hence, in order to protect commercial transactions, Lord Denning added that anyone who acquires title over the goods, in good faith and for value without notice, should get a good title. This Common law principle was later affirmed in the SGA.[689]

However, with the need to install certainty in the law, in order to enable the swift sale of goods transactions, particularly in such sales contract where a seller, with no right over the goods was able to transfer a good title, exception to the general rule was adopted.

These exceptions codified under the SGA[690] are aimed to provide the innocent buyer a greater protection in sale of goods transactions. They include; estoppel, sale by factor, sale by agent, sale under special power, sale in Market Overt, sale under voidable title and sale by the seller or the buyer in possession.

---

684 Arrêt n° 019/2002 du 31 Octobre, 2002.
685 SGA 1893 s 21 (1).
686 Cameroon, Article 2279 (1) CC; Cote d'Ivoire, Article 2279 (1) CC.
687 P. S. Atiyah et al., *The Sale of Goods*, Op. cit., p. 372.
688 [1949] 1 K.B 332, 336–7.
689 SGA 1893 s 21 (1).
690 SGA 1893 ss 21–25

Rules Governing Transfer of Risk Under the Uniform Act

Risk of "*loss*" in a sales context refers to the allocation of financial responsibility for the injury or destruction of goods that occurs while the goods are changing hands from seller to buyer.[691] Goods may become damaged as a result of carrier neglect, theft, or catastrophe such as fire, flood, or shipwreck. From the Middle Ages until the middle of the twentieth century, the risk of loss was borne by the party who had title to the goods. This ancient doctrine was preserved by the Uniform Sales Act of the United States of America (U.S.A.) before the enactment of the American Uniform Commercial Code (UCC).

Any owner of goods faces the possibility that some hazard may occur that will damage or destroy them. A seller holding goods for sale, just as any other owner, must either absorb the loss flowing from such an occurrence or insure against it. Both a seller and buyer know, however, that the economic risk of such a loss will move from the seller to the buyer as an incident of the sales transaction. To identify the appropriate moment for passage of this risk is the task of the law governing risk of loss. That law is currently found in Articles 277 et seq. of the Uniform Act.

Contractual Allocation of Risk

It is customary to speak of three stages, or incidents, in the performance of a contract of sale. These are the transfer of the property, delivery of possession and the passing of the risk. The typical transaction begins with all three "*interests*" vested with the seller who is compelled when all have passed irrevocably to the buyer. The respective transfer may take place simultaneously or in any sequence.[692]

The UAGCL and the SGA share the same position on the passing of risk whereby the passing of risk is tied with the passing of property.[693] This means that, risk passes to the buyer as soon as the property has passed. A cursory reading of some provisions of the Uniform Act reveal that title does not determine risk of loss under the OHADA Uniform Act on General Commercial Law. The Act discards title as the determinant of risk of

691 Mitchell Stocks, Risk of Loss under the Uniform Commercial Code and the Convention on the International Sale of Goods: A Comparative Analysis and Proposed Revision of UCC Sections 2–509 and 2–510', (1993) 87 *Northwestern University Law Review*, pp. 1–49, p. 1.

692 L.S. Sealy, 'Risk' in the Law of Sale, (1972) 31 *Cambridge Law Journal*, pp. 225–247, p. 225.

693 Article 277 UAGCL; SGA 1893 s 22; See Louise Merrett, The Importance of Delivery and Possession in the Passing of Title, (2008) (67) *Cambridge Law Journal*, pp. 376–395, p. 382.

loss.[694] The Uniform Act instead breaks sales transactions into categories based on the factual circumstances of the case. The Uniform Act links the burden of risk with possession. Indeed, for the purposes of the time of the passing of risk, the Uniform Act refers to physical acts of transfer of possession: the '*handing over*'[695] of the goods to a carrier or to the buyer, or '*taking over*' by the buyer. The drafters assumed, not without reason, that the party who has control of the goods is better placed to prevent losses or damages to the goods and, if need be, to limit the harmful consequences and assess the damage. In other words, objective factors such as "*handing over*" and "*taking over*", are determinative. Their relevance reflects the two interrelated premises upon which the risk of loss sections of the Act are built: that risk should rest on the party with control over the goods.

The Uniform Act's approach to risk of loss does not depend upon the inadequate principle of passage of title, an outcome similar to the UCC.[696] Rather, the basic policy behind the Uniform Act's risk of loss provisions is that the risk of loss should fall upon the party most likely to have insured or otherwise taken precautions against such loss. This general policy manifests itself in provisions in which the allocation of risk of loss turns upon such factors as which party has possession of the goods or which party retains the most control over the goods. This general policy is logically sound. For example, one provision of the Act places the risk of loss on the party having possession of the goods.[697]

Default Allocation of Risk

Under the OHADA UAGCL, it is inferable that the risk can pass to the buyer or remain with the seller, regardless of who has possession or control over the goods. In the absence of contrary agreement, Article 278 para.

694 In general, the OHADA Uniform Act on General Commercial Law, like the U.C.C., has avoided determining the passage of risk by the transfer of title or property, providing instead that risk passes on the occurrence of 'concrete commercial events—handing over goods to the carrier and the buyer's 'taking over' physical possession from the seller'—Articles 278 para. 1 and 279 para. 1 UAGCL.

695 This has been translated by the author based on the French version of the Uniform Act.: Article 278 para. 1—Lorsque le contrat de vente prévoit la remise des marchandises à un transporteur, les risques sont transférés à l'acheteur par la remise des marchandises au premier transporteur.

696 Section of 2–509 of UCC; Magaret Howard, Allocation of Risk of Loss Under the UCC: A Transactional Evaluation of Sections 2–509 and 2–510, (1983) (15) *Uniform Commercial Code Law Journal*, pp. 334–372, p. 334

697 Article 278 para. 1 UAGCL.

1 UAGCL allocates risk of loss when the seller has agreed to ship goods by carrier (carriage contract). Carriage contracts can be further subdivided into shipment and destination contracts. Shipment contracts require only that the seller deliver the goods to a carrier, while destination contracts require that the seller ship goods to some named point for tender of delivery to the buyer. To determine the contractual default instances of risk allocation, we first have to determine whether the contract is a carriage or destination contract.

In order to understand the OHADA Uniform Act's allocation of risk of loss when the parties have contracted for shipment of the goods, common delivery terms must be examined if the parties have provided for such a transaction in their contract of sale. These shorthand terms were developed by merchants to distinguish between "*shipment*" and "*destination*" contracts. The law of documentary sales is a product of the custom of the international community of merchants, ship-owners, marine insurance underwriters, and bankers of many countries. It has developed over many centuries as part of the international law merchant. Since the seventeenth century it has gradually been received into the developing national commercial legal systems of most countries. Many of the rules of the law merchant relating to documentary sales are embodied in the definitions of trade terms elaborated by the International Chamber of Commerce[698] and published as INCOTERMS 2010.[699]

In short, a shipment contract requires only that the seller places the goods in the hands of the carrier in order to shift the risk of loss to the buyer. On the other hand, a destination contract places the risk of loss on the seller until the carrier actually delivers the goods to the buyer. By implication, the Uniform Act adopts these common delivery terms and allocates risk of loss according to whether the parties have agreed to a shipment or destination contract.

[698] The International Chamber of Commerce is a global federation of national committees of approximately 65 countries. The U.S. national committee is the United States Council for International Business. Where no national committee has been established, direct membership is available to enterprises as well as business and trade organizations, including chambers of commerce. Direct membership exists in approximately 110 countries, including many in the developing world. Over 50,000 enterprises are represented, either through national committees or by means of direct membership. Enterprises in planned economies of the Soviet Union and Eastern Europe are not represented in the ICC. However, the ICC is formally engaged in a number of cooperative activities with representatives of these countries.

[699] INCOTERMS 2010. INCOTERMS 1980 replaced the original 1953 edition which had been updated in 1967 and 1976. See also International Chamber of Commerce, Guide to INCOTERMS, (1980). The chief rival to INCOTERMS 1980 is the General Conditions for Delivery of Merchandise, developed in 1968 by the Council for Mutual Economic Assistance and revised January 1, 1976.

Shipment Contracts

Article 278 para.1 UAGCL expressly governs sales contracts which require the seller to hand over goods to a carrier for transmission to the buyer. It provides, first, that if the seller '*is not bound to hand over the goods at a particular place*,'[700] the risk passes to the buyer when the goods are handed over to the first carrier. This seems to refer to the passage of risk in all except destination contracts, an inference supported by the legislative interpretation. It appears, however, that in this Article the draftsmen were concerned only with the question whether, in the event of transhipment from one carrier to another, the risk should pass when the goods are handed over to the first or the second carrier.

One of the main issues arising from this provision concerns the meaning of "*hand over*".[701] which appears throughout the Uniform Act. The term denotes a physical act of transfer of possession, meaning that the goods are transferred from the control of the seller to that of the carrier. The reference to the "*handing over*" of the goods constitutes an evident gain in clarity, in which the risk in the goods passed on physical delivery. The seller's liability here will not only be ascertained on grounds of goods delivered but mostly handing over of conforming or non-conforming goods to the buyer. In a situation such as this, the risk should pass to the buyer when he possesses the goods.

In principle, the reading of the above Article distils the idea that the whole transportation is at the buyer's risk. Furthermore, this rule poses problem where the seller uses his own employee(s) to transport the goods for part of the way. In such a case, the risk is split and passes to the buyer only when the goods are handed to the independent carrier who could also be the agent of the buyer. To determine the precise moment at which breakage occurred is a cumbersome task, as is often the case with container traffic of goods. Therefore, it would be of the utmost difficulty to allocate the burden of the loss or damage.

A definitional problem exists with regard to the use of the term "*carrier*" since the term is not defined by the Uniform Act. However, the implication of the Act is that '*carrier*' is used in its normal sense to mean an enterprise in the business of transporting the goods of others for commercial gain. Thus, paragraph 1 of Article 278 would not apply to a seller shipping goods by means of its own vehicles. An interpretative problem is created under a

[700] This is an unofficial translation from the author in accordance with the French version of the UAGCL.

[701] Translated from the French version as 'la remise des marchandises'.

transportation contract which does not explicitly state whether it is a shipment or a destination contract. Foreseeing this problem, the drafters intended that there be a presumption in favour of the will of the parties.

It is important to note here that the OHADA Member States have enacted a Uniform Act on Contracts for the Carriage of Goods by Road,[702] which governs only contracts for the carriage of goods by road. Therefore, it also embraces combined transactions of goods by rail/road transport or road/sea transport, or other combination of road and another type of transport where, to perform a single contract for the carriage of goods by road, a road vehicle containing goods is carried over part of the journey by a non -road vehicle, and the goods are not unloaded from the vehicle.[703] This follows therefore that a carrier being an independent party to the contract of sale between the seller and the buyer, his services may be needed to execute the seller's delivery performance.

Destination Contracts

Under a destination contract, pursuant to Article 251 of the Uniform Act, the risk of loss shifts to the buyer at the place of destination if the goods are duly so tendered as to enable the buyer to take delivery. In this case, tender of delivery to the buyer is accomplished when (1) "*the seller puts and holds conforming goods at the buyer's disposition and gives the buyer any notification reasonably necessary to enable him to take delivery,*" and (2) if the contract requires, the seller tenders the specified documents of title in correct form. Thus, by implication, the seller is responsible for damage or loss in the event of shipment and may be required to pay the buyer damages or to provide the buyer with substitute goods.[704]

From this standpoint, a parallel reading with Article 277 para.1 UAGCL would suggest that the seller is expected impliedly to comply with the requirements of shipment under a destination contract as set forth in Article 252 UAGCL. This may involve for example, C.I.F, ex-ships or F.O.B contracts. To make a proper tender of delivery pursuant to this section, the seller is

---

702 It was adopted on 22 March in Yaoundé (Cameroon) and entered into force on 1st January 2004. By virtue of Article 2-1 of the Uniform Act on Contracts for the Carriage of Goods by Road, a carrier is defined as any individual or corporate entity who assumes the responsibility of carrying the goods from the place of departure to the place of destination, using a road vehicle. see also, Boris Martor,Nanette Pilkington et al., Business Law in Africa, OHADA and the Harmonization Process, Op. cit., p. 220; Peter Schlectriem and Ingebord Schwenzer, Op. cit., p. 347.

703 Article 2 (J); Boris Martor, Nanette Pilkington et al., Op. cit., p. 217.

704 Article 283 UAGCL.

required to tender conforming goods and to give the buyer any notification reasonably necessary to enable buyer to take delivery. Although the manner, time, and place of tender are determined by the contract of the parties, the seller is required to make tender at a reasonable hour and to keep the goods available for delivery for a reasonable period. The seller is further obligated to tender the proper documents of title.[705]

It follows that when the contract of sale requires transportation, the seller is bound to ensure the transportation by concluding the relevant contract including that of the transportation of the goods and insurance.[706] Unless it is not required to insure the goods in transit, the seller is nevertheless bound or requested to provide to the buyer all relevant information necessary for the conclusion of an insurance contract.[707]

In a sense, the application of Article 252 UAGCL produces a somewhat consistent result under either a shipment or a destination contract. In both cases the seller initially begins bearing the risk of loss. Through compliance with the requirements of tender under the applicable Act's provisions, the seller may shift the burden of the risk of loss.

Furthermore, the primary rule related to the place of delivery under the Uniform Act shall be determined by the parties in the contract in question.[708] Hence, if the parties determined the place of delivery to be at the sea port of the buyer's country of residence, then the seller is bound to deliver the goods at the very place stated in the contract. It is therefore contrary to the provisions of the law that the seller in our case rely on the default rule if the contract clearly determined the place of delivery. For parties operating pursuant to a shipment contract, the risk of loss passes upon delivery to the carrier, while under the destination contract the risk does not shift until delivery to the buyer at the place of destination.

Goods Sold in Transit

Under the UAGCL, where the goods are sold in transit, risk passes to the buyer upon conclusion of the contract.[709] As a matter of practice in trade, it is rather uncertain and difficult to determine when the goods get damaged

705 Article 250 UAGCL.
706 Article 252 para.3 UAGCL.
707 Article 252 para.2 UAGCL.
708 Article 250 UAGCL.
709 Article 279 para.1 UAGCL.

while in transit, for the purpose of certainty. The seller is best placed to know the itinerary of the transportation of goods when he must have handed the goods for transmission to the carrier for delivery to the buyer. Thus, the seller bears that risk, if he knew or ought to have known that the goods were lost or damaged and failed to disclose this situation to the buyer.[710]

Which Risks are transferred to the Buyer?

As a matter of fact, it is important at this point to determine the different types of risks which may pass on to the buyer.

Liability for Loss or Damage to the Goods

The Uniform Act does not define the types of risks that it governs. However, inference can be made from the wordings used under the Act. The wording used in the Uniform Act is "*loss or deterioration*"[711] as contained in Article 277 para. 2. Physical risks to the goods including their destruction are covered by the concept of "*loss*".

By analogy, disappearance of the goods, including theft, misplacing the goods, their transfer to a wrong address or person, and mixing up the goods with other goods are included. Assuming that there is guilt of the seller's fault, which is a broad notion that encompasses: (i)-occurrence in transporting the goods from one party to the other; (ii)-in handling the storage, including the risks of natural processes leading to a decline in quality (resulting from whichever cause, like lack of care, bad packaging or from melting, thawing, shrinking, loss of weight or of strength or taste, or appearance).

This situation was vivid during a field trip conducted by the researcher in markets of some big cities in Cameroon: Douala and Yaounde.[712] Most big merchant-sellers of second- hand goods like shoes, for example, find in their bulk of goods damaged shoes and because the risk has already been transferred to them by their suppliers in their respective countries, such as Dubai and China. Consequently, they are unable to return the goods to their suppliers and have no other option than to sell them at relatively cheap prices.

---

710 Article 276 para.2 UAGCL.

711 This is the author's translation of the French version of the UAGCL, which uses the words: "la perte ou la deterioration".

712 The Nkoulouloun and Mokolo markets respectively.

The risk of loss of a document relating to the goods, in my opinion, passes together with the risk for the goods; and the risk-of-loss rules of the Uniform Act apply as easily to documents as to goods. The time and place to hand documents may at times not reach the buyer concurrently. In a case where there exists no agreement to this effect, the delivery of documents may be expected just in time for their use, for taking delivery of the goods in accordance with the trade usage.[713] Thus, if the documents are lost before they are delivered the risk would not be associated to the goods. Consequently, the holding of relevant documents of the goods by the seller does not affect the passing of risk.[714] The buyer should rather contend himself with the remedies for non-conforming delivery of documents, by applying to the courts for avoidance of the contract, which would stop risk relating to those documents from passing.[715]

It is true that the Uniform Act also considers the application of its risk-of-loss rules to legal risk. Legal risk is the risk, through operation of the law where a party would be deprived of the right to make valuable use of the goods.[716] It is uncertain whether legal risk passes together with physical risk. Such risk may occur when an authority intervenes, confiscates, or forbid the possession, intended use or further commercial exploitation of the goods.[717] This authority may be a bailiff. These instances are governed by the OHADA Uniform Act Organising Simplified Recovery Procedures and Measures of Execution.

Delay in delivery (which might occur together with deterioration in the quality of the goods), can constitute a breach of contract that prevents risk from passing. It is a risk associated with contracting to perform by a particular date, and non-performance by that date or performance on another place is simply a breach of contract. Failure to deliver also leaves the risk of loss to the seller.

Damage Caused by the Goods Themselves

The risk of loss for goods sold under a sales contract is altogether different from the risk of damage later caused by the goods sold. The goods sold can

713 Article 254 UAGCL.

714 Article 278 para. 2 UAGCL

715 Articles 281 & 296 UAGCL.

716 Johan Erauw, CISG Articles 66–70: The Risk of Loss and Passing It, (2005) 25 *Journal of Law and Commerce*, pp. 1–13, p. 3 (available on westlaw).

717 Articles 260 & 295 UAGCL.

deteriorate or injure persons or other property. Other damage raises issues of contractual or tortious liability between buyer and seller, or tortious liability *vis-à-vis* third parties whose property are at risk or may suffer economic loss. With respect to contractual liability between buyer and seller, recovery of damage is exclusively based on breach of contract (lack of conformity) and the damages fall under Article 292 of the Uniform Act. This Article provides for full compensation for some well defined losses. A seller's liability for such damages would be based on a breach by delivery of non-conforming goods even though the damage caused, shown to be within the chain of causality, might occur after the time of delivery.[718] The appearance of such damage, of course, could be the first indication that something was wrong with the goods all along. The risk for this damage also passes to the buyer when the delivery is duly made or when the deadline for notice of non-conformity under Article 258 UAGCL has expired.

Claims under tort law, of course, are beyond the scope of the Uniform Act and outside the possible extensions of its principles by way of gap-filling. But even contractual liability for damage caused to other property of the buyer cannot be simply identified with or subsumed under the rules of passing of risk. The Uniform Act's risk-of-loss rules clearly limit their ambit to loss or damage to "*the goods*" (that is, the goods sold) or "*in respect of goods sold.*"

Consequences of the Passing of Risk

In a contract of sale, the transfer of risk has obvious consequences on the parties as well as regarding their respective liabilities for lack of conformity in the goods. The conformity of the goods in accordance with the contract is judged, as a general rule, at the time when risk passes to the buyer. This is the effect of Articles of 255 para.1, 256 and 277 para. 2 of the Uniform Act, which explains that the seller may be liable for lack of conformity which exists at the time or after the time of delivery.

The link between the duty of conformity and the passing of risk underscores that the duty applies regardless of the seller's fault of omission. The general principle underlying the above provisions is that risk passes when the seller gives up physical possession of the goods, either to the buyer or the carrier. It is worth to note that the Uniform Act rejects the theory of risk passing at the time the contract is formed.

---

[718] Article 256 UAGCL.

There are, however, several provisions of the Uniform Act that address the effect of either party's breach on the normal presumption of risk transfer set out in Article 277 para. 1. The basic notion is that the party in breach should bear the risk of loss regardless of whether the breach causes the loss. The purpose of the allocation of risk is to determine which party shall bear loss of or damage to the goods, provided that such loss or damage to the goods, is actually covered by the provisions as to risk.

The Effect of the Buyer's Breach

Price-Risk: The buyer must pay the price despite loss or damage to the goods

The effect of a buyer's breach is controlled by Article 277 para. 2 UAGCL. This Article says that once risk has passed, the buyer still has as duty to pay for the price of the goods. The Article, in a sense, repeats or reaffirms Article 262,[719] which imposes the payment obligation on the buyer.[720] The buyer acquires the price-risk at the moment the seller is divested of the risk of loss. The rule of Article 277 is contractual by nature and relates to the performance of the buyer's obligation to pay. If the buyer breaches before risk of loss has passed to him, the seller may throw the risk of loss on the buyer for a commercially reasonable time to the extent of any deficiency in the seller's insurance coverage. However, risk transfers to the buyer only if the goods are conforming and have already been identified to the contract and the buyer is obliged to pay the agreed price.

If the loss or damage to goods occurs after the parties have performed their obligations and while the goods are under the control of the buyer, the rule that the buyer loses the value is self-evident. This reflects the economic risk after purchase, a matter beyond the scope of the Uniform Act. Once risk of loss has passed, the buyer has the price-risk, meaning the buyer must pay even though the goods in his possession are damaged or lost. Article 277 para.2 so states, but the same Article also introduces the possibility of transferring the performance—risk back to the seller if the loss or damage is due to the

[719] The forerunner of Article 256 is Article 225 of the previous Uniform Act. Equally, see Article 36 of the CISG.

[720] For the convenience of the reader, Article 66 of the CISG reads: 'Loss of or damage to the goods after the risk has passed to the buyer does not discharge him from his obligation to pay the price, unless the loss or damage is due to an act or omission of the seller'.

seller's "*act*".[721] Thus, the seller may find his obligation to care, to repair and eventually to redeliver, all reborn again-with no clear time limit. In effect, the buyer can claim damages for the seller's wrong under Article 281 UAGCL. The rule simply imposes the burden of proof on the buyer regarding his eventual claims for compensation.

Article 277 para. 2 also covers damage or loss after the passing of risk, but flowing from old defects that existed before the passing of the risk and the buyer did not reveal them during the prescribed periods.[722] It is appropriate that the buyer should be on the look; generally, for post-delivery losses. Article 277 para. 2 indeed contemplates that there has been a fault by the buyer in notifying the seller and consequently only the buyer must pay the price. The provision explains that the buyer enjoys no automatic exceptions and finds no automatic liberation from its payment obligation because of loss or deterioration occurring after risk of loss and delivery have passed. Article 277 para. 2 looks like it introduces a principle of "pay first", discuss later. The rule simply imposes the burden of proof on the buyer regarding his possible claims for compensation.

The Effect of a Seller's Breach

Risk Can Stay with or Return to the Seller's Act or Omission

There is, furthermore, mitigation to the strictness of the rule of Article 277 para. 2 UAGCL. This relief comes from the last words of this Article, providing that the buyer is discharged from the obligation of paying the price in case "*the loss or deterioration is an act of the seller.*"[723] This is good measure in preventing abuse by the seller. But the vague wording seems not to introduce the fault concept into the Uniform Act as in tort.

The exception in the last words in Article 277 para. 2 can be interpreted broadly or narrowly. The drafting literally allows the buyer to suspend or withhold payment for a variety of reasons connected to the behaviour of the seller.

---

[721] The French version of that Article reads: "La perte ou la détérioration des marchandises survenue après le transfert des risques ne libère l'acheteur de son obligation de payer le prix que si événements sont le fait du vendeur". Like under the CISG, what could mean by the seller bearing the risk of loss or damage due to its "act" requires clarification.

[722] See also, in this regard, Articles 256, 258 & 259 UAGCL.

[723] The final text of the CISG unlike in some other Statutes refers only to the seller's own "actions and omissions" contained in Article 66.

When the exception applies, presumably, the buyer's obligation to pay the whole price or to pay part of it is postponed or even waived, and the obligations of the seller are reborn in part or entirely. It is conceivable, in this situation, that neither of the parties carries the risk. But taking a dynamic view of the 'transfer of risk', it looks more logical to decide that risk simply stayed with the seller. If the seller has tendered non-conforming goods that gives rise to a right of revocation to the buyer[724], the risk of loss remains on the seller until there is a remedy to the situation or if the buyer accepts the goods. The goods need only fail in any respect to give the buyer the option of rejecting the whole, accepting the whole, or accepting any units and rejecting the rest. Under Article 289 UAGCL, the buyer may accept the non-conformity and claim damages for the missing part(s) of the goods.

If the seller was to replace the lost or damaged goods with substitute goods, then the obligation to pay the price would be back on the buyer. It could be said that the rules of transfer of risk in this context highly requires the collaboration of both parties based on the principle of good faith.[725] If the premise of the argument changes, for example, if the buyer supplies materials for the manufacture of the goods, or he plays a role in selecting the goods or materials for them, or if the buyer's knowledge and skills are superior to the sellers, then the validity of the argument is weakened, and the allocation of risk changes, since there are now elements which are outside the seller's sphere of influence which can affect the assessment of lack of conformity to the contract. The conformity of the goods to the contract now falls within the buyer's sphere of influence—*caveat emptor* shifting the risk to the buyer for any defect in the goods tendered to the seller for manufacture.[726]

Before the risk with regard to goods passes and in order to assure conforming delivery, the seller must procure the goods, must preserve them, repair them if necessary and duly bring them to the point of delivery; and if they are lost or undergo accidental damage during this process, he must resupply them because his obligations remain unchanged.

If the risk is still with the seller and loss occurs due to an impediment not within the seller's control (*force majeure*), then the loss is the seller's. Theoretically, both seller and buyer can lose. But the seller's risk of being liable for the buyer's damages beyond the value of the goods is alleviated by Article

[724] Article 281 UAGCL.

[725] Akuété Pedro Santos and Jean Yado Toé, *OHADA Droit Commercial Général*, Op. cit., p. 441.

[726] René Franz Henschel, 'Conformity of Goods in International Sales Governed by CISG Article 35: Caveat Venditor, Caveat Emptor and Contract Law as Background Law and as a Competing Set of Rules', (2004) *Nordic Journal of Commercial law*, pp. 1–21, p. 4.

294. This suggests that the seller is not liable for non-performance if there is *force majeure.*

Conclusion

Overall, the Uniform Act's approach to the complicated commercial area of risk of loss marks a vast improvement. The Act's rules are, for the most part, refreshingly simple.

Furthermore, the Act's approach to risk of loss is based upon sound, practical commercial policies. Under the Uniform Act, allocation of risk of loss depends not only on the legal concept of passage of title. The general principle of the Uniform Act's risk of loss provisions is to place the risk of loss on the party who has control of the goods or is most likely to have insured or otherwise taken precautions against damage to the goods.

Control theory in its most obvious sense- that is, physical possession—dictates that risk of loss should fall on the party having actual possession of the goods. The Uniform Act's drafters believed that the party with control over the goods, because of physical possession, is more likely to insure them. This assumption cannot operate, however, when goods are not in the hands of either the seller or buyer. The Uniform Act will place risk of loss on one of them, but that party will not have become cognizant, through possession, of the need to insure. Control is not the only indicator of likelihood that a party will insure goods. The Act, which passes risk of loss in such cases from the seller to the buyer at the moment the latter receives the goods, produces a result consistent with both the insurance premise and the concept of control in its physical possession sense.

Article 278 para.1 UAGCL sets out the method of allocating the risk of loss when it is a carriage contract. When the parties have contracted for the transportation of goods under a shipment contract, through a carrier, risk of loss passes to the buyer when the goods are duly delivered to the carrier. If a destination contract is involved, the risk of loss shifts when the goods are duly tendered to the buyer as specified in the contract of sale. The basic rule covering the bailment situation (which has not been covered by the UAGCL) is that the party having control over the bailee bears the burden of the risk of loss. When neither a transportation contract nor a bailment contract is involved, the general rule for the seller shifts the risk to the buyer when the buyer actually receives the goods. Significantly, the parties may avoid the application of Article 278 altogether by contractually agreeing to their own method of risk of loss allocation. Regrettably, the Uniform Act has made mention of bailment contracts which is a worthy topic in commercial sales relating to the passing of risk.

7

LIMITS OF THE SELLER'S LIABILITY FOR NON-PERFORMANCE

Introduction

Commercial impracticability, a defence in a breach of contract action, is triggered when an external event such as a flood, death of the promisor, or change in the law disrupts a contractual relationship.[727] What are the bases of the excuses for impossibility, frustration, impracticability, or hardship? What are the value judgments that have guided legislators and courts in these areas? In the Common law systems, contract liability is no-fault liability, yet some leeway for an excuse has been allowed. Although in some Civil law countries, fault is perceived to have a greater role in contract liability than in the Common law, the discussions of these excuses do not seem affected in any important way by ideas related to fault or its absence.

One trend of thought about the foundation of these excuses stems from one of the principal underpinnings of contractual obligations. Contract liability stems from consent. If an event occurs that is totally outside the contemplation of the parties and the event drastically shifts the nature of foreseen contractual risks, is there truly consent? Under this line of thinking, one can infer that the parties did not intend that performance would have to be rendered if an unexpected event would create a radical change in the nature of performance. If the parties have not addressed the event ex ante and if the disruption is

[727] Daniel T. Ostasa & Frank P. Darr, Understanding Commercial Impracticability: Tempering with Community Fairness Norms, (1996) 27 *Rutgers Law Journal*, 343, p. 1.

so severe that requiring strict performance appears to be harsh and unfair, then the courts may grant relief by rescinding the contract or reforming the contractual language. Distinguishing events that warrant excuse from those that do not is no easy matter. If this inference is sound, one can conclude that the contract did not cover the unexpected event that has occurred. Under this reasoning, the court must then supply a term to cover an omitted case. Thus viewed, relief for impossibility or hardship does not interfere with freedom of contract. If this is so, the next question is how is the court to fill the gap and provide for the omitted case? A useful analogy is cases decided on the basis of mistake of fact. The distinction is that the doctrine of mistake is applicable only if there is a mistake as to a material existing fact, while ordinarily impossibility, frustration, and hardship relate to future events.

Public international law has long recognised the principle of *rebus sic stantibus*, an implied term in every treaty that it will cease to be binding when the facts and conditions on which they were based have fundamentally changed. This implied term has its origins in the Roman law of contract. The full Latin text is: *Contractus qui habenttractum succesivum et dependentiam de futurum, rebus sic stantibus intelligentur*. Freely translated, the phrase is: "*Contracts providing for successive acts of performance over a future period of time must be understood as subject to the condition that the circumstances will remain the same.*"[728]

All contracts involve risks. Some contracts are almost purely aleatory[729], which do not afford any basis for liability by reason of delay in accepting it or the want of care in dealing with it. If one sells shares of stock on the stock exchange that person does not have the so-called "*short sale,*" it is a contract of pure risk, and I can conceive no circumstance (absent fraud, duress, or other vitiating cause) in which a court should relieve the seller or buyer from a total loss, even if unexpected and unforeseeable events disrupted the market. On the other hand, in the more typical contract involving the sale of goods, which is our concern here, each party expects to gain from the contract and each party understands that the other party also expects to gain. In such a contract, neither party expects to gain from the other's loss, although both realise

---

728 David Bederman, The 1871 London Declaration, Rebus Sic Stantibus and a Primitivist View of the Law of Nations, (1988) 82 *American Journal of International Law* 1.

729 Standardised contracts are frequently contracts of adhesion, they à prendre ou à a laisser. An insurance contract is a contract of adhesion par excellence. Martha Simo Njikam, *Insurance Law In England and Cameroon—A Comparative Study—With Specific Reference to Motor Vehicle Insurance*, (Ph.D Thesis, Sheffield University, 1986) p. 51, (unpublished); Friedrich Kessler, Contracts of Adhesion—Some Thoughts about Freedom of Contract, (1943) 43 *Columbia Law Review* 629.

that such an imbalance may occur. Involved are cultural beliefs about unjust enrichment and unjust impoverishment. At Common law, several kinds of events produce an almost automatic excuse for non-performance: death of a person who is to personally perform, supervening illegality of a performance, and the destruction of the subject matter.

When one goes beyond all the above events, relief is most justified if unexpected events inflict a loss on one party in a contract of sale and provide a windfall gain for the other, or where the excuse would save one party from an unexpected loss while leaving the other party in a position no worse than it would have without the contract.

The General Structure of Impracticability under the Uniform Act

The Uniform Act on General Commercial law's impracticability rules[730] are generally drawn from Article 294, which provides:

A party is excused from his duty to render performance if he can prove that it is made impracticable without his fault by the occurrence of an event, namely; due to a third party or the occurrence of a *force majeure*. A *force majeure* entails events which happen beyond the party's control and which could not be reasonably foreseeable. However, there is no exemption if the failure to perform has been caused by a third party appointed by the defaulting party to perform all or part of his contractual obligations.[731]

Inherent in these general statements of excuse are four elements: (1) performance has become impracticable; (2) the non-occurrence of the cause of impracticability was due to *force majeure*; (3) the party asserting the excuse is without fault; and (4) the party seeking excuse did not assume greater obligations in the contract.

This chapter will now proceed with a more detailed review of the relevant provisions. First, *force majeure* will be discussed followed by a discussion of the provisions concerning hardship.

---

730 The effect of a finding of impracticability is likewise stated generally in the American Uniform Commercial Code, Section 2-615.

731 The author's translation.

Force Majeure (Impossibility of Performance)

Force majeure originates from the roman concept *vis major* meaning a greater or superior force.[732] The concept of *force majeure*, though alien to the Common law, is an established doctrine in French Law which relieves a promisor from responsibility for non-performance in certain circumstances. Although having a close affinity with the Common law doctrine of frustration, it is somewhat narrower in its relieving effects.[733] However, in Common law jurisdictions, *force majeure* is not contained in any of the common law statutes nor used as a defence. It is rather used in the area of contractual liability where it is known as *force majeure* clauses.[734]

Although there is no authoritative definition of the term *force majeure*, it is mostly used in legal practice to excuse a party from liability if some unforeseen event beyond the control of that party prevents him from performing his obligations under the contract. After a contract is made, a party bound under that contract may run into obstacles that make his performance impossible. When such is the case, that party is not liable for any damage that may result from his failure to perform.[735] That is the doctrine of *force majeure*. For that doctrine to prevail, however, performance by the obligor must be truly impossible. In the traditional approach of the Uniform Act, there is *force majeure* only when the performance of an obligation becomes absolutely impossible because of obstacles that the obligor could neither foresee nor resist. An obligor, in that conception, must honour his signature or his word at any price. He is bound to employ all his efforts and resources, and even face the collapse of his business if necessary, in order to perform his obligation. His diligence, in other words, must be absolute and perfect, regardless of the magnitude of the increase in physical or financial effort that unforeseen events or changes in circumstances may require of him in order to perform, and also regardless of the collapse of his expectations when such events or changes, without making impossible the performance he promised, deprive him from obtaining the reasonable advantage in contemplation of which he bound himself to perform.

---

[732] Henry Campbell Black, *Black's Law Dictionary*, (Bryan A. Garner ed.), 8th ed., West Group, 1999) p. 1567.

[733] Nicholas Barry, Force Majeure and Frustration, (1979) 27 *American Journal of Comparative Law*, p. 231.

[734] M. Schmidt Kessel & Katrin Mayer, *Spervening Events and Force Majeure*, (Jan. M. Smits ed., Edward Elgar Publishing, 2006) p. 689.

[735] Saul Litvinoffa, Force Majeure, Failure of Cause and Théorie de l'Imprévision, (1985)49 (1) *Lousiana Law Review*, pp. 1–25, p. 1.

In French legal writing, *force majeure* is referred to, and explained under, the theory of cause. In the civilian tradition no '*consideration*' is needed to make a promise enforceable, but a cause must be found at the root of every obligation in order to make it binding. That cause is the motive, or end, or reason, or purpose for which a party binds himself. If that cause fails, the obligation fails also. From that vantage point, *force majeure* prevents parties from attaining realisation of the end for which they entered the contract. Connection between cause and *force majeure* is, thus, direct. Such a direct connection amply justifies a broadening of the basis of *force majeure*, especially in view of the fact that a strict approach to impossibility is the result of interpretation rather than a clearly formulated rule.[736]

The provisions on *force majeure* are rigid under the Uniform Act. Nothing less than total impossibility will suffice as a predicate for an excuse. There must have been an "*impediment*[737] *beyond [the seller's] control*" and the seller "*could not reasonably be expected to have taken the impediment into account at the time of the conclusion of the contract or to have avoided or overcome it or its consequences.*"[738] Let us analyse the quoted language.

"Impediment beyond [the party's] control"

The Uniform Act addresses the exoneration of liability due to an impediment beyond control.[739] Like the CISG, the Uniform Act associates the issue of performance impediment with *force majeure*.[740]The text as in the case of *force majeure* is silent with respect to instances of contractual "*impediments*". However, more clarifications on this can only be drawn from domestic law rules.[741] However, the Uniform Act provides that the party will be exempted from further performance whenever such performance is caused by either a third party or *force majeure*.[742] The event beyond his control that may explain the seller's failure is that obstacle which, in spite of the seller's having exercised all the care and diligence he owed under the contract, suddenly appeared to obstruct his performance and is such that it could be avoided or overcome only

[736] Ibid.; p. 7.
[737] This is the author's translation. The French version of the UAGCL uses the word empechement.
[738] Article 294 UAGCL.
[739] Article 294 Uniform Act; Article 79 CISG.
[740] Ibid.
[741] Article 237 of the Uniform Act.
[742] Article 294 of the Uniform Act; Alain Fénéon, L'influence de la CVIM sur le Nouveau Droit Africain de la Vente Commerciale, (2005) 853 *Penant*, pp. 464–517, p. 511.

by means superior to those at his disposal or superior to those the contract required him to employ. Such an event is a *force majeure* that, in this light, appears as marking the limit or borderline of the obligation. The expression '*force majeure*' indicates, by itself, a comparison between the magnitude of the obstacle and the diligence owed, and clearly means that situation or event which exceeds the scope of such diligence.

What if the impediment is caused by the party's financial failure? Neither Article 294 UAGCL, nor the commentary to it, refers to this kind of impediment. Under American Law, it is quite clear those financial impediments provide no excuse; these are regarded as "*subjective*" rather than "*objective*" impossibility and both the courts and legal writers are unanimous that subjective impossibility provides no excuse, whether or not it was the result of conditions outside the control of the obligor. It is generally believed that the risk of financial ability to perform is such a basic assumption underlying all contracts that it cannot be excused, except by a decree in a bankruptcy proceeding. It is hard to believe that this general belief is suspended in international trade. Consequently, the phrase "*beyond [the party's] control*" should be given a broad meaning so that it will be deemed that financial health is always within a contracting party's control.

"*[The party] could not reasonably be expected to have taken the impediment into account at the time of the conclusion of the contract*". This phrase raises the issue of foreseeability.

Foreseeability

The issue of foreseeability is a difficult one. Anyone who has read a bit of history or who has lived for three or more decades of the twentieth century can foresee, in a general way, the possibility of war, revolution, embargo, plague, terrorism, hyper-inflation and economic depression, among the other horrors that have afflicted the human race. If one reads science fiction, one learns of the possibility of new terrors that have not yet afflicted us, but involve possibilities that are not pure fantasy. The following notion of unforeseeability seems real-an event so unlikely to occur that reasonable parties see no need explicitly to allocate the risk of its occurrence, although the impact it might have caused would be of such magnitude that the parties would have negotiated over it, had the event been more likely.

The view that the seller assumes the risk of only contingencies that were foreseen (or virtually certain to occur) is consistent with the limited obligation view of contractual risk assumption intended by Article 294 UAGCL. It is a relatively narrow basis for risk assumption, yet it has much to recommend it. If the seller has not protected himself with a contract clause against this kind of contingency, the reasonable expectation is that his promise to deliver is not conditioned on the non-occurrence of the contingency. Further, the narrow view avoids much of the criticism levied against the looser standard of foreseeability. The narrow view is also consistent with traditional excuse theories based on injury to the goods and governmental actions as discussed above, for in the usual case, these are events which are not perceived at the time of contracting to be virtually certain to occur.[743]

One might object that this narrow view permits a seller to escape too easily from his contractual obligations. The response to this objection is that the seller is not automatically excused under article 294 UAGCL if the contingency were unforeseen. First, the contingency must also have rendered the seller's performance commercially impracticable. The effect of the narrow view of risk allocation, therefore, is to shift the emphasis in many disputes from the question of basic assumption, the content of which is often quite elusive and unpredictable, to the question of what effect the contingency has had on the seller's performance, which can be quantified to produce workable rules of thumb that will guide the resolution of disputes.

Second, even if the contingency were unforeseen and did render the seller's performance commercially impracticable, the seller is not excused under article 294 if the contingency were a '*business risk*.' This concept of '*business risk*' is best understood through what Llewellyn intended subsection 2–615(a) of the American Uniform Commercial Code to accomplish.[744] Llewellyn wished to liberalise excuse in primarily two areas. The first area concerned events causing failure of a specific source of production or supply assumed by both parties but not made an explicit contract term.[745] The second area covered events causing general changes in business conditions. Though the point is more implicit than explicit, the drafts comments to Section 2–615 indicate that Llewellyn intended to liberalise excuse only for events that affected sellers generally, and not for events that

[743] John D. Wladis, Impracticability as Risk Allocation: The Effect of Changed Circumstances upon Contract Obligations for the Sale of Goods, (1988) 22 *Georgia Law Review* 503, p. 12.

[744] Llewellyn, Comment on Section 6–3 (S.88)—*Merchant's Excuse by Failure of Presupposed Facilities or Conditions*, comments 1 and 2 (n.d.) in The Llewellyn Papers, file J–IX (2)b and in A.L.I. ARCHIVES, supra note 2, drawer 198 (reproduced in the Appendix of this Article by John D. Wladis), Op. cit. Similarly, Article 282 UAGCL Llewellyn became chairman of the Section on Uniform Commercial Acts in 1937.

[745] Similarly, Article 282 UAGCL.

affect just an individual seller. This is a similar view found in Article 292 of the UAGCL where the seller could only be excused for reasons of his inability to produce goods. This is not a general problem but particular to an individual seller in this circumstance. Thus, for example, the text would excuse a cannery from a contract to sell canned salmon if an event, such as war, caused a general shortage of cans, but he would not excuse a cannery if its inability to perform were caused by its having obtained from a reliable source, cans which later were found to be defective and thus unusable for canning. The idea that sellers are responsible for their own singular misfortunes is not new. It probably reflects a tacit commercial understanding that these risks are business risks of the seller, even if they were unforseen and beyond his reasonable control. The only exceptions to this view seem to be injuries to production facilities or sources of supply, assumed by both parties at the time of contracting.[746]

Further, even if the event is general in effect, it will not excuse unless it directly affects a material part of the seller's performance; events interfering with incidental parts of the performance will not necessarily excuse. Similarly, events that cause only indirect interference with the performance of the seller, such as failure of his credit facilities, are business risks and will not excuse him.

It is difficult to believe that judges in reviewing the "*factual*" question of foreseeability can refrain from taking into account the larger consequences of a finding of foreseeability. Referring to the Civil Code, these instances include unexpected, unforeseen and unavoidable external events.[747] Civil law takes into consideration issues of *force majeure*, hardship known under the principle of imprevision[748]—theory of unexpected circumstances. Both in common and civil law countries, once the impediment due to an event beyond the parties' control has occurred, its effect depends on the terms of the *force majeure* clause in the contract. It is common for *force majeure* clauses to provide that performance is suspended for a period prior to the parties' obligations being

[746] John D. Wladis, *Impracticability as Risk Allocation: The Effect of Changed Circumstances upon Contract Obligations for the Sale of Goods*, Op. cit.

[747] Cameroon, Articles 1147, 1148, 1150 CC; Côte d'Ivoire, Article 1147.

[748] Imprévision was applied many other times by the Conseil d'État. In all cases the contract involved is one governed by public law, such as a contract of concession entered into between a public entity and a private company for services of a public nature to be rendered by the latter, that is, a contract strictly governed by administrative law under the French system. Under imprévision, the party whose performance became exceedingly more onerous because of unforeseen circumstances is awarded compensation—indemnité—aimed at restoring the altered equilibrium of the contract.

totally discharged.[749]

Temporary Force Majeure

In contractual language, Article 282 of the Uniform Act provides instances where the seller's impediment to perform is only temporary, and the excuse shall have effect for such period as is reasonable having regard to the effect of the impediment on the performance of the contract. It can be deduced from this text that the seller's inability to perform may be temporary as a result of such impediments beyond his control, namely; (i) a serious inadequacy in its ability to perform; or (ii) insolvency. Basically, the seller's inability to perform may be due to some economic embarrassment leading to a halt in further manufacturing goods to supply to the buyer; which are issues beyond his control. These are events which could fall under cases of *force majeure*.

The doctrine of impossibility, temporary *force majeure* or otherwise, does not inhibit the buyer's ability to cancel the contract, by applying to the courts for an order authorizing it to defer performance of his own obligations. Temporary impossibility gives rise to prospective inability to perform. Although the seller may be excused by temporary impossibility, the prospective inability will normally give the buyer a power to suspend performance by court order and demand assurance of due performance. However, under the Uniform Act, if the seller is not able to provide assurance of due performance during an appropriate extension of time for performance to retender goods, the buyer may cancel the contract despite the impossibility that may provide a defense in an action for damages.[750] In this case, if the impediment relates to the cost of replacing the goods by the seller due to the seller's failure, the buyer shall be entitled to the difference of the cost of replacing the goods and the agreed contractual price.[751]

Financial *Force Majeure*

Although a change in the economic value of the goods will not render them non-conforming, such a change may amount to '*financial force majeure*' giving the buyer an exemption from remedies.

---

[749] Mezatio Sylvestre, *L'Adaption du Contrat aux Circonstances Economiques*, (Mémoire de Maitrise, Université de Yaoundé, 1991) pp. 117,118.

[750] Article 283 para. 2 UAGCL.

[751] Article 292 UAGCL.

Article 294 acts as an exception to a party's liability for damages; it does not affect the question of whether a seller has breached the conformance duty. However, by its nature, this provision restricts the seller's duty to provide conforming goods; indeed, it could be described as competing with or potentially serving to undermine Article 255 of the Uniform Act. Article 294 is examined here because of its potential to render market-based factors de facto conformance characteristics. For example, Article 294 may be relevant where there has been a drastic change in consumer demand or market prices for the goods. A seller might argue that making delivery and receiving the price in these circumstances would be so unprofitable as to amount to an '*impediment*'. If this argument was successful, the seller would therefore be exempted from damages for failing to perform these obligations.

The application of Article 294 in such circumstance is unclear. A dramatic change in circumstances may constitute an '*impediment*': Article 294 encompasses economic impediments, but only those that are comparable to non-economic (physical) impediment.[752] Some cases indicate that a change in market prices will never amount to an impediment. In one arbitral case, it was stated that '*change in market conditions cannot serve as an excuse for the buyer to avoid payment for the goods*'. Similarly, the Oberlandesgericht Hamburg rejected an argument that a change in market prices amounted to an impediment, stating that a party bears the risk of adverse price fluctuations.[753] The court in that case said that market factors would only be an impediment if the goods were no longer available. In another case, the same court considered a seller's argument that a market shortage of the goods amounted to an '*impediment*'. The Court found this insufficient, noting that '*[t]he owed class of goods was undoubtedly not exhausted.*' The court characterised the facts as an increase in the market piece rather than a shortage and did not consider this an impediment.

In *Société Romay AG v. SARL Behr France*,[754] the buyer '*invoked the collapse of the automotive market*', which reduced the buyer's resale price to '*less than half the price of the goods supplied by the seller*'. According to the Court, the buyer would succeed if it established that the change in the market caused

[752] John O. Honnold, *Uniform Law for International Sales under the 1980 United Nations Convention* (1997), 477.

[753] See also 1996, Bulgarian of Chamber of Commerce and Industry, 11/1996 (Steel ropes' case), available at <http://cisgw3.law.pace.edu/cases/98021bu.html>; 11th June 1997; Tribunal of International Commercial Arbitration at the Russian Federation Chamber of Commerce and Industry, 255/1994, available at http://cisgw3.law.pace.edu/cases/970611rl.html.

[754] *Société Roamy AG v. SARL Behr France* 2001, Cour d'Appel Colamr, in CLOUT No. 480, available at <http://cisgw3.law.pace.edu/vcases/010612fl.html>.

a "*necessity*" which would allow him [the buyer] to terminate the contract'. On the facts, this was not the case. The requirement in Article 294 that the market change must be unforeseeable was also not satisfied, despite a 50 per cent fall in the resale price. The Court emphasised that '*price fluctuations, even sudden and significant, are not exceptional*' in international markets and that it is up to the parties to build economic risk management into the contractual framework.

The weight of case law shows that it is at least arguable that market factors may constitute an impediment within the meaning of Article 294. Thus, a sudden drop in the market value of goods may allow a seller to refuse to make delivery without consequence, if two criteria are satisfied: first, the drop in value must be unforeseeable; second, the drop in value must have an effect on the buyer that it could not reasonably have avoided. In such a circumstance, the seller would/may be exempted but liable to pay damages.

Although the existing case law focuses on the question of foreseeability, a seller might also argue that the buyer ought to have taken steps to avoid the effects. In trades where production imputs are susceptible to prove volatility, it is common to mitigate the risk of such exposure through future trading and hedging instruments.[755] If a seller established that a buyer could reasonably have been expected to prevent the financial impediment from arising by hedging against the economic risk, the buyer would be unable to rely on the exception in Article 294.

The OHADA rules for the burden and passing of risk discussed in this chapter raise interesting issues with respect to non-physical characteristics of the goods. For such characteristics, an allocation of risk based on physical delivery of the goods seems rather arbitrary. Goods conforming at the time the contract is concluded may be rendered non-conforming by adverse market events before time of delivery, which may result in non-conformance. However, the distinction between market-based characteristics of the goods and the economic value of the goods is problematic. The boundary between these concepts must be determined according to the facts of each case, with reference to the intent of the parties and the sphere of influence principle. However, to maintain economic policy objectives such as arbitration in the market of goods, Courts and tribunals should not allow Article 294 to render purely price-based factors to become a *de facto* conformance requirement.

---

[755] G. David Haushalter, Financing Policy, Basis Risk, and Corporate Hedging: Evidence from Oil and Gas Producers (2000) 55 *The Journal of Finance*, pp. 107–152.

Governmental Licenses and Permits

In national or international sales, giant businessmen in Africa and around the world today through their agents sell a variety of goods (cocoa, cotton, groundnut, consumer products, machinery, building materials etc.). In addition, private importers or exporters buy from or sell to foreign manufacturers or companies. The execution of such sales or purchase transactions often entails shipment and a lot of other transactions from or to an African country port. Under these circumstances, the seller is commonly under the duty to supply the goods to the buyer by providing the buyer with the necessary documents related to the goods in view to ensure its transportation as may be agreed in the contract or in accordance with trade usages.[756]

Similarly, the seller as provided by the Uniform Act is required to deliver the goods in question together with relevant documents appropriate for means of transacting such goods.[757] If the agreement provides for transport, the seller must take the appropriate steps for the goods to be delivered to the place agreed with the buyer.[758] From this standpoint, the seller is under the duty to ensure that the means of transportation used are appropriate in the circumstances and provide the necessary documents related to the goods to ease the delivery of the goods to the buyer at the place indicated. In fact, the transportation of the goods in question may concern sales at a distance within the OHADA zone and such cross border sales frequently require the issue of a license if the goods are to be exported and imported. As a matter importance, licence could be considered to be one of the documents related to the delivery of the goods to the buyer's country or another place of delivery agreed by the parties.

In the context of international sales, it has been advanced that the seller must procure an export licence and the buyer, an import licence.[759] Although with some exception, this position has also been followed by INCOTERMS.[760] In addition, when it is for the buyer to collect the goods, it must also obtain the export licence.[761] But where it is for the seller to bring the goods, it must also

[756] Franco Ferrari, Trade Usage and Practices Established between the Parties under the CISG, (2003) 5 *International Business Law Journal*, pp. 571-576.

[757] Article 250 UAGCL; Franco Ferrari, Op. cit.

[758] Article 252 para. 2 UAGCL.

[759] Ingeborg Schwenzer, *Commentary on the UN Convention on the International Sale of Goods (CISG)*, Op. cit., p. 526.

[760] Except 'Ex Works' (EXW) and 'Delivery Duty Paid' (DDP).

[761] Similar position under in the INCOTERMS 'Ex Works' (EXW) but not in case of FAS nor FCA.

have to obtain the import licence.[762]

If, however, the lack of approval in obtaining an export licence or a permit by the seller makes the contract impossible to perform by prohibiting the exportation of the goods constituting the contractual object who is to blame? Certainly, this is an important topic in domestic trade and a more complex one in international trade. Permits may be needed from more than one State or there may be licensing requirements of which one or both parties may be unaware. The burden of applying for any necessary governmental approval is cast on the party who has its place of business in the State whose approval is required, but only if the other party has no place of business in the State. In any other case, for example, when neither party has, nor both parties have, a place of business in the State, the party whose performance requires permission must take the necessary measures.[763] Where both parties' performances are subject to the same approval requirement, and neither or both parties have a place of business in the State, the provisions are silent on the question of who must apply for the necessary permission.

From a reading of the provision of the Uniform Act, it is the seller in this context who has the duty to contract (by application) for the approval and must exercise best efforts by applying for the approval is to be obtained.[764] As elsewhere in this Uniform Act, there is an emphasis on communication. Unless information regarding the need for approval is generally accessible, the existence of the need for permission must be disclosed by the seller whose duty it is to obtain it.[765] Failure to disclose is a breach of the obligation of good faith inherent in all negotiations. Similarly, if the approval is granted or denied, the seller must, without undue delay, notify the buyer. Failure to notify constitutes a breach of contract.

What are the consequences of refusal of an approval of a document related to the goods which has been diligently sought by the seller? The text is not totally clear. One reading is that if the contract is subject to export licence, permits or governmental approval, it is as though no contract ever came into being if such official documents are not obtained by the seller due to certain

762 Similar position under in the INCOTERMS 'Delivery Duty Paid' (DDP).

763 This is the spirit of Article 252 UAGCL requiring the seller to provide the buyer with all information necessary to obtain insurance cover for the goods during carriage.

764 Article 252 UAGCL.

765 Ibid.

reasons beyond his control.[766] This could be considered to be an impediment which the parties would have avoided if they knew of it. This makes approval in this context similar to the French concept of la cause, if not identical with, that of English law namely,consideration; such view being that the disappearance of the common end of the parties puts an end to the contract. The lack of approval makes the contract impossible to perform in the case of non-delivery by the seller because the seller would perform his obligation if he knew of this impediment. The rights of the seller are governed by the rules governing contractual breaches[767], including the defence of *force majeure*.

Failure of 'Cause' under the Uniform Act: Unexpected Circumstances, Contract Dissolution, and Failure of 'Cause'

The Uniform Act contains several examples of situations where a contract may be dissolved because of a sudden change of circumstances. Thus, in the case of delivery of goods to the buyer, if it appears that after the agreement has been reached the party (seller) will not perform part of his obligations, because of either a serious inadequacy to manufacture goods or insolvency[768], it will be understood that based on those circumstances the seller even though was able to perform, was disrupted by unforeseen events and could be used by the seller as an excuse for non-performance.

In all those situations the Uniform Act insinuates a foundation for *théorie de l'imprévision* which are cases of *force majeure*. In all of them the common feature is the frustration of the purpose, or the disappearance of the reason, for which the transaction was made—the failure of its cause, a failure brought about by a change in circumstances that frustrates the parties' motives or expectations. Indeed, at civil law, an obligation is closely dependent upon the existence, the possibility, and the nature of the contemplated end. Moreover, after its birth, the life of an obligation is subjected to the materialisation of the pursued end because, if the end is not attained, the binding force of the obligation is not recognised. An obligation is valid only insofar as the end contemplated by the parties is susceptible of being attained. A promise has no binding force when it is no longer conducive to the end contemplated by the

[766] Joseph M. Perilloa, Force Majeure and Hardship under the UNIDROIT Principles of International Commercial Contracts, (1997) 5 *Tul. Int'l & Comp.* L. 5. pp. 20-21; David Thomas, Frustration and Force Majeure: A Hard Line in English Law, (2011), 6 (2) *Construction Law International* 21, pp. 1–13, p.2.

[767] Articles 281–284 UAGCL.

[768] Article 281 UAGCL.

promisor. As a matter of necessity, the obligation disappears together with its cause.

Hardship

It is usually difficult to draw a line as to what amounts to hardship as opposed to *force majeure*. As an attempt, *force majeure* as seen above, occurs when the performance becomes impossible whereas hardship occurs when performance becomes much more cumbersome but not impossible. In practice, hardship can be illustrated in a situation where the performance of the contract becomes more onerous for the performing party. It is therefore quite distinct from a *force majeure* situation. Therefore, by definition, hardship is the occurrence of events that fundamentally alter the equilibrium of the contract resulting in an excessive burden being placed on one of the parties involved.[769] This can either be because the cost of the party's performance has increased or because the value of the performance a party received has diminished.

Hardship is not perceived as a legal concept under the Uniform Act. The Uniform Act, just like the CISG,[770] addresses only the issue of *force majeure*. It provides no equivalence to this concept by totally avoiding the use of '*hardship", in fear, presumably, not to end up being culturally linked with any contracting States*' domestic law.[771]

Hardship requires a change in circumstances so severe and fundamental that the promisor cannot be held to his promise in spite of the possibility of performance. If an unforeseeable event, not within the control of the disadvantaged party and the occurrence of which was not a risk assumed by the disadvantaged party, occurs or becomes known after contracting, and the equilibrium of the contract is fundamentally altered for either party because of an increased cost of performance or the decrease in value of the performance to be received, hardship results.[772]

[769] Article 6.2.2 UNIDROIT; Article 6.2.1 to 6.2.3 of the preliminary draft of OHADA Uniform Act on Contract Law; UCC s 2–615.

[770] Peter H. Schlechtriem & Ingeborg Schwenzer, *Commentary on the UN Convention on the International Sale of Goods (CISG)*, Op. cit., p. 809–810.

[771] Emmanuel S. Darankoum, Op. cit., p. 514, 518. In the Civil law system, hardship does not apply in Civil and Commercial law matters. Where the contract is subject to the jurisdiction of the Droit Administratif (Administrative Law) then the theorie de l'imprevision allows the court to relieve the promisor where the economic basis of the contract has disappeared.

[772] Sarah Howard Jenkins, Exemption for Non-performance: UCC, CISG, Unidroit Principles-A Comparative Assesment, (1998), 72 *Tulane Law Review*, pp. 1–12, p. 5.

The criteria required for exemption applicable under the Uniform Act are: an unforeseeable event or contingency, beyond the party's control, and the occurrence of which was an unassumed risk.[773] Unlike the UCC and the CISG, the Uniform Act mandates good faith, constructive renegotiation between the parties to adapt the contract to the unforeseen circumstances. This can be inferred from the event where the seller has tendered defective goods or only part of the whole goods. Here, the parties, in the first instance, are allocated the responsibility to resolve the disequilibrium or to fill the gap in their agreement. Only after an unsuccessful attempt for a reasonable time may the buyer request the intervention of a court[774] or claim damages[775]. In practice, these instances which could be deciphered from the text of the Uniform Act must be understood to be situations of hardship in which the seller may find them burdensome to fulfil or further the performance of its obligations towards the buyer.

As a corollary to the above instances, regard can also be had by looking at the provision of Article 282 of the Uniform Act which also carries some instances where the seller may be unable to execute his obligations after the conclusion of the contract. These events may be where the seller lacks sufficient production capacity or lacks means (may be in case of insolvency) to continue production. All together, these events could be justifiably understood to be obstacles to the seller's performance which may occur or become known to him during or after the conclusion of the contract.

The above events do not render the seller's performance impossible t as it is with *force majeure* and impossibility. In fact, the above adverse change of circumstances will not amount to impossibility and cannot discharge the seller from future performance.[776] The spirit of the OHADA Law here is to strengthen the contractual bond between the seller and the buyer by either paving the way for a possibility to the seller to request for additional time with the buyer due to the delay in carrying out performance or apply to the court to adapt the contract with a view to restoring its equilibrium.

The purpose of exonerating the seller from these radically changed circumstances is geared at avoiding extreme and unreasonable difficulty, expense, injury or loss which may prevent performance of the contract thereby causing some injury to the buyer.[777]

[773] Article 294 UAGCL.
[774] Article 283 para. 2 UAGCL.
[775] Article 289 UAGCL.
[776] M. Schmidt-Kessel & Katrin Mayer, Op. cit., p. 689.
[777] Malaurie, Op. cit., p. 382,385.

However, whenever the performance has become impossible or where the party's obligations under the contract have been radically transformed by the changed circumstances, the contract may be discharged by the court under the doctrine of frustration as it is at Common law[778] or may be terminated. This will not free the seller from paying damages or interests to the buyer.[779]

Development Risks

Another angle of the story connected to this issue of hardship could be drawn from the defence of development risks which the seller could seek for excuse based on the facts of the case. One of the most important defences and understandably, one of the most controversial elements in the British Consumer Protection Act, 1987, is the so-called development risks defence under section 4 (1). The subsection provides:

> *that the state of scientific and technical knowledge at the relevant time was not such that a producer of the products of the same description as the product in question might be expected to have discovered the defect if it had existed in his products while they were under his control.*

By this defence, liability for defective products can be avoided by the seller, that is, in the capacity of a producer, proving that the defect could not have been discovered in the light of the existing state of scientific and technical knowledge. It appears, therefore, that the liability, after all, depends on the conduct of the producer (seller). This is similar to the American state-of-the art defence.[780]This defence though not specified under the Uniform Act, can be situated within some of its provisions. The seller's failure to deliver goods with defects[781] and his inability to replace the goods within the stipulated time period accorded by the buyer[782] could be explained as a result of some development risks. It may be deduced that if the seller is the producer of the goods he delivered to the buyer, some defects inherent in the goods would have been due to his inability to discover those defects during production when the goods were still under his possession. Thus, some development

[778] G.H. Treitel, Op. cit., p. 847.

[779] Articles 281and 296 UAGCL.

[780] 'State-of-the-art' and 'development risks' may be synonymous but not exactly identical. The former is associated with the current technological development in a particular industry, whereas the latter relates to defects which are undiscoverable.

[781] Articles 257–259 UAGCL.

[782] Articles 283–284 UAGCL.

risks may have been inevitably difficult for the seller's discovery. This does not absolve entirely the seller from liability because the buyer is entitled to request the court for settlement of damages.[783]

However, one cannot seriously argue against the contention that the application of the development risks defence inevitably introduces the tort of negligence through the "*back door*", which is not under the domain of the Uniform Act. Indeed, when the defence is raised, the material question before the court is reduced to whether or not the seller's conduct was reasonable.

Although it may happen that sellers could use this tool as an escape route in not performing their obligations as they are reasonably expected to do thereby bringing dissatisfaction to the buyer, it could also be an allay for sellers to flood the markets with defective products and block compensation for victims in a regime of strict liability.[784] Thus the defence should be given a restricted interpretation by the courts.

The Effects of Hardship

If performance has become excessively onerous, the party so burdened is entitled to request cure to the performance to adapt the contract to the changed circumstances. The request should be made without "*undue delay,*" but a delayed request is not automatically excluded. The seller under the Uniform Act may be granted additional time by the buyer where the seller was liable for lack of conformity for defective goods.[785] Presumably, from an understanding of the text, if the seller's non-performance as a result of hardship, the claim could be justified and the buyer could act in good faith to adapt the contract by providing an additional time to alleviate the burden.[786] In the event the seller does not respect the agreement, the buyer may apply to the court for damages.[787]

An important question is whether the party who claims hardship may suspend performance until the contract is modified by agreement or by the court. From the reading of the text, it is consistent with this view in

[783] Article 281 UAGCL.

[784] Samgena D. Galega, Op. cit., p. 258.

[785] Article 283 UAGCL.

[786] 'Good faith' means 'honesty and the observance of reasonable commercial standards of fair dealing in the trade' in Allan E. Farnsworth, 'The Concept of Good Faith in American Law', (1993) Centro di studi e recherché di diritto comparator e straniero, Roma, p. 3.; Peter Schlechtriem, '3 Good Faith in German Law and International Uniform Laws', Centro di studi e recherché di diritto comparator e straniero, Roma, 1997.

[787] Article 281 UAGCL.

stating that suspension of performance by court order is permissible only in extraordinary circumstances, that is, where the seller's act is a serious one.[788] Another instance under the Uniform Act is where the buyer may withhold performance in an event where he refuses to take delivery of goods (may be due to lack of conformity), by keeping the goods until the seller reimburses his expenses incurred for their safety.[789]

If the court finds that legally redressable hardship exists, it can terminate the contract, or revise it to restore the equilibrium of the contract. The text insinuates that the court has great flexibility in its power to terminate the contract upon the buyer's request. The termination may be estimated by having regard to the seriousness of the case as the court deems just.[790] It should be noted that in many cases, the reliance interest of the buyer not burdened by hardship ought to be redressed.

At Common law, the doctrine of frustration encompasses all situations of changed circumstances. A contract is frustrated where, after the contract was concluded, events occur which make performance of the contract impossible, illegal or something radically different from that which was in contemplation of the parties at the time they entered into the contract. A contract which is discharged on the ground of frustration is brought to an end automatically by the operation of a rule of law, irrespective of the wishes of the parties.[791] In *Mazin Eng. Ltd v. Tower Aluminum (Nig) Ltd.*,[792] it was held that once the court confirms that the contract has been frustrated, there is no room for breach of contract as the frustration is none of the parties' fault.

Impossibility

Supervening impossibility of performance could also discharge a seller from his obligations. The maxim "*lex non cogit ad impossibilia*" meaning that the law will not compel the doing of the impossible is a guiding rule recognised in most Civil and Common Law systems. It has been said that what is "*impossible*" depends partly on the state of technology, and partly on the amount of trouble and expense to which one is prepared to go to achieve it.[793]

---

788 Ibid., para. 2

789 Article 272 UAGCL.

790 Article 282 UAGCL.

791 Ewan Mckendrick, Op. cit., p. 308.

792 [1993] 5 NWLR (Pt.295).

793 G.H. Treitel, Op. cit., p. 809.

When the parties enter into in a contract, the performance of the contract sometimes becomes impossible due to certain events: events or situations in which, by all means, the performance of the contract is not accomplishable. In English law, this situation is treated under the doctrine of frustration.[794] Most legal systems, mainly civil and common law jurisdictions, have followed the maxim "*lex non cogit ad impossibilia*" meaning that the law will not compel the doing of the impossible.

Under the Uniform Act, a party to a contract will not be liable for failure of performance of his obligation if he proves that the event that led to the impossibility of performance was beyond his control.[795] The Act goes ahead to mention the instances which provoke the impossibility of execution ofthe contract.[796] Referring to the Civil Code, these instances include unexpected, unforeseen and unavoidable external events.[797] Furthermore, the Uniform Act provides that the party will be exempted from further performance whenever such performance is caused by either a third party or *force majeure*.[798]

Although it is not easy to list all instances where the principle can operate, courts so far have identified the occurrence of frustration sometimes from the nature of the contract or the circumstances surrounding such contract. It follows that impossibility can be classified under subjective or objective impossibility. Subjective impossibility is related to factors such as death[799] or illness[800] whereas objective impossibility means that the performance of the contract cannot be accomplished. This includes carrying out a contract that has become illegal because the law has changed or the subject matter of the contract is destroyed. Article 294 of the Uniform Act is silent on this issue.

Impact of the Behaviour of the Party not in Breach

The Uniform Act provides for situations where as a result of the events causing the non-performance by the seller of his obligations, the party not in breach,that is, the buyer is in fact expected to take all reasonable measures

794 In Nigeria, the doctrine of frustration was established in the leading case of *Mazin Engineering Ltd. v. Tower Aluminium (Nigeria) Ltd.*, Op. cit. Decision based on the English Case of *Taylor v. Caldwell* (1863) 3 B & S 826; A Similar decision was held in the Nigerian case of *Akanmu v. Olugbode* (2001) 13 WRN 132.

795 Article 294 UAGCL.

796 Article 294 para. 2 UAGCL.

797 Cameroon, Articles 1147, 1148, 1150 CC; Côte d'Ivoire, Articles 1147, France, Article 1150 CC.

798 Article 294 UAGCL.

799 *Stubbs v. Holywell Railway Co.* (1867) Lr 2 Ex. 311.

800 *Robinson v. Davison* (1871) LR 6 Ex. 269.

which might result in minimising the loss.[801]

As an explanation to that, the buyer is not expected to take any measure preventing the impossibility or *force majeure*, before its actual occurrence but rather it may help reduce the amount of damages which might be awarded against the seller being the defaulting party.[802] Hence, the buyer might mitigate either by the purchase of substituted good or stop further performance which might prevent the loss.[803]As a matter of fact, the behaviour of the buyer in such circumstances could only be determined on a case by case basis.

Conclusion

Despite the similarity of language and factors to be established, a party desiring to rely on exemption for non-performance under the Uniform Act is confronted with a continuum of exemptions rather than identical opportunities for relief. Greater leeway and flexibility of exemption and remedial rights are granted in the Uniform Act. The Uniform Act limits exemption to impracticability of performance. Impracticability (and its historic predecessor's impossibility and frustration) present an interesting problem for courts and scholars. Events or situations which render the impossibility of the seller to further his duty of conformity are "*impediments*", impossibility, *force majeure* and hardship. Although it is not easy to make an exhaustive list of where these principles can operate, the Uniform Act so far have identified the occurrence of certain events which may radically change the circumstances of the contract or the nature of the contract itself.

Consistent with economic theory, the Uniform Act defer to individual autonomy by strictly enforcing express allocations of risk. Transaction costs are reduced by providing precedents that discourage opportunistic behaviour and avoid cost to the non-breaching party (buyer). When a disruptive event has not been addressed by the parties ex ante, and neither party is at fault, the Uniform Act uses equitable notions based on community fairness norms to divide the loss between innocent parties. The result is a set of precedents that combines efficiency and fairness in a pragmatic and tractable way. It should be noted that in many cases, the reliance interest of the buyer not burdened by those disruptive events are redressed in addition, due to the impact of these events on the buyer, the latter is still in fact expected to take all reasonable

801 Article 293 para. 1 UAGCL.

802 Article 293 para. 2 UAGCL.

803 Article 292 para. 1 & 2 UAGCL.

measures which might result in minimising the loss.

However, proposed revisions to Chapter V of the Uniform Act suggest that, thought should be given to providing parity between buyers and sellers under the express terms of the statute. The formulation is too general. Currently, sellers are entitled to exemption when performance becomes impracticable but not impossible. Buyers may have some right to exemption under Article 294 but clearly have a right under Article 282 UAGCL to resort to the doctrine of frustration of purpose. This, however, requires near total frustration before an exemption can be granted. This difference in standards is inconsistent with prevailing international practice and will thereby limit the exportability of the OHADA laws to other countries. The burgeoning global marketplace, the growing interdependency among sovereign nations on the international trade of goods, and the impact of modern computer and telecommunications technologies that facilitate transnational and global contracting strongly suggest that the current initiative to modernise Article 294 should be more global in its focus in an effort to encourage the harmonization of the commercial law of the sale of goods by also assessing parties' non-performance based on these issues in the course of commercial transactions.

8

REMEDIES FOR BREACH OF CONTRACT BY THE SELLER

Introduction

In most legal systems, whether Common law or civil law jurisdiction, upon formation of a contract of sale, parties are bound to perform their respective obligations. When a contracting party fails to perform or wrongly performs his obligation under the contract, the aggrieved party is thereupon entitled to seek relief on the basis of the breach of contract. Generally, the purpose of awarding relief upon breach of contract is to either enforce the natural purpose of the contract or to put the parties in the situation they would have been, if the contract had been properly performed.

Depending on the system of law or the type of remedy sought, there are some remedies that may be exercised only unilaterally, some need to be granted by court order and some others are only granted at the discretion of the court.[804] Moreover, in particular circumstances, equitable remedies will also be awarded whenever adequate to ensure justice.

The Uniform Act contains a comprehensive system of remedies for aggrieved buyers which pre-empts remedies available under domestic sale laws. The purpose of this chapter is to explore the consistent scheme set up by the Uniform Act in determining non-conformity and the remedies available to the buyer in the case of non-conformity. Article 281 is the leading provision of Part V, Chapter 1 ("*General Provisions*") of the new amended Uniform Act.

The system of remedies under the UAGCL follows are by and large Civil Law inspired whereby upon breach of contract, specific performance is the primary remedy available to the aggrieved party aimed at compelling the breaching party to perform his obligation. It is only when all attempts to

[804] Andrew Burrows, *Torts and Breach of Contract*, (2nd edition, Butterworths, London 1994) p. 1.

compel performance are ineffective or inadequate that a judicial decree will be granted either for the award of damages or the avoidance of the contract.

Under the UAGCL, the remedy of specific performance is broad. In favour of the buyer, it can be used against the seller in failing to perform any of his duties. In applying for specific performance, the buyer may require the seller to repair the goods,[805] substitute them,[806] or withhold performance,[807], an additional period of time may also be granted for the seller to complete performance of his obligations under the contract.[808] Although the buyer has the right in certain circumstances of the breach to reduce the purchase price,[809] the seller's right to cure is meant to take over the latter's right.

On the other hand, the seller has not been provided the opportunity to grant to the buyer an additional period of time to perform his obligation.[810] In practice, the injunction to pay is most likely used when the seller intends to recover payment from a breaching buyer, in a sales contract. However, it is worthy to point out that although the injunction to pay can be used in a sales contract, as per Uniform Act Organising Simplified Recovery Procedure and Measures of Execution (UASRPME),[811] it remains a seller's means of remedy.[812]

When the breach of contract is so severe that a contracting party will be substantially deprived (anticipatory breach)[813] or is substantially deprived (actual breach) of what he is expecting under the contract, the remedy of avoidance is the appropriate remedy. As a general rule, once fundamental breach is satisfied, the aggrieved party is entitled to the remedy of avoidance.[814]

Under the UAGCL, upon exercising any of the remedy available to him due to the breach of contract, the buyer may still have the right to claim damages alongside. For example, the buyer may claim both repair and damages or he may avoid the contract and claim damages. Any claim for damages in these circumstances is restricted to compensate the loss that the other remedy has not been able to compensate. In any case, the award of damages is equal to the loss incurred or to the profit by the aggrieved party.

---

805 Article 283 para. 1 UAGCL.

806 Article 283 para. 2 UAGCL.

807 Article 282 UAGCL.

808 Article 283 UAGCL.

809 Article 288 UAGCL.

810 Article 283 UAGCL.

811 Articles 1–18 UASRPME; CA Abidjan, Ch. Civ. & Com. No. 644, 11–6–2004 : A. A. G. c/ STE KPMG, et autre ; (www.ohada.com, Ohadata J–05–338). Obs. Jimmy Kodo.

812 Akuété Pedros Santos & Jean Yado Toé, *OHADA Droit Commercial Général*, Op. cit., p. 427.

813 Article 281 UAGCL.

814 Articles 281 & 296 UAGCL.

The remedies of avoidance, damages and injunction to pay are judiciary that is, awarded by the competent court on petition by the aggrieved party. Whereas, the remedy of specific performance is unilateral and the aggrieved party does not need a court order to exercise his right upon breach.

Also, it should be noted that the breaching party will be exonerated from the breach of contract if the failure is caused by force majeure, an act of a third party or an impediment beyond the breaching party's control.[815]

Similarly, the remedy of avoidance of the contract is also as broad in application as the remedy of execution performance. By way of explanation, the remedies of execution performance and avoidance of the contact remain mutually exclusive to the aggrieved party. To be accurate, the aggrieved party has the choice between one of these two remedies in order to be reinstated in the position he would have been in, had the contract been properly performed.[816] As a general rule, the decree of one excludes the award of the other. In particular, the test of the availability of the avoidance remedy is the absence of the provision to that effect.[817]

Whenever a contracting party has suffered loss on the breach of contract, he is entitled to sue for damages. It is immaterial whether one of the first two remedies has been granted or not.

Common Law Approach in Comparism with OHADA

Upon breach of a contractual obligation, the basic remedy is the award of damages, aside from avoidance or rescission of the contract which to be accurate do not amount to remedies.[818] Damages are a monetary sum, fixed by the court to compensate the aggrieved party. The *raison d'être* of damages as a primary remedy is to put the aggrieved party in the same financial situation he would have been in, had the contract been properly performed.[819] It is only when the court believes that damages in a contractual situation is not the adequate remedy for the relief that equitable remedies such as specific performance or injunction come into play.

[815] Article 282 UAGCL.

[816] P. Havenga, M. Havega et al., *General Principles of Commercial Law*, (6th edition, Juta, Cape Town 2007) p. 127.

[817] C. G Van Der Merwe, et al., *Introduction to the Law of South Africa*, (Kluwer Law International, 2004) p. 264.

[818] P. S. Atiyah, *Atiyah's Introduction of the Law of Contract*, Op. cit., p. 371.

[819] G.H. Treitel, Op. cit., p. 17.

With regard to equitable remedies, specific performance is an order of the court aimed at ensuring the natural performance of obligations the parties agreed on at the time of the conclusion of the contract. In the SGA, the remedy of specific performance concerns action for breach of contract related to specific or ascertained goods. An injunction is similarly an order of the court aimed at ensuring the performance of a negative obligation. The negative obligation might be an order of the court making it an obligation to perform (proprietary injunction) or not to perform (mandatory injunction).

In particular, in a sale of goods contract, the SGA provides certain remedies, aside from the specific performance and damages, upon breach of contract. These include the self-help or non-judiciary remedies which are not money compensatory, rather, are attached to the goods and might remedy the seller in circumstances of the buyer's breach. These remedies include the seller's right of lien; the seller's right of stoppage of goods in transit, and the seller's right to resale the goods. Under the right of lien for instance, the unpaid seller is entitled to keep possession of the goods until the buyer performs his part of the obligation. The right of lien at common law may be the equivalent remedy of suspension of contract in the civil law world. With regard to the right of stoppage of goods in transit, once the buyer becomes insolvent and the seller has already handed over the goods to the carrier for the buyer, the seller has the right to stop the goods in transit until payment or tender of the price.[820] Moreover, despite the seller's notice to resell the goods, where the goods are perishable and the seller remains unpaid, he is entitled to resell the goods and claim damages for any breach incurred in this process.[821]

Specific Peformance

Under the UAGCL, the remedy of specific performance is considered as the "*natural*" or primary remedy upon breach of contract.[822] The purpose for a contracting party to compel performance of the contract is nothing but to ensure the proper execution of the contract despite the breach.[823] In other words, the reason of the claim is to place the aggrieved party in the position he would have been if the obligation from the other party was fully performed.

820 A.G Guest, *Benjamin's Sale of Goods*, Op. cit., p. 906.

821 Ibid., p. 938.

822 Akuété Pedros Santos & Jean Yado Toé, Op. cit., p. 420.

823 Donald Harris & Denis, *Contract Law Today Anglo-French Comparisons*, Op. cit., p.249.

Whether the breach of contract occurs as a result of the non-performance or bad performance, the UAGCL provides for the remedy of specific performance which can be exercised by a contracting party to enforce the natural performance of the contract be it the complete or partial fulfillment of his obligations.[824] Hence, it is submitted that the buyer's right of specific performance is unrestricted as it includes all seller's obligation without exception.[825] However, this is not the case for the seller's right for specific performance toward the buyer's breach of contract. It follows that according to the UAGCL, the seller's right for specific performance to the buyer is restricted to grant to the latter an additional period of time to perform his obligation.[826] In case the buyer in a contract of sales fails to pay the price, the seller is rather entitled to take an action for an injunction to pay as per the UASRPME.[827]

When the breach of seller's obligation amounts to a fundamental breach, instead for the buyer to petition for the avoidance of the contract, he may still use the option, for instance in case of non-conformity of the goods, to require specific performance from the seller to supply substituted goods.[828] But when the breach is less severe, that is, does not constitute a fundamental breach, then the specific performance may require the seller either to repair the goods,[829] withhold performance[830] or an additional time may be granted for the seller to complete performance of his obligation.[831]

There are instances at Common Law where the remedy of damages turns inadequate in favour of a decree of specific performance. Specific performance at Common Law is an equitable remedy. It is issued at the discretion of Common Law court, particularly when the Common law remedy has been found inadequate or with inappropriate relief.[832] In fact, as per JSC in *Universal Vulcanizing (Nig.) Ltd. v. I.U.T.T.C.*[833] specific performance is aimed at constraining a contracting party to do that which he has promised to do. Moreover, it is a remedy for breach of contract provided by equity to meet those cases where the common law remedy of damages is inadequate.[834]

[824] Article 281–282 UAGCL.

[825] Akuété Pedros Santos & Jean Yado Toé, Op. cit., p. 420.

[826] Article 286 UAGCL.

[827] Article 1–18 UASRPME; CA Abidjan, Ch. Civ. & Com. No. 644, 11–6–2004: A. A. G. c/ STE KPMG et autre, Op. cit.

[828] Article 283 para. 1 UAGCL.

[829] Article 283 para. 2 & 284 UAGCL.

[830] Article 282 UAGCL.

[831] Article 283 para. 2 UAGCL.

[832] G.H. Treitel, *The Law of Contract*, Op. cit., p. 22.

[833] [1962] NWLR 73. *Similar statements were also made in Afrotech v. MIA* [2001] 6 WRN 65.

[834] Michael Furmston, *Cheshire, Fifoot and Furmston's Law of Contract*, Op. cit., p. 797.

As it is the case in most Common Law jurisdictions, it is also a settled law in majority of the Common Law courts in Africa that on a claim for specific performance, courts have the power to award damages either in addition to or in lieu of the specific performance. It is immaterial in this case whether damages have specifically been claimed or not.[835]

Anticipatory Breach

Generally, when a party in a contract expressly or by conduct informs the other that he will not be able to, or does not intent to perform part or some of his obligation[836] or when it is clear that he will not perform his obligation under the contract,[837] this amounts to anticipatory breach.

Under the UAGCL, the buyer can petition to the competent court in order to cancel the contract, if it appears, after the agreement has been entered into, that the seller will not perform a material part of his contract, due to certain reasons.[838] The buyer may apply to the court to obtain an order authorising it to defer performance of his own obligations.[839] However, it is important to note that an action for anticipatory breach under the Uniform Act unlike at Common Law is judiciary. These actions are directly not exercised between the parties.

If the buyer claims that there has been a breach of the contract, he must take all appropriate measures to mitigate its damages. If he fails to do so the seller may request a reduction in the damages payable, equivalent to the amount of damage that could have been avoided.[840]

If the buyer elects to hold the contract open, the duty to mitigate is deferred, when the seller has committed a serious breach, the buyer thereafter keeps the contract open to his peril.[841]

The seller may be exempted from liability if he can prove that his failure to perform was due to an, event beyond his control.[842] However, the seller cannot be exempted if the failure to perform has been caused by a third party

[835] *Ibedewelu v. Lawal* [1971] 1 All NLR; *Universal Vulcanizing (Nig.) Ltd. v. I.U.T.T.C*, Op. cit.
[836] Dennis Campbell, *Remedies for International Sellers of Goods*, (Yorkhill Law Publisher, 2008) p. 647.
[837] Article 281 UAGCL.
[838] Article 282 para.1 UAGCL.
[839] Article 282 para. 2 UAGCL.
[840] Article 293 UAGCL.
[841] Article 281 para. 1 UAGCL.
[842] Article 294 UAGCL.

appointed by the seller to perform all or part of his contractual obligations.

It follows that anticipatory breach is subject to the fundamental breach on the one hand and the high probability that there will be non-performance of the obligation by a contracting party on the other hand. By way of explanation, the non-performance must cause detriment to the other party to the extent that the aggrieved party is substantially deprived of his expected interest under the contract. Moreover, the foreseability of the breach must be established in order to prove that the material breach be committed. Bankruptcy for instance is a flagrant situation which may satisfy this requirement. It is generally admitted that the degree of probability of the breach required for an action of anticipatory breach is higher than that of the remedy of the right to withhold performance as discussed under the remedy of specific performance.[843]

Avoidance of the Contract

Material Breach

Sales of Goods' provisions in the UAGCL define material breach[844] as a breach that causes detriment to the other party to the extent that the aggrieved party is substantially deprived of his expected entitlement under the contract.[845] Exception is made to this rule if the failure to perform is due to an act of a third party or to force majeure.[846] In the official commentary of the OHADA provisions, it is made clear that for a fundamental breach to take place, the requirements regarding the importance of the detriment and the requirements of foreseeability must be satisfied.[847]

It follows that there is material breach when there is a deprivation of a party's expectations under the contract due to a detriment caused by the other party to the contract. The deprivation of expectation shall be substantial, i.e. affecting the very nature of the contract. The gravity of the detriment suffered by the aggrieved party must have affected the nature of the common intention of the parties, so much so that if the event could have been foreseen, the aggrieved party would never have entered into a contract. In short, the

---

843 Akuété Pedros Santos & Jean Yado Toé, Op. cit., p. 411.

844 Under the former UAGCL, fundamental breach is known as "essential breach" or "manquement essentiel" in the authoritative text.

845 Article 282 UAGCL.

846 Ibid.

847 Joseph Issa-Sayegh et al., *OHADA Traité et Actes Uniformes Commentés et Annotés,* Op. cit., p. 296, (Commenting on former Article 248 UAGCL).

importance of the detriment caused to the aggrieved party shall be therefore so fundamental to cause the breach.

Even if the detriment has been so grave as to deprive the aggrieved party of its expectations under the contract, the principle of fundamental breach will not be considered fulfilled without the foreseeability requirement of the breach.

Similar to foreseeability of damages under the civil code,[848] the determination of the foreseeability of the detriment for the fundamental breach under the UAGCL is a question of fact and not of law: Was the detriment foreseen or foreseeable by the defaulting party at the conclusion of the contract? Is the question to be answered as to determine what foreseeability is all about in the UAGCL.

OHADA's leading literatures suggest that the detriment will be considered foreseeable in two circumstances.[849] First, if the defaulting party knew or ought to have known of the gravity of the detriment.

This might result from non-performance or wrong performance of his obligation. Secondly, the defaulting party (seller) knew that in case of non-performance which led to the gravity of the detriment, the defence following which the act was that of either a third party or was due to an event of force majeure cannot be satisfied. Hence, the foreseeability requirements for fundamental breach will be satisfied once the above two conditions are fulfilled.

It is paramount for the parties to the contract to disclose to each other all relevancies they have or expect from the contract to be considered in their respective performance of obligations. Upon failure to disclose, the detriment caused will not be held foreseeable. But, if such requirement is fulfilled, contrary to the CISG position,[850] the detriment caused to the aggrieved party will be held foreseeable. Unless the detriment was caused by a third party or an event of force majeure, the aggrieved party will be exonerated from being considered in breach. In other words, there is no fundamental breach if the breach is caused by a person other than the parties to the contract or if the breach comes as a result of a force majeure event.[851] However, the direct effect of fundamental breach under the UAGCL is the avoidance of the contract.

848 Cameroon, Article 1150 CC; Côte d'Ivoire, Article 1150 CC; France, Article 1150 CC.
849 Akuété Pedro Santos & Jean Yado Toé, Op. cit., p. 413, 414.
850 Articles 25 & 79 (1) CISG.
851 Articles 282 & 294 UAGCL as opposed to Articles 25 & 79 (1) CISG.

The fundamental breach provision stated in the UAGCL does not provide any examples of events that would constitute a fundamental breach. Instead, it defines fundamental breach in terms of the detriment to the injured party based on the injured party's contractual and other expectation interests. However, unlike the CISG, the UAGCL reduces uncertainty in the definition of fundamental breach by providing instances which will not amount to a fundamental breach: third party acts and *force majeure*. These constitute measures of exoneration from the fundamental breach.[852] But the exoneration does not include a third party appointed by the defaulting party to perform part or the entire obligations under the contract on its behalf.[853]

In Common Law jurisdictions, fundamental breach, unlike any other breaches, refers to a breach which goes to "*the root of the contract*"[854] or which results in performance "*totally different from that which the contract contemplates*" with the effect of depriving the aggrieved party from achieving the main purpose for which he contracted for and entitle the aggrieved party to sue for damages.[855] In this sense, the breach shall be related to a fundamental term, a breach of condition or a breach of condition which constitutes the reason of the aggrieved party (buyer) to put an end to the contract. However, as to the question of what term or condition amounts to fundamental a breach, it is a question of construction depending on every particular case.

In the leading case of *Suisse Atlantique Société d'Armement Maritime S.A v. N. V. Rotterdam scheKolen Centrale*,[856]a case that was latter reaffirmed on appeal by Lord Denning in the House of Lords decision in *Photo Productions Ltd. v. Securicor Transport Ltd.*[857] It was held that a fundamental breach in a contract is a breach of a fundamental term, i.e. a breach of condition that "*goes to the root of the contract*". Also, the two cases reaffirmed that fundamental breach is strictly a question of construction of the contract. Therefore, a fundamental breach is therefore found only through examining the reasonable intentions of the parties at the time of entering into contract.

---

852 Article 294 UAGCL.

853 Article 295 UAGCL.

854 *Suisse Atlantique Société d'Armement Maritime S.A v. N.V. Rotterdamsche Kolen Centrale*, Op. cit.

855 J. Ademola Yakubu, *Law of Contract in Nigeria*, Op. cit., p. 259.

856 Op. cit, (per Lord Reid).

857 [1978] 1 W.L.R 856.

Avoidance of the Contract in case of Non-Delivery

Delivery of the goods is an obligation of the seller and in case of failure to deliver; the law provides remedies for the buyer.[858] Non-delivery of the goods means that the goods do not reach the buyer. In other words, no matter the means used, the goods did not arrive to their destination as stated and agreed upon by the parties in the contract of sale.

Sales law under the UAGCL summarises all available remedies to the buyer in cases of circumstances resulting from the seller's breach.[859] What constitutes the seller's breach in both the CISG and the UAGCL is similar.

Under the two laws, avoidance of the contract by the buyer is the consequence for the seller's breach of obligation to deliver the goods.[860] *Prima facie*, non-delivery of the goods entitles the buyer to avoid the contract.[861]

When the delivery has not been fulfilled as required under the contract, the buyer may fix an additional period of time for performance.[862] The extended period of time shall be reasonable to allow the seller to complete his obligation to deliver in the light of all circumstances surrounding the transaction.[863] During this period, the buyer is not allowed to take any action of remedy for breach of contract against the seller's failure of the initial delivery.[864] But, he does not lose his right to sue for damages.[865] Hence, the seller may avoid an action for a non-fundamental breach of contract provided he delivers conforming goods within the additional time granted.[866] However, if after the additional time is granted to the seller,[867] and he notifies the buyer that he will not be able to deliver within the extended allocated time frame, the buyer has the right to take an action for breach against the seller.[868] It follows therefore that the seller's breach for non-delivery may amount to a material breach.

If the seller's initial failure to comply with the delivery obligation satisfies the requirement of a fundamental breach, the buyer may immediately take

858 Articles 285–290 UAGCL.

859 Article 282 UAGCL.

860 Articles 255–259 UAGCL.

861 Article 283 UAGCL.

862 Ibid.

863 Boris Martor et al, *Business Law in Africa, OHADA and the Harmonization Process*, Op. cit., p. 64.

864 Article 283 para.3 UAGCL.

865 Article 284 UAGCL.

866 Articles 283 para. 3, 257 UAGCL.

867 Article 283 UAGCL.

868 Article 284 UAGCL.

an action for fundamental breach, without granting the additional period for performance.[869] It follows therefore that the non-delivery obligation is not precluded from giving rise to an action for fundamental breach and finding an immediate right to an action of avoidance.[870]

However, it should be pointed out that whenever there is a breach of an obligation of the seller, with the exception of non-delivery, the buyer may only avoid the contract when the breach is fundamental.[871] It is also relevant to note that upon the seller's breach due to failure to deliver, avoidance of the contract can only be made possible through a petition by the buyer to the competent court:[872] Avoidance of the contract due to failure to deliver is therefore judicial under the Uniform Act as opposed to the unilateral avoidance under the CISG.[873]

Avoidance of Contract in case of Tender of Non-Conforming Goods

Under the UAGCL, if the seller tenders goods not conforming to the contract- for example, because they do not correspond with the contract stipulations or are unmerchantable or unfit for the known purpose- the buyer may: (i) reject the goods and, if the seller is not able or willing to re-tender substitute goods in due time, treat the contract as repudiated, and sue for damages for non-delivery.[874]

The effect of the of the buyer's lawful rejection of the goods is to make the case one of non-delivery. It is worth to mention that since there is a contractual duty on the part of the seller not to deliver non-conforming goods,[875] the buyer on avoiding the contract, can, it is implied, include as part of his claim any expenses rendered futile in connection with the re-delivery[876] as agreed with the seller, for example, the costs incurred in taking possession of the goods and installing them prior to rejection.[877]This applies even though the risk has passed and the goods have been lost or damaged. Thus, the effect of the remedy of avoidance is to throw back the risk upon the

---

869 Ibid.

870 Article 281 UAGCL.

871 Article 282 UAGCL.

872 Article 281 UAGCL.

873 Boris Martor et al, Op. cit., p. 64.

874 Article 283 para. 2 UAGCL.

875 Article 255 UAGCL.

876 Article 283 para. 2 UAGCL.

877 Roy Goode, *Commercial Law*, Op. cit., p. 377

seller.[878] The seller who collects or delays in collecting the goods after notice of rejection is liable in damages for storage costs in a warehouse for example, incurred by the buyer.[879]

The basis on which damages may be considered in the event of lack of conformity is whether the goods are bought for use or resale. A first element which should be taken into account is measuring the possibility for the buyer to still make use of the goods or resell them. No fundamental breach is to be found when the buyer can still satisfactorily resell the goods in a normal business environment without incurring any inconveniences. Because of the commercial necessity to resell the goods, the fact that the buyer might be forced in this situation to resell the goods at a lower price is not to be considered, in itself, an unreasonable inconvenience or difficulty. Likewise, the unreasonable difficulty may also stem from that the goods were produced in a country different from the one agreed upon the contract, and subjected at the time to an international embargo: the buyer in this case has to prove unreasonable difficulties in trading the goods in his own country.[880] Apart from the possibility of reselling the goods, the buyer can still seek to be reimbursed for loss of income-profit and for any expenditure incurred in taking reasonable steps in either procuring the temporary use of comparable goods or the loss of deprivation of the use of the asset or the period of the delay in view to mitigate the loss.[881]

In another respect, the rejection may also relate to the part of the non-conforming goods. Article 288 of the Uniform Act allows for partial avoidance of the contract for non-delivery or non-conformity of only a part of the goods. In fact, the buyer who accepted part of the goods is precluded from rejecting the rest is not conforming to the contract. The buyer is expected to accept part while only entitled to claim for damages relating to the non-conformity part(s) of the goods. In some cases, the buyer cannot be compelled to accept a fresh delivery as to the part rejected, for he is not obliged to accept delivery by installments.[882] However, because of some commercial necessity the buyer may decide to accept a fresh tender of the non-conforming part of the goods if the seller is still within the contract

[878] Slyvain Bollée, Theory of Risks in the 1990 Vienna Sale of Goods Convention (1999–2000), *Pace Institute of International Commercial Law*, (available at cisgw3.law.pace.edu), pp. 245–290, p. 57.

[879] Article 272–274 UAGCL.

[880] Anna Veneziano, *Non-Conformity of Goods in International Sales; A Survey of Current Caselaw on CISG*, Op. cit., p. 57.

[881] Roy Goode, *Commercial Law*, Op. cit., p. 376.

[882] SGA 1979 s 31.

period.[883] The reason for this is that in every contract there is an implied condition that the party undertaking an obligation shall continue to be willing and able to perform up to the date of performance. If, therefore, the seller's contract evinces either an intention to repudiate or an inability to perform,[884] the buyer is entitled to treat the contract as repudiated by what is usually termed anticipatory breach.

Avoidance of the Contract in case of Non-Conforming Documents

What rather constitutes "*documents*" in the UAGCL has not been defined.[885] But the seller's duty to deliver under the Uniform Act is thus not a distinct and isolated obligation but encompasses all the seller's obligations with respect to the goods, including delivery of conforming documents related to the goods. This makes it clear that if the seller is to avoid a breach of the delivery obligation, it must ensure that the documents themselves conform to the goods in question. In this case, the seller's failure to deliver the conforming documents at the time and in the manner prescribed in the contract or by the trade, gives the buyer the right to reject the contract and claim for damages.[886] In other words, the buyer's rejection of the non-conforming goods due to improper documents over the goods exposes the seller to an immediate action for payment of damages as of breach of contract. With regard to the conformity of the documents, the general rule is that failure to deliver or delivery of non-conforming documents is treated in the same way as the delivery of non-conforming goods.[887] This is so because UAGCL treats documents as an essential part of the goods and therefore, any missing part of the goods opens an action for the buyer to reject or request for the re-tender of that missing item of the goods.[888]

However, it remains a fact that delivery of non-confirming documents is considered as material to the sale.[889] This is often the case when the goods

[883] At common law, this is known as the right to cure. This was illustrated in the case of *Borrowman Phillips & Co. v Free & Hollis* (1878) 4 QBD 500.

[884] Article 281 UAGCL.

[885] The SGA refers to the documents of title which have the same meaning as they have in the Factor Acts. Then, it lists the documents falling within its generic and makes it clear that they are documents used in the ordinary course of business as proof of the possession or control of goods.

[886] Article 282 UAGCL.

[887] Akuété PedroSantos & Jean Yado Toé, Op. cit., p. 390.

[888] Article 289 UAGCL.

[889] Article 254 UAGCL; Joseph Issa-Sayegh et al., Op. cit., p. 290; Bills of lading, warehouse warrants for instance have been acknowledged to be of relevance in modern sales.

are delivered to a buyer who intends to resell them but they were delivered without the vital documentary title contrary to the contract, although the seller in this case had knowledge of the importance of the documents of title of the goods. It may also be the case of the delivery of an engine which cannot be used without the documents (guidelines and usage notice of the goods). Unless otherwise agreed, the documents need be handed over only in exchange for payment, for prima facie payment and delivery are concurrent conditions[890] and here the delivery obligation is satisfied by the furnishing of the documents. Even though the purpose of documents as understood under the UAGCL may be for the seller to arrange for the transportation of the goods typically to sales at distance,[891] the main consideration here is for the buyer to be entitled to obtain possession and have a legitimate right to use the goods for commercial purpose with respect to the type and place of business.[892]

Rejection, on the other hand, does not necessarily place the seller in breach at all as regards its primary delivery obligation,[893] for unless the improper delivery signifies the seller's intention or incapacity to perform (and thus constitutes an anticipatory breach), rejection simply produces non-delivery and the seller may still have time to re-tender in conformity with the contract (unless otherwise agreed with the buyer), or the buyer may simply claim for damages.[894] The taking of the goods must be distinguished from acceptance of the goods.

As to the seller's breach under the Uniform Act,[895] the buyer may be granted an additional time frame to remedy the breach.[896] However, unlike with the seller, the buyer's additional time must not cause to the seller an unreasonable delay or inconvenience or any doubt as to the payment of the price.[897]

Procedure of Avoidance

Under the UAGCL, fundamental breach caused by either contracting party[898] and failure by the seller or buyer to perform any of its obligations or

[890] Articles 262 & 267 UAGCL.
[891] Article 252 UAGCL.
[892] Articles 234 & 235 UAGCL.
[893] As to the fact that the delivery must conform to the contract.
[894] Article 282 UAGCL.
[895] Article 283 para. 3 UAGCL.
[896] Article 283 para.2 UAGCL.
[897] Article 285 UAGCL. Joseph Issa-Sayegh et al., Op. cit., p. 298.
[898] Article 281 UAGCL.

failure to perform after an additional time gives rise to the avoidance of the contract.[899] However, with the exception to late delivery, it should be pointed that, non-performance by a party within the additional time offered to cure the breach does not generally meet with the requirement for petition to avoid the contract.[900]

The process of avoidance under the UAGCL is judicial.[901]As a matter of fact, it is expressly clear that OHADA is for the judicial process of cancellation of the contract,[902] as well as the anticipated action for avoidance when before the date of the performance of the contract, it appears that one party will not fulfill an essential part of its obligation due to some circumstances beyond its control.[903]

The buyer may apply to the court for cancellation of the contract if the seller's breach of the contract is a serious one provided the buyer had notified the seller of his decision. The buyer nevertheless retains all other remedies, such as the right to claim damages or a reduction in price.

However, in the UAGCL, the time for an action to petition the competent court for avoidance of the contract has not been defined.[904] However, apart from those specifically spelt out in articles 258[905] and 259[906] UAGCL, all claims on commercial sales must be filled within two years, failing which they will elapse.[907]

In Common Law jurisdictions, avoidance of the contract takes place immediately when one of the contracting parties shows an intention, express or implied, not to proceed with the contract.[908] But if a party's acts or conducts are implied, a reasonable person test is used to determine whether or not the implied acts or conducts lead to the conclusion that the party in question did not intend to fulfil his obligations under the contract. After the English case of *Mersey Steel & Iron Co. v. Naylor Benzon & Co*,[909] this position was reaffirmed in some more recent cases in Africa.[910]

---

899 Articles 283 & 284 UAGCL.
900 Akuété Pedro Santos & Jean Yado Toé, Op. cit., p. 424.
901 Article 281 as opposed to the unilateral procedure of avoidance under Article 49 CISG.
902 Article 281 UAGCL.
903 Article 282 UAGCL.
904 Joseph Issa-Sayegh et al., *Traité et Actes Uniformes Commentés et Annotés*, Op. cit., p. 285.
905 In the case of apparent defect of conformity
906 In the case of hidden defect of conformity.
907 Article 301 UAGCL.
908 K. L. Igweike, Op. cit., pp. 191–192.
909 [1884] 9 App. Cas. 434.
910 *Westav v. Sokoto State Governement & Ors* [2001] 1 WRN 113 p. 125.

It may occur when either contractual parties by words or conducts refuses to perform their obligations under the contract. If it happens, the other party is therefore released from other obligations under the contract and therefore entitled to sue. This position is well illustrated in the leading authority of *Cort v. Ambergate, & Railway Company,*[911] where the plaintiff had a contract to deliver a certain fixed number of goods to be manufactured to the defendant. After the plaintiff had delivered a certain quantity, the defendant informed the plaintiff that he should not deliver anymore as the remaining part was no more desired. It was held that it was unnecessary for the plaintiff to try and deliver the remaining part since the contract was avoided. He could merely maintain an action without attempting to further manufacture and deliver the remaining goods.

If the aggrieved party wishes to accept the breach and terminate the contract, it must do so unequivocally and without undue delay. Delay on its own is not fatal, provided the innocent party does not do anything to affirm the contract in the interim, and it is prudent to put it on record that the innocent party objects to the conduct. When a contract is to be avoided for inadequate reasons, the avoiding party must provide a valid reason existing at the time he is avoiding the contract as a justification of the avoidance. There must be a direct link between the fact justifying the avoidance and the avoidance itself.

Where it appears that the avoidance is justified by a genuine reason, the defence must be raised as soon as possible. But if the aggrieved party has knowledge of its right to avoid the contract and he keeps on with the contract, he will automatically lose his right to avoid the contract as this will constitute a waiver of action.[912]

Delivery of Substitute and Repair of Goods

If the goods do not conform with the contract the buyer as an alternative to avoidance, may require delivery of substitute goods.[913]The buyer may require repair of the goods by the seller, unless this is unreasonable having regards to all circumstances.[914]

If this is possible, the buyer may require the seller to remedy the lack of conformity by repair and fix an additional period of time for this purpose. If

911 [1851] 17 QB 127.

912 *Panchard Preres SA v Establshment General Grain Co.Ltd* [1970] 1 Llyod's Rep. 53.

913 Articles 258, 259, 283 para. 2 UAGCL.

914 Article 282 UAGCL.

the goods perish before the defect is repaired, the buyer may resort to other remedies with respect to the seller's breach of contract because repair is no longer workable. This solution follows from Article 283 para. 2 and 3 of the Uniform Act, which applies where the buyer has fixed "*additional period of time for performance by the seller of his obligations*" and may be expanded, by analogy, to cases in which such period has not been fixed. A different solution would encourage the buyer to avoid the contract than to accept a less drastic course, the repair of the goods.[915]

It follows therefore from the above discussion that three conditions must be satisfied for the buyer to exercise his right upon the seller's breach: (i) There must be non-conformity of the goods according to the contractual provisions, (ii) the breach of conformity must be a fundamental breach (that is for full avoidance by the buyer) and (iii) the request to substitute the good must be within a reasonable time frame allocated for such a breach and be complied with. In the second case, upon the seller's breach due to non-conformity of the goods at delivery, the buyer may request the seller to remedy the non-conformity by repair.[916] In his claim, the buyer must comply with the requirements of notice and the time frame.[917]

Also, the law has provided for the seller an opportunity to cure his breach (replacement of the goods or repair of non-conforming goods) before[918] and after the date of delivery provided the buyer agrees.[919] This opportunity is often called self-execution. For instance, if the breach is about the delivery of the missing part or quantity of the goods or substitution of the goods, in case of an anticipated delivery, the seller's willingness to remedy the breach amounts to a self-execution.[920] In other words, the seller needs not to give notice for remedy, provided the remedy takes place before the fixed date for delivery. However, the attempt to remedy may give rise to damages if it causes to the buyer unreasonable inconvenience or additional costs.

The availability of such a choice of the performance-oriented buyers' remedy suggests that the Uniform Act favours remedies that preserve the contractual bond in contrast to remedies that involve termination of the contract (that is, avoidance).

---

915 Sylvain Bollée, *Theory of Risks in the 1990 Vienna Sale of Goods Convention*, Op. cit.

916 Article 257 UAGCL.

917 Article 258 UAGCL.

918 Articles 257 & 290 para. 1 UAGCL ; Charles Mba-Owono, *Non-conformité et vices cachés dans la vente commerciale en droit uniforme africain*, Op. cit., p. 122.

919 Article 283 (2) UAGCL.

920 Ingeborg Schwenzer, Op. cit., p. 606; Akuété Pedro Santos & Jean Yado Toé, Op. cit., p. 422.

The issue of failed repair should also be considered here. Accordingly, if the buyer wants to rely on an unsuccessful repair by the seller in an attempt to deliver the missing part(s) of the goods as stipulated in Article 283 para 2 and 3 UAGCL, it must give notice of the fact that the lack of conformity failed, and this is irrespective of any notice already given before delivery of the repaired goods. Even though the seller may remedy the breach at its own expense, the buyer can, however, oppose to this or claim for damages ensuing from the delayed performance.[921]

The issue of the seller's act to repair or substitute goods may seem doubtful on the part of the buyer with respect to the character or quality of the goods.. A buyer might naturally be skeptical of repair work that the seller is forced to do under an order of a court or arbitral tribunal. This or the alternative of avoiding the contract and purchasing substitute goods eliminates doubts about the quality of repair work performed by the seller that has delivered non-conforming goods. Of course, if the seller has repair capabilities not possessed by others, and the buyer cannot easily avoid the contract and replaces the goods, forcing the seller to repair pursuant to Articles 257 and 283 para.1 and 2, of the Uniform Act may be the buyer's only practical course, but such cases, apparently are rare.

In addition, the buyer might well be concerned with the delay of waiting for a court or arbitral tribunal to order the seller to repair.[922]

Furthermore, it is, however, regrettable to conceive some difficulties which may be related to the seller's duty to make a fresh tender of goods in which conforms to the contract, in view to remedy its breach of lack of conformity. Is the buyer bound to accept the goods tendered? In fact, it is hard to justify an obligation for the seller of selecting different goods to be delivered or to perform a second delivery with conforming goods. That would mean to substitute the performance of an obligation which does not exist; where would such an obligation come from? In addition, how many times should the seller correct his proper delivery to bring the result up to the expectations of the buyer? How long would it take for professional traders to include in their written general conditions an exemption from

---

[921] Article 284 UAGCL.

[922] Harry M. Flechner, Buyers' Remedies in General and Buyers' Performance-Oriented Remedies, (2005–2006) 25 (339) *Journal of Law and Commerce*, pp. 339–347, p. 343, (available online at www.heinonline.org).

such an obligation in order to safe time in business dealings?[923] As a matter of fact, time is of essence here on the part of the commercial buyer in his business. It is, however, regrettable that opportunity has not been taken to revisit the OHADA Uniform Sales Act by including express provisions as to this right of retender, a right which mitigates the impact of an improperly motivated rejection by the buyer while at the same time tending to avoid economic waste.[924]

Obviously, according to the OHADA Law, the buyer is not quite deprived of all protection. He may avail himself of the guarantee provided by a default rule that grants him the right of complaining of the defects existing at the moment of the conclusion of the contract,[925] or from the time of delivery[926] within a short term of time and to start an action in court within the time limit of one year from the delivery.[927]

Reduction in Price

Likewise, the right for the buyer to reduce the price applies with respect to all the non-conforming goods, whether they have subsequently perished or not. If the goods do not conform to the contract the buyer may reduce the price in the same proportion as the value that the goods actually delivered bears to the value that conforming goods would have had at that time.[928] In order to calculate how to reduce the price, courts need to interpret the two elements of the aforementioned proportion.

As to the first element—"*value of the goods actually delivered*".[929] This would mean that the value of the goods accepted.[930]

Turning to the second element of the proportion in order to quantify the price reduction as regard to the "*value that conforming goods would have had*"—would be determined by the price agreed upon by the parties.[931]

923 Silva Ferreri, Remarks Concerning the Implementation of the CISG by the Courts. (The Seller's Performance and Article 35), (2005–2006) 25 *Journal of Law and Commerce*, pp. 223–239, p. 224, available online at www.heinonline.org.

924 The right to retender given by s 2–508 of the UCC could be useful here.

925 Article 1477 of the Italian Civil Code also strengthens this point in ordering the seller to "... deliver the good(s) in the condition which it was at the moment of the sale."

926 Article 256 UAGCL.

927 Article 259 para.1 and2 UAGCL.

928 Article 288 UAGCL; Charles Mba-Owono, Op. cit., p. 126.

929 Article 292 para. 2 UAGCL; Section 2–714 (2) of the UCC.

930 Section 2–714 (2) of the UCC also contains the same meaning.

931 Article 292 para. 1 UAGCL.

Suspension of Payment

The non-fulfilment by the seller of any obligation to tender goods of conformity to which the duty of payment is correlative entitles the buyer to suspend payment until the obligation has been performed. According to the UAGCL, the exact time the buyer has to pay is located at the time thereupon the seller makes available to him either the goods or the documents representing the goods.[932] In other words, payment and delivery must be made simultaneously.[933] Thus, otherwise agreed, payment and delivery are concurrent conditions, and the buyer need not tender payment unless and until the seller has properly performed his own obligations to the contract. This provision seems to secure both parties: it allows the seller to remain in control of the goods until the buyer pays and on the buyer's part, he will not proceed with the payment until delivery of the right goods. At times, payment of the price may be conditioned: depending on the circumstances of each case, the seller may condition delivery of the goods or handing over of the documents on payment of the purchase price[934] or the buyer may condition payment of the price after examination of the goods.[935]

From this standpoint, it is therefore clear that both parties enjoy under these provisions the right of retention. In particular, the buyer's right of retention is evidenced by the fact that he will only release payment when the goods are placed at his disposal. Moreover, the buyer's right may sometimes be extended when he has to examine the goods before acceptance.[936]This situation evidently signifies that either physical possession or such form of constructive possession is afforded the buyer a reasonable opportunity to examine the goods. Also, in accordance with Article 272 of the Uniform Act, the buyer exercises an extended right of retention of title by keeping control over the undesired goods until the seller reimburses the expenses he incurred for their safety.[937] This is a typical condition for securing performance by the seller against retention of the goods. Moreover, if the contract of sale requires transportation of goods, the seller usually takes the risk to forward the goods to the buyer by himself or through his agent with the related documents as

932 Article 266 UAGCL.

933 This is a similar position at Common Law as per Sale of Goods Act 1979, s 28.

934 Ibid.

935 Article 267 para. 2 UGACL.

936 Article 267 para. 2 UAGCL.

937 Article 272 UGACL ; Akuété PedroSantos & Jean Yado Toé, Op. cit., p. 405; Ingebod Schwenzer, *Commentary on the UN Convention on the International Sale of Goods (CISG)*, Op. cit., p. 852.

well[938]. The buyer in this case may decide to retain the documents and send back the goods to the seller in case he finds any defects in the goods. Such a measure is to either hold the seller to act accordingly or reimburse any money paid representing the price of the goods. In other words, the title over the goods will be retained by the buyer until the goods are in conformity to the contract stipulation.

Right to Damages: Damages to other Goods of the Buyer

Damages are one of the remedies available for breach of contract.[939] In the UAGCL and common law systems, the reason for awarding damages is to compensate, and nothing more. Damages for breach of contract usually aim to fulfill the aggrieved party's expectations by putting him into as good a position he would have been in if the contract had been properly performed.[940] In practice, the principle of full compensation under the UAGCL is meant to include all pecuniary losses that the aggrieved party would have incurred under the contract, in addition to all actual losses but for the breach.[941] The test is whether it is sufficient for the aggrieved party to prove that he has suffered non-performance from his counter party as a result of the breach or if he also has to prove that the loss was suffered as a consequence of the non-performance. Both tests will be used in the assessment of damages.

As a general rule under the Uniform Act, in matters of sale where an aggrieved party accepts and has been granted avoidance of the contract due to a serious breach of the duty of performance,his claim may give way to a request for payment of damages.[942] In this event, the buyer may claim damages for the seller's lack of conformity of goods. The measure of damages would be estimated on the loss directly and naturally resulting, in the ordinary course

938 Article 250 UAGCL.

939 Ewan McKendrick, *Contract Law*, Op. cit., p. 829.

940 Andrew Burrows, Op. cit., p.16; Pascal Nguihe Kante, La Prise en Compte des Attentes Légitimes du Cocontractant en Droit Privé des Contrats, (2008) (12) *Annales de la Faculté des Scieces Juridiques et Politiques,* Université de Dschang, p.35; Nicholas B., *The French Law of Contract*, Op. cit.,p. 225. For tort, damages usually aim to put the plaintiff into as good a position as he would have been in if no tort had been committed. Whereas the payment of damages for a breach of a tort "is essential to the maintenance of the tort system as an effective, credible deterrent to negligence", without some kind of punishment for the defendant, there is no reason, other than a matter of conscience, for him not to commit that tort again. Providing the guilty party with a punishment is a way of deterring unsafe conduct.

941 Akuété Pedros Santos & Jean Yado Toé, Op. cit., p. 417.

942 Article 281 UAGCL.

of event, from the breach of the contract, and in the case of breach of the warranty as to the quality of goods, this is *prima facie* the amount by which the value of the goods as contracted exceeds their value in the state in which they are delivered.

Damages may also be granted also when repair is made at the seller's expense, that is, the cost incurred to redress the defective goods.[943]For example, the buyer having received the conforming goods with delay[944] or the goods may be non-conforming; some costs may have been incurred by the buyer in the transportation of goods twice or for conserving the goods in a warehouse.[945]

Consequential loss claims may well arise upon the acceptance of the goods which prove defective. At common law, such claims will be governed by the rule laid down in the judgment of the case of *Hadley v. Baxendale*[946] whereby the measure of damages is the estimated loss directly and naturally resulting in an ordinary course of events from the buyer's breach.

Restitutionary Remedy

Unlike reliance interest, which focuses on the costs incurred by the non-breaching party, or expectation interest, which is concerned with the gains and losses that full performance of the contract would produced, restitution as a remedy for breach looks to the benefits conferred by one party on the other. Restitution's concept of "*benefit,*" however, is elusive. It may be understood as requiring an increase in the wealth of the receiving party. In that event, one of the primary purpose of restitution is to avoid unjustly enriching one person at the expense of another.[947]

Restitution under the UAGCL is retroactive, which is the direct effect of the cancellation of the contract of sale.[948] In the first place, when a contracting party has either performed his obligations in whole or partially under the contract, in application of the rule of restitution, that party shall claim from the other party refund of what he had delivered or paid in performance of the

943 Article 292 (1) and (2) UAGCL.

944 With respect to Articles 258 and 259 UAGCL.

945 Article 272 UAGCL.

946 [1854] 9 Exch 341.

947 Eric G. Anderson, The Restoration Interest and Damages for Breach of Contract, (1994), 53 *Maryland Law Review*, pp. 1–64, p.6.

948 Joseph Issa-Sayegh, et al., *Traité et Actes Uniformes Commentés et Annotés*, Op. cit., (Commenting on former Article 270 of the former Uniform Act) p. 300.

contract.[949] A mutual restitution as such binds both parties, and not just the breaching party whose non-performance led to avoidance of the contract. As such, the effect of cancelling a contract of sale under the Uniform Act does not exonerate the parties from paying any damages due.[950] That is to say, each party must restore in return for restitution by the other.[951] As a consequence of the avoidance, the contract disappears as never existed between the parties. This restitution remedy is based on the net benefit conferred upon the breaching party by the victim. Thus, it is a routine element of restitutionary remedies for breach that the aggrieved party also must restore the value of any benefits received from the party in breach. Such mutual restoration as the case under the Uniform Act, might suggest that the goal of the restitution remedy for breach of contract is to return the aggrieved party to the *status quo ante*.[952]

It therefore appears that restitution may be partial. This may be due to the fact that the seller has partially performed his obligations or because of some other reasons such as impossibility to perform, the buyer could take a legal action to recover what is due based on a restitutionary remedy.[953]

Once the recission of the contract is effective, restitution shall take place immediately so as to comply with the effect of avoidance, aimed at putting parties in the position they would have been had there never been a contract between them. In effect, it follows that there will be no restitution if there has not been performance by either contracting party. If there has been performance, by either both or one party, restitution may take place.

Strictly construed, the idea of restitution interest under the Uniform Act in returning the parties to their pre-contractual positions persists. It is expressed in the event where the goods expected to be restored must be refunded in the state in which the buyer had received them at the formation of the contract.[954] But if before the restitution the goods are no more available or are destroyed, the restitution will take place by money compensation.[955] The value of the goods shall be that the goods had at the making of the contract.[956]

[949] Article 297 UAGCL.

[950] Article 296 UAGCL.

[951] Article 269 UAGCL; Ingeborg Schwenzer, op cit, p .1106.

[952] Eric G. Anderson, Op. cit., p. 6; Akuété Pedro Santos & Jean Yado Toé, Op. cit., p. 415.

[953] Articles 281 para. 2, 282 & 296 UAGCL.

[954] Articles 283 & 298 UAGCL.

[955] Remy Cabrillac, *Droit des Obligations,* (7 édition, Dalloz, 2006) p. 80.

[956] Article 273 para.2 UAGCL.

The purpose of restitution under the Uniform Act is to prevent one party to the contract to unjustly be enriched against the other party who has performed his obligation under the contract. In order to avoid such a situation under the contract, the law requires the party who has received or benefited from performance, to compensate the other party's performance,[957] in addition to the benefit earned for the received performance.[958]

In addition, if there had been any expenses on the maintenance of the goods to be returned, the buyer who is the beneficiary of the restitution shall be compensated for such expenses incurred.[959] Also any expenses incurred by the buyer before restoring the goods shall be refunded. Otherwise, if the goods restored are defective, damages may be awarded to the aggrieved party.[960] However, in the event where the contract has been cancelled, the seller shall refund any interest gained from the price paid for the goods before restoration of the goods by the buyer.[961] It means, therefore, that parties are required to disclose all profits earned from the goods, as it shall be returned in compensation to the other party. The interest starts from the day of the payment thereof.

Reliance Interest

The reliance interest takes its bearing from the "*sunk costs*" of the aggrieved party. When protected, it compensates a party for losses or harms that were incurred or suffered based on the assumption that the promise of the breaching party would be kept. The modern understanding of the reliance interest derives from the article by Fuller and Perdue, which generalised that it puts the injured party in the position he would have occupied had the contract not been formed, provided that the reliance damages do not exceed the expectation interest.[962]

Accordingly, it could be supposed that the purpose of awarding damages under the Uniform Act (though it is more of an expectation interest), is based on the claim of reliance interest in placing the aggrieved party in the position in which it would have been if he had not relied on the due performance of the

957 Article 297 UAGCL.
958 Article 300 UAGCL.
959 Article 272 UAGCL.
960 Akuété Pedro Santos & Jean Yado Toé, Op. cit., p. 415.
961 Article 300 UAGCL.
962 L. L. Fuller & William R. Perdue, The Reliance Interest in Contract Damages, (1936) 40 (52) *Yale Law Journal*, pp. 1–27, p. 2.

contract.[963] For instance, where the contract of sale has ended and the buyer has made a purchase in replacement of the contract of the goods, or the seller has resold the goods, the buyer is entitled to claim damages on the basis of the difference between the contract price and the cost of the replacement or the resale. Thus, what may turn to be the expectancy interest of the buyer in reliance of the contract could be recoverable under a claim of reliance interest. With reference to conventional contract law, the buyer's reliance damages are protected, which are less than its expectation damages, because its profits cannot be proven with sufficient certainty.[964] As a result, the aggrieved party is put back to the position prior to the contract being made as opposed to the position as if the contract where successfully made. It therefore means that reliable interest is taken to be, "*losses caused*" (*damnum emergens*), and "*gains prevented*" (*lucrum cessans*) generally falls within the scope of the Uniform Act. In the first place, though reliance ordinarily results in "*losses*" of an affirmative nature (expenditure labour and money) it is also true that opportunities for gain may be forgone in reliance on a promise. Hence the reliance interest must be interpreted as at least potentially covering "*gains prevented*" as well as "*losses caused*". Obviously, certain scruples concerning "*causality*" and "*foreseeable financial interest*" which the aggrieved party would have regardless of the breach are suggested to constitute the reliance interest under the Uniform Act.[965] It is enough for present purpose to note that there is nothing in the definition of the reliance interest itself which would exclude items of this sort from consideration.

Expectation Interest

The contractual expectation interest traditionally is conceived in terms of a promisee's expectation of receiving the promised benefit of the contract.[966] It is, as a matter of fact, clear that the things which the law of damages purports to "*measure*" and "*determine*"—the "*injuries*" and to ascertain whether the plaintiff has included the "*items of damage*" in his complaint.[967] One finds here the normal rule of contract damages which is expectation interest. This refers to the award to the promisee the value of the expectancy.

[963] Article 292 UAGCL; Akuété Pedro Santos & Jean Yado Toé, Op. cit., p. 417.

[964] Eric G. Anderson, *The Restoration Interest and Damages for Breach of Contract*, Op. cit., p.6.

[965] Akuété Pedro Santos & Jean Yado Toé, Op. cit., p. 417.

[966] Steven J. Burton, Breach of Contract and the Common Law Duty to Perform in Good Faith, (1980) 94 *Harvard Law Review*, p. 1.

[967] L.L. Fuller & William R. Perdue, *The Reliance Interest in Contract Damages*, Op. cit., p. 1.

The purpose of awarding expectation interest under the Uniform Act is generally to award profit to the buyer had it been that the seller had performed its delivery obligations.[968] In other words, this measure of awarding damages under the Uniform Act rotates around the idea a breach is deemed when it substantially deprives a party of the benefit that it is legitimately entitled to expect under the contract if the buyer had performed his own obligations. We can, to be sure, understand that the "*compensation*" here seems to be appropriate because the seller's breach deprived the buyer of the expectancy. Thus, it is convenient to say without any doubt that the Uniform Act is basically in favour of expectation interest than any other type of damages.

Thus, by way of explanation, the purport of expectation interest under the Uniform Act suggests that where the contract has been cancelled and the buyer has made a purchase in replacement of the goods or the seller has resold the goods, the buyer's damages shall be estimated from the difference between the contact price and the price of the replacement of the purchase or the resale, as well as all other damages to which it may be entitled. The aim of the Uniform Act is to put the buyer in as a good position as it would have occupied had the seller preformed his promise. The interest protected in this case is purely the expectation interest of the buyer. In his article, Professor Burton argues that expectation interest also encompasses the expected costs to the promisor, which consist of opportunities forgone at the time of contract formation. This cost perspective articulates an operational standard of good faith performance.[969]

A reason which may be advanced for the Uniform Act protecting the expectancy of the buyer may be found in the much-discussed "*will theory*" of contract law. This theory gives way for the agreement of contracting parties to be enforceable by the law. Thus, if any party to this contract violates any term, the law is there to compel the defaulting party to perform his obligations as set up by the parties. This theory reinforces the notion that every contract create a "*right*" which needs to be enforceable by the courts. Under such a rule, the penalty for violating the norm established by the contract would simply consist in being compelled to compensate the aggrieved party for detrimental reliance.

Again, from the economic standpoint, the Uniform Act can be appraised for protecting the expectation interest for purposes of the existing economic environment and to enhance the reliance on business agreements. Basically,

[968] Article 292 UAGCL.

[969] Steven J. Burton, Op. cit.

the breach of a promise renders an actual diminution of the buyer's assets, in the sense that the latter had not "*used*" the property which the contract represents. Expectations of future values, become for commercial purposes, present values to the buyer,[970] because he needs it for possible or future commercial uses.

Concrete and Abstract Calculation of Damages

Under the UAGCL, concrete calculation of damages is meant to quantify loss based on the difference between the contract price and the price of the substitute transaction.[971] However, requirements such as avoidance of the contract, time and substitute transaction must be satisfied to enable concrete calculation of damages in accordance with the UAGCL.

The first requirement is that there must be avoidance of the contract,[972] which as an effect, discharges the parties from their obligations related to the contract , that is, one party to the contract, the buyer in our case, must have avoided the contract, and should have notified the seller of the avoidance as required.[973] It suggests that the right time of assessment is shortly after the avoidance of the contract.

But it may also be admitted that the notice prior to avoidance turns unnecessary when it becomes a fact that the seller will definitely not perform his obligations under the contract due to certain factors beyond his control.[974] Accordingly, the buyer usually takes all appropriate measures to mitigate his damages. If it fails to do so, the seller may request a reduction in the damages payable, equivalent to the amount of damage that could have been avoided.[975]

As it may be the case, the prices on the market may be relevant to determine whether or not a cover transaction was concluded in accordance with the Uniform Act. Generally, it is accepted that the cover purchase is to be concluded by a third party. Under the CISG, with a similar inference from the provisions under the UAGCL, it could be possibly true that if the buyer produces the substituted goods himself, this will not be regarded as a cover purchase and the buyer will have to rely on the general provision of damages

---

[970] L. L. Fuller & William R. Perdue, Op. cit., p. 4.

[971] Article 292 UAGCL.

[972] Article 296 UAGCL.

[973] Article 281 UAGCL.

[974] Articles 282 & 283 UAGCL.

[975] Article 282 para. 2 UAGCL.

to be reimbursed of his expenses incurred on the substituted goods.[976] It is however required that the goods suit the contract goods description. However, the market price could also be taken into consideration here.

Once these requirements are fulfilled, the buyer may claim as damages the difference between the contract price and the price of the substituted goods. The provision also entitles the buyer to claim any additiona loss such as the cost of transportation of the goods, examination by an expert or any other loss falling within any recoverable loss under the Uniform Act.[977]

Unlike the CISG,[978] UAGCL is silent on the abstract calculation of damages, neither have scholars discussed the matter deeply. However, the position at common law is quite distinct as the abstract calculation of damages is well considered than the concrete calculation of damages.[979] Abstract assessment of damages is all about the market price at which substitute goods could be obtained if in a contract of sale the seller fails to deliver the goods.[980] However, in addition to the concrete assessment of damages as pointed out under the UAGCL, if the breach is as the result of the buyer's non-performance for instance, the concrete assessment of damages will be based on the amount for which the seller resold the goods and the abstract calculation will remain based on the market price.[981]

Interest

As a general rule, the law does not impose a statutory or Common law obligation to pay interest upon default.[982] Interest calculated in terms of money if a breaching party fails to pay is unknown in Common law countries.[983] Rather, delay in payment, as agreed in the contract would entitle the aggrieved party to claim and recover from the lost incurred.

At Common Law, it is submitted that there are four exceptions where a contracting party can claim interest. These include: (1) Common law courts

[976] Article 291–293 UAGCL; Article 74 CISG; Ingeborg Schwenzer, Op. cit., p.1017.

[977] Articles 270 & 272 UAGCL.

[978] Article 76 CISG.

[979] G.H. Treitel, *The Law of Contract*, Op. cit., p. 47.

[980] Ibid., p. 44.

[981] Ibid., pp. 45–6; Hugh Beale, et al., Op. cit., p. 845.

[982] *President of India v. La Pintada Cia Navegacion SA* (No. 2) [1985] 1 AC 104, (1984) 2 All ER 773.

[983] *William v. Reynolds* (1865); 6 B & s 495; Michael Furmston, *Cheshire Fifoot and Furmston's Law of Contract*, Op. cit., p. 777.

have discretionary power to award interest on a case to case basis and provided the money was owed at the time the proceedings were instituted, or when statutes provide the payment of interest; (2) where the court in analysing the case in dispute, finds out that the parties have implicitly agreed on the interest,[984] (3) where there is an express term in the contract providing for interest in specific circumstances,[985] (4) where interest is claimed as a special damages as per the landmark case of *Hadley v. Baxendale*.[986]

The UAGCL on its part provides rules on the duty to pay interest, particularly when a contracting party fails to pay the contract price. Although the UAGCL does not fix the interest rate, it gives reference to the application of domestic law. In addition, it gives guidelines as to how it shall be calculated and how it is dispatched.[987] It starts running from the moment the notice is dispatched. The notice must be written, no matter the means. It is suggested that a formal written letter can constitute a notice. However, to be addressed, it must be dispatched as a registered mail; the notice shall be so addressed along with an acknowledgement receipt.[988] It should be noted that although most of the provisions of the UAGCL derive from the CISG, the latter is silent as concerns the time at which interest starts accruing.[989] Moreover, the CISG does not either provide the interest rate.[990]

In the OHADA member States, parties in a sale of goods contract are required to pay the interest due as per the UAGCL.[991] The law states that whenever any of the parties fail to pay the contract price or any other sum of money owed, he is under the duty to pay the interest of the sum owed. Hence, the obligation to pay interest on any sum as interest may occur from the contractual obligation.[992]

In particular, if the avoidance of the contract turns effective, during the restitution process, the buyer is given an opportunity to claim for the interest of the purchase price, while claiming for the refund of the very purchase price. The interest so claimed is as important to the buyer as it starts running not

---

[984] *Minter v. Welsh Health Technical Services Organisation* (1980) 13 BLR 1.

[985] Michael Furmston, Op. cit., pp. 777–778.

[986] Op. cit.

[987] Article 291 UAGCL.

[988] Article 263 para. 2 UAGCL.

[989] Ingeborg Schwenzer, Op. cit., p. 1055.

[990] Ibid., p. 1054.

[991] Article 291 UAGCL.

[992] As opposed to the default rules, contractual parties may agree on the contract on terms and condition related to the payment of interest.

from the day of the avoidance but, from the day of the payment thereof.[993] Here the payment of interest is mandatory once the payment is not fulfilled as required. It is immaterial whether failure to pay was caused by a prejudice or there was no notice of payment.[994]

Mitigation

The UAGCL lays down the duty to mitigate the loss.[995] In fact, the duty to mitigate as provided by the Uniform Act on sales is to the effect that the party relying on the breach of contract cannot recover damages in respect of a loss which ought to have been avoided.

Our concern here is that, as a general rule, no sanction is attached to a breach of the duty to mitigate by the buyer. But rather the buyer who relies on the breach of the contract, but fails to mitigate the loss due to the breach, may have as a consequence, a reduce amount of his recovery, if the seller do request.[996]

Regarding the aforementioned rule, it is also important to consider the scope of the decision to mitigate. To the UAGCL, the duty to mitigate applies regarding all the reasonable measures that the party relying on the breach should undertake in order to mitigate the loss. What then amounts to reasonable measures? These are those acts that an ordinary businessman in a position of the party claiming damages would have taken to protect the business.[997]

Conclusion

This chapter reveals that the Uniform Act on General Commercial Law contains a comprehensive system of remedies for aggrieved buyers which pre-empts remedies available under domestic sales laws. This chapter has explored the consistent scheme set up by the Uniform Act in determining non-conformity and the remedies that the buyer can resort to in the case of non-conformity. Most remarkably, this chapter revisits the expectation and restitution interests; concepts that are instrumental in shaping our

993 Article 300 UAGCL.

994 Joseph Issa-Sayegh et al., Op. cit.,p. 301.

995 Article 293 UAGCL.

996 Article 293 para. 2 UAGCL.

997 Ingeborg Schwenzer, Op. cit., p. 1045.

understanding of contract remedies embodied in the UAGCL in view to bring relief to the commercial buyer. A superior model is bipolar, with the expectation interest standing opposite the restoration interest. These two interests—one pulling toward the economic equivalence of full performance and the other toward the replication of the *status quo*—constitute the alternatives that determine the measure of damages for seller's lack of conformity under the OHADA Uniform Act on General Commercial Law. However, interest rates are also an additional compensation alongside payment of damages to the buyer where necessary.

9

GENERAL CONCLUSION

This study on this area of Commercial Law (specifically on sale of goods) appears to be very timely in view of the legal and socio-economic problems resulting from the quality of goods being sold in our marketplaces. The standpoint is that trade amongst countries of the OHADA treaty, such as Cameroon and other major countries like China and U.S.A. keep on building-up every day, so will the volume of related disputes arise over the sale of the goods. Consequently, there is need to gain familiarity with the legal structures in place likely to guide the transactions between commercial persons. The issue of goods to be sold by sellers in conformity with the contractual terms is widely considered to embrace different facets of the goods under a contract of sale. It ranges from the quality itself to the quantity, packaging, labelling, description, to name a few. There is no denial as to the fact that there is a widespread of defective products which continuously flood our markets. Yet, it is difficult to determine whether the sellers' liability for supplying defective goods makes good business sense or it is just part of business practices. However, this study has demonstrated that there should be strict liability of sellers of goods, through the imposition of adequate implementation of the laws in place in view to ensure that sellers adequately fulfill their contractual obligations in supplying goods of conformity to the contractual terms in their business relationship with commercial buyers. Consequently, this will press on manufacturers who stand behind the goods they sell to be more cautious in ascertaining the conformity of their goods during the production phase. This justification arises from the absolute sellers' liability's roots in the duty of conformity. Today, the commercial buyer's protection is gaining ground because of the increasing recognition of the indispensable but vulnerable position which the commercial buyer occupies in the production process. Thus, the consumer's interest is also incidental to this preoccupation.

The concept of '*conformity*' under the OHADA Uniform Act on General Commercial Law must be addressed with a lot of legal ingenuity as it is common for the quality or description of the goods to incorporate some elements that are not part of the physical goods forming the subject of the contract of sale between the seller and the buyer. In particular, courts should consider whether it is appropriate in the context of the OHADA Uniform Act to define this term according to a dichotomy between the physical and non-physical things that could form the object of a contract of sale. The exercise of this duty must be compatible with common trade usages. Such requirements as ethical values, Good Manufacturing Practices, domestic and international standards of goods should not be seen as novel. Certain intellectual property concepts such as trademarks and copyrights should also be taken into consideration as being attributes of goods forming part of a sales agreement. In spite of the fact that the prime consideration in determining the seller's obligation under the OHADA Uniform Act on General Commercial Law is the intention of the parties, requirements to the reputation of the goods in the market places must also be upheld especially when doing business within a cross-border sales context.

As this duty is expansive, imposing an absolute liability for defects that exist when risk passes to the seller, it is critical for the parties to clearly articulate the aspects of the goods that they intend to form a part of the conformance duty. This is especially for goods such as consumer goods, where marketing and brand issues are highly relevant to the usability of the goods.

This study supports the fact that the principal inadequacies of the Common Law principle of *caveat emptor* should in modern commerce be translated to *caveat venditor* according to which the seller and not the buyer should strictly beware. This is the cornerstone of the seller's duty of conformity under the Uniform Act on General Commercial Law. The prevailing norm should be caveat venditor. The justification for this posture is informed by the changes which the logic behind *laissez-faire* untenable such as advances in information and technologies, the increasingly fragmented supply chain and the utter situation of modern consumer goods and services. The situation is exacerbated by marketing practices such as false and misleading advertisement, all of which compromise the commercial buyer and his customers to make an informed purchase decision.

Apart from the Uniform Act on General Commercial Law in which provides for compensation to the commercial buyer because of the seller's breach of his contractual obligations, the virtue of the criminal law in protecting the interests of commercial buyers cannot be overstated. However, the general absence of the possibility of individual compensation under the Uniform Act renders the law an ineffectual tool for protecting the interests of commercial buyers. Commercial buyers are also usually particularly concerned with what direct measures can serve the important function of making good some specific loss or injury which they may have personally incurred or suffered from an act or omission of the seller or manufacturer. Failure by the criminal law to address the commercial buyer's loss under the Uniform Act means that the commercial buyer is confined to his rights in a civil claim based on contract. Though this may seem effective, if penal sanctions simultaneously applied for compensating the commercial buyer in addition to the available remedies on the Uniform Act, this will stand as a more robust measure in affording relieve to an aggrieved buyer.

It is trite to remark that however well-conceived and drafted legislation may be its impact ultimately hinges on the effectiveness of its enforcements. Arguably, because of the complexity of the issues involved in the strict application of sellers' liability for non-conformity goods, this thesis supports the fact that the primary responsibility for enforcement should be attributed to government administrative agency. The infrastructure of such an agency already exists in most African countries such as in Cameroon: the Ministry of Trade and Commerce as well as the Department of Price and Control, attached to the Ministry of Economy. There is no doubt that its personnel have received formal training in dealing with businessmen, farmers and consumers for over a decade now. Because of the legal training most of them have acquired they are conversant with sale practices. The control of quality of goods is not new to them. They should vehemently apply the legislations by being objective in reporting their observations in the field free from any bribery or corruption. This thesis proposes that as in developed countries, the tasks of these administrative agents should not be occasional but regular. In some big shops, offices of State agents should be implanted in order to receive and control deficient goods detected by buyers. Individuals may also lay their complaints to the agents who must act on such complaints. All that is required is a reinforcement of the existing enforcement machinery which already has a wealth of knowledge and also sound fact- finding machinery.

The government should also enhance its implementation of rules on importation of goods through our airports, seaports and border frontiers. Standardisation and quality control in most OHADA countries such as Cameroon is still very poor. We are witnessing each day an increase in sub-standard products into our marketplaces. Custom officials should double their task in controlling the entry of the quality of goods imported into the country. A stricter application of this measure will curtail the amount of poor and dangerous state of goods which fraudulent sellers may import from other countries where such goods have been banned because of non-conformity to certain standards.

Governments of Countries to the OHADA treaty should enhance their interventionist role in industries through quality control and quality assurance of goods and services. A major reform effort calls for the stricter application of quality control of goods in industries in conformity with the ISO–International Standard Organisation. Quality control emphasises testing of products to uncover defects, and reporting to management who make the decision to allow or deny the release of these goods to the purchasing public. On the other part, quality assurance would attempt to improve and stabilise production, and associated processes, to avoid, or at least minimise, issues that led to the defects in the first place. This success can be attained as well if all quality departments in companies operating in the OHADA Countries approach quality with an open mind, then it would improve the quality process.

In this same line of reasoning, government should channel the sales and distribution of some particular kind of goods through the creation of some governmental marketing boards. This suggests that such a measure could help in assuring the quality of goods for exportation through a systematic conduct of testing the goods which they will receive from local producers. Such is the case at this point of agricultural produce, namely; cocoa and coffee. This will be a deliberate attempt to spread the considerable financial benefits of distributing its products and acting as a watch-dog against unnecessary inflation of prices of goods which are not in conformity with the regulations in place.

Another important institution which could be copied in Cameroon for example, is that of the Consumer Ombudsman, an office created by the Swedish Market Court Act, 1970. Such an institution should be impartial by acting as a watch-dog, the '*grievance man*', checking the mal-practices of sellers of goods in the markets. It should be recalled that the existence of association of traders in our various markets have not proven their effectiveness in redressing this problem of influx of deficient goods in the marketplaces. The creation of a National Consumer Ombudsman would oversee the application of the legislation designed to protect commercial transaction of goods. Such a measure will press on producers of who stand behind the goods they sell to be more cautious in the quality of the goods they manufacture. This institution should also be given powers to issue injunctions against businessmen who use contract terms to escape liability which are prohibited by legislation.

Finally, the individual consumer could act as an advocate for the improvement of the quality of goods in the markets requiring vigorously for specific redress from the government and the courts, because the thrust of the legislative proposals given above is to protect consumers through the imposition of adequate implementation of the sellers' liability for defective goods they sell to commercial buyers. The courts should continue to adjudicate on cases stemming from sale contracts where redress is sought. Hence, there is still room for enforcement of the proposed legislation by the courts.

As information technology purveys globalisation of trade and commerce, OHADA member States need to effectively implement their laws on the sale of goods in order for these countries to strategically position themselves to be competitively relevant. This depends to a greater extent on the quality of the goods it purports to offer in the rush of markets at the international trade level. This discussion on some salient interpretation of its provisions on sale of goods makes a serious case for conscious steps to be initiated effectively at Executive, Judiciary and Legislative planes.

If the Cameroon government in striving to achieve economic growth by the year 2035 and the OHADA treaty in its effort to catch sustainable development and predictability of business in its Member countries, then this research must be given close attention. As globalisation purveys the rush for markets of goods, countries to the OHADA treaty must strategically position themselves to be legally assertive through the adequacy application of the law. At a time when aid and grants to Africa are being drastically reduced, it is imperative that OHADA Member Countries devise means to be economically independent. A very powerful weapon is through trade of goods of meaningful quality as especially as The African Growth and Opportunity Act (AGOA), 2000 offers almost uninhibited access to the United States market, a market comprising more than 200 million potential consumers. Yet this important OHADA legislation on Sale of goods is still little known to most business men.

That is why most of the law's provisions of the Uniform Act are to be tested in practice.

It is hoped that this study has shown how much out of touch the sale of goods under the OHADA Law as practised in Cameroon is with the economic and social conditions that prevail in the country. Given the importance of sale of goods, both as an instrument for the realisation of social justice and also as an instrument for the furtherance of economic development, this fact ought to generate serious concern and attempts must be made to correct this situation.

BIBLIOGRAPHY

Textbooks

Akuété Pedro Santos and Jean Yado Toé, *OHADA Droit Commercial Général,* Bruylant, Collection Droit Uniforme Africain, Bruxelles, 2002.

Alfandri, E, *Droit des Affaires,* Litec, Paris, 1993.

Andrew Burrows, *Remedies for Torts and Breach of Contract,* 2nd edition, Butterworths, London, 1994.

Andrew, Geddes, *Product and Service Liability in the EEC,* The New Strict Liability Regime, Sweet & Maxwell, London, 1992.

Anne-Catherine, Imhoff- Scheier, *Protection du Consommateur et Contrats Internationaux,* Librairie de L'Université George & Cie S.A., Genève, 2002.

Arthur, Hartkamp, *Martijn Hesselink, Ewoud Hondius et al., Towards a European Civil Code,* 3rd Edition, The Netherlands, Kluwer Law International, 2004.

Athanase, Foko, *Le Statut du Commerçant dans l'Espace OHADA,* P.U.A., Collection Vade-Mecum, Yaoundé, 2005.

Barry, Nicholas, French Law of Contract, Butterworths, London, 1982.

Beale, Hugh Hartkamp, Arthur, Kotz, Hein and Tallon, Denis, *Cases, Materials and Text on Contract Law,* Hart Publishing, Oxford, 2002.

Benabent, A., Les Contrat Civils et Commerciaux, 5éme Edition, Monchrestien, Paris, 2001.

Benjamin, K. Lesinger, *Fundamental Breach Considering Non-Conformity of the Goods,* Paris, Sellier, European Law Publishers, 2007.

Bianca, C.M. and Bonnell, M.J. et al., *Commentary on the International Sales Law the 1980 Vienna Sales Convention,* Giuffrè, Milan, 1987.

Boris, Martor, Nanette, Pilkington et al., *Business Law in Africa, OHADA and the Harmonization Process,* 2nd edition, London, GMB Publishing Ltd., 2002.

Brice, Dickson, *Introduction to French Law,* Pitman Publishing, London, 1994.

Bricks, Helene, *Les Clauses Abusives,* Tome CLXXV, L.G.D.J., Paris, 1982.

Busch, Danny, Honduis, Ewoud, Kooten Van, Hugo et al., *The Principles of European Contract Law and Dutch Law, A Commentary,* Kluwer Law International, 2002.

Catherine, Elliot and Frances, Quinn, *Contract Law,* 4th edition, Longman, 2003.

Collin P.H., *Dictionary of Law,* 3rd edition, Peter Publishing, 2000.

Dennis, Campbell, *Remedies for International Sellers of Goods,* Yorkhill Law Publisher, 2008.

Donald, Harris and Denis Tallon, *Contract law Today, Anglo-French Comparisons,* Clarendon Press, Oxford, 1991.

Dutilleul, F. and Delebecque, P., *Contrats Civils et Commerciaux,* 5éme Edition, Dalloz, Paris, 2001. ,

E.E. Uvieghara, *Sales of Goods (and Hire Purchase) Law in Nigeria,* Mathouse Press Ltd., Ibadan, 1996.

Ewan Mckendrick, *Contract Law Text, Cases and Materials,* 3rd edition, Oxford University Press, 2008.

Ewan Mckendrick, *Contract Law, New York,* 6th edition, Palgrave Macmillan, 2005.

Ezejoifor et al., *Nigerian Business Law,* Sweet and Maxwell, London, 1982.

Fénéon, A. & Gomez, R.J., *Le Droit de la Vente Commercial,* No. 2, Cahiers Juridiques et Fiscaux de l'Exploitation, CFCE, 1998.

Fréderic, Leclerc, *La Protection de la Partie Faible dans les Contrats Internationaux, Etude de conflits de lois,* Bruylant, Bruxelles, Belgique, 1995.

Freud, Kahn, and Rudden, Levy, *A Source-Book on French Law,* 3rd Revised Edition, Oxford, Clarendon Press, 1991.

G.H. Treitel, *The Law of Contract,* London, 10th edition, Sweet and Maxwell, 1999.

Gerard Cornu, *Vocabulaire Juridique,* 8éme édition, Presses Universitaires de France, 1987.

Guest, A.G. et al., *Benjamin's Sale of Goods,* Sweet and Maxwell, London, 2002.

Henri & Léon Mazeaud et al., *Obligations, Théorie Générale, Leçons de Droit Civil,* 9éme édition, Montchrestien, 1998.

Hewitt, S.W., *Manufacturers' Liability for Defective Goods,* BSP Professional Books, 1987.

I.E. Sagay, *Nigerian Law of Contract,* Spectrum Law ed., 2nd edition, Spectrum Books Limited, 2007.

Igweike, K.I., *Sales of Goods, Nigerian Commercial Law,* Mathouse Law Books, Lagos, 2001.

J. AdemolaYakubu, *Law of Contract in Nigeria,* Mathouse Press Limited, 2003.

Jacques, Ghestin, *Conformité et Garanties dans la Vente* (produits mobiliers), L.G.D.J., Paris, 1983.

Jason, Chuah, *Law of International Trade,* 3rd edition, Sweet & Maxwell, London, 2005.

Jean-Marie, Nyama, *Eléments de Droit des Affaires Cameroun—OHADA,* Collection Apprendre, Presse de l'UCAC, Yaoundé, 2002.

Jérôme, Huet, *Contrats Civils et Commerciaux, Responsabilité du Vendeur et Garantie contre les Vices Cachés,* Litec, Paris, 1987.

John, O. Honnold, *Uniform Law for International Sales,* The Netherlands, 3rd Edition, KLuwer Law International, 1999.

Jolowicz, J.A., et al., *Winfield and Jolowicz on Tort,* 9th edition, Sweet and Maxwell, London, 1971.

Joseph, Issa-Sayegh, and Jacqueline, Lohoue-Oble, *Harmonisation du Droit des Affaires,* Bruylant, Bruxelles, 2002.

Joseph, Issa-Sayegh, et al., *OHADA Traité et Actes Uniformes Commentés et Annotés,* 3éme édition, Juriscope, 2008.

Josette, Nguebou, *Le Droit Commercial Général dans l'Acte Uniforme OHADA,* Presses Universitaires d'Afrique, Yaoundé, 1998.

Lawson, F.H., et al., *Introduction to French Law,* 3rd edition, Clarendon Press, Oxford, 1967.

Martha, Simo Tumnde et al., *Unified Business Laws for Africa, Common Law Perspectives on OHADA,* (ed. Claire Moore Dickerson), 2nd edition, IEDP, London, 2012.

Michael, Bridge, *The Sale of Goods,* Oxford University Press, London, 2003.

Michael, J. Trebilock, *The Limits of Freedom of Contract,* Havard University Press, 1993.

Nayhak, Kumar, Rajendra, *Consumer Protection Law in India, An Eco-Legal Treatise on Consumer Justice,* Sweet and Maxwell Ltd., London, 1991.

P. Havenga, M. Havega, R. Kelbrick, M. McGregor, H. Schluze, K. Van Der Linde, *General Principles of Commercial Law,* 6th edition, Juta, Cape Town, 2007.

Patrick, Atiyah, *The Rise and Fall of Freedom of Contract,* Clarendon press, Oxford, 1979.

Patrick, S. Atiyah, John Adams, Hector Macqueen, *The Sale of Goods,* 12th Edition, Longman, Pitman Publishing, London, 2010.

Paul Peter & Jerry C. Olson, *Consumer Behavior and Marketing Strategy,* 2nd edition, Homewood, 1998.

Paul-Gérard, Pougoué and Yvette-Rachel, Kalieu Elongo, *Introduction Critique a l'OHADA,* P.U.A., Yaoundé, 2010.

Paul-Gérard, Pougoué et al., *Encyclopédie du Droit OHADA,* Lamy, Paris, 2011.

Peter, Schlectriem & Ingebord, Schwenzer, *Commentary on the UN Convention on the International Sales of Goods* (CISG), 2nd (English) Edition, C.H. Beck Ohg, Germany, 2005.

Philippe, Malaurie, Laurent Aynes et al., *Les Obligations, Defrénois,* Paris,

2003.

Philippe, Malaurie, Laurent, Aynes and Pierre-Yves, Gautier, *Les Contrats Spéciaux,* 3éme edition, Defrénois, Paris, 2007.

Phillippe Van De Wiele, *La vente d'Immeubles, 2*éme éditions, DeBoeck Université, 2001.

Reinhard, Zimmermann and Simon Whittaker, *Good Faith in European Contract Law,* Cambridge University Press, U.K. , 2000.

Remy Cabrillac, *Droit des Obligations,* 7éme édition, Dalloz, 2006.

Rippert, G. and Roblot, R., *Traité de Droit Commercial,* 16éme édition, L.G.D.J., Paris, 2000.

Roy, Goode, and Herbert Kronke, *Transnational Commercial Law,* UK, Oxford University Press, 2007.

Roy, Goode, *Commercial Law,* 3rd edition, LexisNexis and Penguin Books, England, 2004.

Schmidt-Kessel, M. and Katrin, Mayer, M., *Spervening Events and Force Majeure,* Edward Elgar Publishing, Jan. M. Smits ed., 2006.

Simmonds, N.E., *Central Issues in Jurispudence, Justice, Law and Rights,* 2nd edition, Sweet & Maxwell, London, 2002.

Sutton, K.C.T., *Sales and Consumer Law in Australia and New Zealand,* 3rd Edition, The Law Book Company Limited, 1983.

Articles/Monographs

Adam, M. Giuliano, (2000) Non-conformity in the Sale of Goods between the United States and China; The new Chinese Contract Law, the Uniform Commercial Code, and the Convention on Contracts for International Sales of Goods, 18 *Florida Journal of International Law*, 331.

Adrian, Chandler and James Devenney, (2004) Mistake as to Identity and the Threads of Objectivity, 3 *Journal of Obligations and Remedies*, pp. 7–22.

Adjita, Akrawati Shamsidine, (2002) L'interprétation de la Volonté des Parties dans la Vente Commerciale (OHADA), 841 *Penant*, pp. 473–524.

Alain, Fénéon, (2005) L'influence de la CVIM sur le Nouveau Droit Africain de la Vente Commerciale, 853 *Penant*, pp. 464–517.

Alain, Fénéon, & Antoine, Delabière, (1998) Présentation Générale de l'Acte Uniforme sur le Droit Commercial Général, 827 *Penant*, pp. 136–144.

Allan, E. Farnsworth, (1988) Review of Standard Form or Terms under the Vienna Convention, Vol. 21, *Cornell International Law Journal*.

Alvine, Longla Boma, (2011) Consumer Protection: A Cameroonian Perspective 8(2) *The African Law Review*, pp. 47–62.

Anna, Veneziano, (1997) Non-Conformity of Goods in International Sales; A Survey of Current Case law on CISG, 1 *International Business Law Journal*, pp. 39–62.

Antonio, J. Senagore, (2010) The Benefits of Limiting Strict Liability for Used-Product Sellers, 30 *Northern Illinois University Law*, pp. 1–34.

Arthur, Best & Alan R. Andreasen, (1977) Consumer Response to Unsatisfactory Purchase: A Survey of Perceiving Defects, Voicing Complaints, and Obtaining Redress, 11 *Law & Society*, pp. 701–742.

Benedict, Sheehy, (2005–2006) Good Faith in the CISG: The Interpretation Problems of Article 7, *Pace International Law Review* (*Review of the Convention on Contracts for the International Sale of Goods* (CISG)).

Bolgar, (1972) The Contract of Adhesion: A Comparism of Theory and Practice, 20 *American Journal of Comparative Law*, pp. 53–78.

Boyd, H arper W. and Claycamp, H., (1966) Industrial Self-Regulation and the Public Interest, 64 *Michigan Law Review*, pp. 1239- 1254.

Camilla, Baasch Andersen, (1998) Reasonable Time in Article 39(1) of the CISG—Is Article 39(1) Truly a Uniform Provision? *Review of the Convention on Contracts for the International Sale of Goods* (CISG), Kluwer Law International.

Caroline, London and Michael Llamas, (1994) Packaging Laws in France and Germany, 6 (1) *Journal of Environmental Law*, pp.1–22.

Charles, Mba-Owono, (2000) Non-conformité et Vice Cachés dans la Vente Commerciale en Droit Uniforme Africain, 41 *Juridis Périodique*, pp. 107–127.

Charles, T. LE Viness, (1943) Caveat Emptor Caveat Venditor, 7 (3) *Maryland Law Review*, pp.177–200.

Claire, Moore Dickerson, (2011) Informal-Sector Entrepreneurs, Development and Formal Law: A Functional Understanding of Business Law, Vol. 59, *American Journal of Comparative Law*, pp. 159–226.

Danie,l T. Ostasa & Frank P. Darr, (1996) Understanding Commercial Impracticability: Tempering with Community Fairness Norms, 27 *Rutgers Law Journal*, 343.

David Slawson, (1971) Standard Form Contracts and Democratic Control of Law Making Power, 86 *Harvard Law Review*, 829.

David, Bederman, (1988) The 1871 London Declaration, Rebus Sic Stantibus and a Primitivist View of the Law of Nations, 82 *American Journal of International Law*, 1.

David, G. Haushalter, (2000) Financing Policy, Basis Risk, and Corporate Hedging: Evidence from Oil and Gas Producers' 55(1) *The Journal of Finance*, pp.107–152.

David, Thomas, (2011) Frustration and Force Majeure: A Hard Line in English Law, 6 (2) *Construction Law International* 21, pp. 1–13.

Edouard, Gnimpieba Tonnang, (2006) Le Nouveau Régime Juridique des Exportations entre les Etats d'Afrique Centrale: Entre Reformes Laborieuses et Influences Européennes, 857 *Penant*, pp. 433–483.

Eid, Rawach, (2001) La Validité des Clauses exonératoires de Responsabilité et la Convention de Vienne sur la Vente Internationale de Marchandises, *Revue Internationale de Droit Comparé.*

Elizabeth, I. Hack, (2007) Pharmaceutical Global Marketing Practices: Increased Scrutiny Ahead? 343 *Food and Drug Law.*

Emmanuel, S. Darankoum, (2005) La Pérennité du Lien Contractuel dans la Vente Commerciale OHADA: Analyse et Rédaction des Clauses, 845 *Penant.*

Eric, G. Anderson,(1994) The Restoration Interest and Damages for Breach of Contract, 53 *Maryland Law Review*, 1, pp. 1–64.

Eric, H. Steele, (1975) Fraud, Dispute and the Consumer: Responding to

Consumer Complaints, 123 *U. Pa. L. Rev.*, 1107, 1108.

Ernst, Rabel, The Nature of Warranty of Quality, (1950) 24 (3) *Tulane Law Review*, pp. 273–287.

Fone, Anne Marie,(1998) Le Secteur Informel Camerounais au regard du Doit Commercial, Tome 2, *Annales de la Facultés des Sciences Juridiques*, Université de Dschang.

Franc, R. Kennedy, (1966) Foreword to Symposium on Consumer Protection 64 *Michigan Law Review*, 1197.

Francis, B. Palumbo, (2001) The Role of the State as a Drug Purchaser, *Food and Drug Law Journal*, 266.

Francis, Fourment, (1997) Défauts Cachés de la Chose Vendue que Reste-t-il de l'Action en Garantie des Vices Cachés?, 3 *Revue Trimestrielle de Droit Economique*, pp. 416–419.

François, Anoukaha, (2001) L'Incompatibilité d'Exercice d'une Activité Commercial dans l'Espace OHADA: le cas du Cameroun, *Annales de la Faculté des Sciences Juridiques et Politiques, Tome* 1, Vol.5, Université de Dschang.

Franck, L. Mechem, (1928) Implied and Oral warranties and the Parol Evidence Rule, 12 (3) *Minnesota Law Review*, pp. 209–224.

Franco, Ferrari, (2003) Trade Usage and Practices Established between the Parties under the CISG, 5 *International Business Law Journal*, pp. 571–576.

Franklin, E. Crawford, (2002) Fit for its Ordinary Purpose? Tobacco, Fast Food, and the Implied Warranty of Merchantability, 63 *Ohio State Law Journal.*

Frederich, Kessler, (1964–1965) The Protection of the Consumer under Modern Sales Law, 74 *Yale Law Journal*, 262.

Friedrich Kessler, (1943) Contracts of Adhesion-Some Thoughts about Freedom of Contract, 43 *Columbia Law Review*, 629, pp. 629–642.

Gaston, Kenfack Douanji, (1998) Les Conditions de la Création dans l'espace OHADA d'un Environnement Juridique favorable au Développement, *Penant.*

George, A. Akerlof, (1970) The Market for 'Lemons': Quality Uncertainty and the Market Machanism, 84 (3) *The Quarterly Journal of Economics*, pp. 488–500.

George, Gleason Bogert, (1923–1924) Express Warranties in Sales of Goods, 33 *Yale Law Journal*, 14, pp. 14–32.

George, Gleason Bogert & Eli, E. Fink, (1930–1931) Business Practice Regarding Warranties in the Sale of Goods, 24 *Illinois Law Review*, pp. 400–417.

Gomez J.R. (1998) Un Nouveau Droit de la Vente Commercial en Afrique, 827 *Penant*.

Gustavo, Vieira da Costa Cerqueira, (2005–2006) Defective Performance in Contracts for International Sale of Goods: A Comparative Analysis between the Brazilian Law and the 1980 United Nations Convention on Contracts for the International Sale of Goods, *Pace International Law Review*.

Harry, M. Flechner, (2005–2006) Buyers' Remedies in General and Buyers' Performance-Oriented Remedies, 25 *Journal of Law and Commerce*, pp. 339–647.

Ingeborg, Schwenzer, (2007) Buyer's Remedies in the Case of Non-Conforming: Some Problems in a Core Area of the CISG, 101 *Am. Soc'y Int'il Proc.*, 416.

Jennifer, A. Lazo, (2007) The Life-Saving Medicines Export Act: Why the Proposed U.S. Compulsory Licensing Scheme will fail to Export Any Medicines or Save Any Lives, 33 (1) *Brooklyn Journal of International Law*.

Joern, Rimke, (1999–2000) Force Majeure and Hardship: Application in International Trade Practice with specific regard to the CISG and the UNIDROIT Principles of International Commercial Contracts, *Review of the Convention on Contracts for the International Sale of Goods* (CISG).

John, D. Wladis, (1988) Impracticability as Risk Allocation: The Effect of Changed Circumstances upon Contract Obligations for the Sale of Goods, 22 *Georgia Law Review*, 503, pp. 1–98.

John, Erauw, (2005) CISG Articles 66–70: The Risk of Loss and Passing It, 25 *Journal of Law and Commerce*, pp. 1–13.

Joseph, M. Perilloa, (1997) Force Majeure and Hardship under the UNIDROIT Principles of International Commercial Contracts, 5 *Tulane International & Comparative Law*, 5, pp.1–18.

Joseph, Nzalie Ebi, (2002) Reflecting on OHADA Law Reform Mission: Its Impact on certain aspects of Company Law in Anglophone Cameroon, Tome 2 *Annales de Faculté des Sciences Juridiques et Politiques, Université de Dschang*, pp 97–119.

Kabir, Masson, (2009) Paradox of Presumptions: Seller Warranties and Reliance Waivers in Commercial Contracts, 109 *Columbia Law Review*, 503, pp. 1–32.

Karl, N. Llewellyn, (1936) On Warranty of Quality, and Society, 34 (5) *Columbia Law Review*, pp. 689–744.

Karl N. Llewellyn, (1931) What Price Contract – An Essay in Perspective, 40 *Yale Law Journal*, pp. 1–41.

Kelner, J., (1970–1971) The Fault System, the Courts and the Consumer Revolt, 8 *San Diego Law Review*, 75.

Kristian, Maley, (2009) The Limits to the Conformity of Goods in the United Nations Convention on Contacts for the International sale of Goods (CISG), 12 *International Trade & Business Law Review*, 82, pp. 83–126.

L.L. Fuller & William R. Perdue, (1936) The Reliance Interest in Contract Damages, 40 *Yale Law Journal*, pp. 1–27.

Larry, Dimatteo et al., (2004) The Interpretive Turn in International Sales Law: An Analysis of Fifteen Years of CISG Jurisprudence, 24 *Northwestern Journal of International Law and Business*, pp. 299–392.

Loiuse, Merett, (2008) The Importance of Delivery and Possession in the Passing of Title, 67 *Cambridge Law Journal*, pp. 376–395.

Magaret, Howard, (1983) Allocation of Risk of Loss under the UCC: a Transactional Evaluation of Sections 2–509 and 2–510, Vol.15, *Uniform Commercial Code Law Journal*, pp. 334–372.

Michael, Joachim Bonell, (2008) The CISG, European Contract Law and the Development of a World Contract Law, Volume 56 *American Journal of Comparative Law*.

Mitchell Stocks, (1993) Risk of Loss under the Uniform Commercial Code and the United Nations Convention on Contracts for the International Sale of Goods: A Comparative Analysis and Proposed Revision of UCC Sections 2–509 and 2–510, 87 *Northwestern University Law Review*, 1415, pp. 1–49.

Nathan, Isaacs, (1934) The Industrial Purchaser and the Sales Act, *Columbia Law Review*, pp. 262–272.

Nicholas, Barry, (1979) Force Majeure and Frustration, 27 *American Journal of Comparative Law*, 231.

Nsie E., (1999) La Formation de la Vente Commercial en Afrique, 829 *Penant*.

Olu, Fasan, (2003) Global Trade Law: Challenges and Options for Africa Vol. 47, 2 *Journal of African Law*.

Pascal, Nguihe Kante, (2008) La Prise en Compte des Attentes Légitimes du Cocontractant en Droit Prive des Contrats, Tome 12, *Annales de la Faculté des Sciences Juridiques et Politiques, Université de Dschang*, pp. 33–69.

Pekins, Rollins M., (1919–1920) Unwholesome Food as a Source of Liability, 5 (6) *Iowa Law Bullentin* 86, pp. 86–111.

Peter, Schlechtriem, (1993) Good Faith in German Law and in International Uniform Laws, *Centro di Studi e Ricerche di Dritto Comparato e Straniero*, Roma.

Peter, Schlechtriem, (2007) Non-Material Damages-Recovery under the CISG? 19 *Pace International Law Review*.

René, Franz Henschel, (2004) Conformity of Goods in International Sales Governed by CISG Article 35: Caveat Venditor, Caveat Emptor and Contract Law as Background Law and as a Competing Set of Rules, *Nordic Journal of Commercial Law*, pp. 1–21.

Richard, J. Barbar, (1975) Government and Consumer, 64 *Michigan Law Review*.

Robert C. Brown, (1938) The Liability of Retail Dealers for Defective Food Products, 23 *Minnesota Law Review*, 585, pp. 585–611.

Robert, Koch, (1998) The Concept of Fundamental Breach of Contract under the United Nations Convention on Contracts for the International

Sale of Goods Contracts, *Review of the Convention on Contracts for the International Sale of Goods* (CISG).

Roger, Mevoungou Nsana, (2000) Les Obligations du Vendeur de Marchandises dans l'Acte Uniforme OHADA,1 (2) *Revue Africaine des Sciences Juridiques*, Université de Yaoundé II, pp. 6–19.

Roscoe, Pound, (1908–1909) Liberty of Contract, *Yale Law Journal.*

Saidov, Djakhongir, (2004–2005) Causation in Damages: The Convention on Contracts for the International Sale of Goods, the UNIDROIT Principles of International Commercial Contracts, the Principles of European Contract Law' *Pace International Law Review* (*Review of the Convention on Contracts for the International Sale of Goods* (CISG)), European Law Publishers.

Samgena, D. Galega, (2004) Strict Liability for Defective Products in Cameroon? Some Illuminating Lessons from Abroad, 48 (2) *Journal of African Law*, pp. 239–270.

Samgena, Galega & N. Kangha, (2004) Cameroon and the Trade Growth and Opportunity Act (AGOA): Trade, Investment and Other Benefits, Vol. 4, No. 1, *Journal of Applied Social Sciences*, University of Buea.

Samuel, J. Stoljar, (1952), Conditions, Warranties and Descriptions of Quality in Sale of Goods, Volume 15, 15 *Modern Law Review*, pp. 425–445.

Samuel, Williston, (1911) Liability for Honest Misrepresentation, Vol. 24 (6) *Harvard Law Review*, 1911, pp. 417–439.

Sandeep, Goplan, (2004) The Creation of International Commercial Law: Sovereignty Felled?, *San Diego International Law Journa*l.

Sarah, Howard Jenkins, (1998) Exemption for Non-performance: UCC, CISG, Unidroit Principles—A Comparative Assessment, 72 *Tulane Law Review*, pp. 1–12.

Saul, Litvinoffa, (1985) Force Majeure, Failure of Cause and Théorie de l'Imprévision Louisiana Law and Beyond, (1985), 49 *Louisiana Law Review*, 1, pp. 1–25.

Sealy, L.S., (1972) Risk in the Law of Sale, 31 *Cambridge Law Journal*, pp. 225–247.

Silva, Ferreri, (2005–2006) Remarks Concerning the Implementation of the CISG by the Courts. (The Seller's Performance and Article 35), Vol. 25 *Journal of Law and Commerce*, pp. 223–239.

Slyvain, Bollée, (1999–2000) Theory of Risks in the 1990 Vienna Sale of Goods Convention, Pace Institute of International Commercial Law, pp. 245–290.

Sone, A. Ewang, (1997) Brewed Drinks unfit for Human Consumption can Warrant for Liability, 29 *Juridis Périodique*.

Steven, J. Burton, (1980) Breach of Contract and the Common Law Duty to Perform in Good Faith, 94 *Harvard Law Review*.

Stigler, G. J., (1961) The Economics of Information, 69 *Journal of Political Economy*, 213.

Taiwo, A. Oriola, (2002) Consumer Dilemmas, The Right to Know, Safety, Ethics and Policy of Genetically Modified Food , *Singapore Journal of Legal Studies*, 514, pp. 514–573.

Todd, S. Lowry, (1976) Bargain and Contract Theory in Law and Economics, 10 (1) *Journal of Economic Issues*, pp. 1–22.

William, L. Prosser, (1943) The Implied Warranty of Merchantable Quality, 27 *Minnesota Law Review*, pp. 117–168.

Walton, H. Hamilton, (1931) The Ancient Maxim Caveat Emptor, 40 (8) *Yale Law Journal*, pp. 1133–1187.

Theses/Dissertations

Atangcho, Nji Akonumbo, *Foreign Direct Investments and Legal Policy Options in Cameroon*, Ph.D. Thesis, (unpublished), University of Yaounde II, Soa, 2008.

Ayonghe L.S., *A French-English Glossary of Terms related to OHADA, Masters Dissertation in Translation*, ASTI, University of Buea, 2003.

Edie Diabe Pascal, *Contract of Sale of Goods under the OHADA Uniform Act on General Commercial Law, The Common Law and the CISG: A Comparative Study*, Masters Dissertation, University of Dschang, 2011.

Joseph Dione Ngute, *Standardzised Contracts in a Bi-Jural State: The United Republic of Cameroon*, Ph.D.Thesis, University of Warwick, Law School, 1982.

Marie, C. Kamwe Mouaffo., *L'Obligation de Conformité dans la Vente Commerciale en OHADA*, D.E.A. Dissertation, Université of Dschang, 1999.

Martha, Simo Njikam, *Insurance Law in England and Cameroon- A Comparative Study—With Specific Reference to Motor Vehicle Insurance*, Ph.D. Thesis, (unpublished), Sheffield University, 1986.

Noel, Thierry Kanchop, *Le Secteur Informel a l'Epreuve du Droit des Affaires OHADA*, Mémoire de D.E.A., Université de Dschang, 2008.

René, Njeufack, Temgwa, *La Protection de la Concurrence dans la CEMAC*, Thèse de Doctorat, (unpublished), Université de Dschang, 2005.

Roland, Djieufack, *The Nature of Agency relationship under the OHADA Uniform Act on General Commercial Law and Common Law: A Comparative Study*, D.E.A. Dissertation, University of Dschang, 2004.

Sylvestre, Mezatio, *L'Adaption du Contrat aux Circonstances Economiques*, Mémoire de Maitrise, Université de Yaoundé, Octobre 1991.

Urbain, Olanguena Awono, *Liberte du Commerce et de L'industrie au Cameroun*, Thèse de Doctorat de 3é cycle, (unpublished), Université de Yaoundé, 1982.

Conference Papers/Reports/Presentations

Allan, E. Farnsworth, The Concept of Good Faith in American Law, Centro di Studi e Ricerche di Dritto Comparato e Straniero, Roma, 1993.

Cameroon Growth and Employment Strategy Paper, Reference Framework for Government Action over the Period 2010–2020.

Ewoud, H. Hondius, Protection of the Weak Party in the Law of Contract, in Proceedings of the symposium of Dutch and Japanese Laws Compared, Publications of the International Center for Comparative Law and Politics, No.3, The University of Tokyo, 1993.

Foneris, X., Harmonizing Commercial Law in Africa: the OHADA, in Governance, Development and Globalization, University of Warwick.

Jacob, S. Zigel, New Developments in International Commercial and Consumer Law, Proceedings of the 8th Biennial Conference of the International Academy of Commercial and Consumer Law, Hart Publishing, Oxford, 1998.

Jean, Claude James, La Vente Commerciale OHADA, Précurseur d'un Droit Harmonise des Contrats ? in Actes du Colloque International de Libreville sur Les Pratiques Contractuelles d'Affaires et les Processus d'Harmonisation dans les Espaces Régionaux, organisé par l'Ecole Régionale Supérieure de la Magistrature du 26–28 octobre a Libreville, Gabon, 1ere édition, Juin 2012.

Jean-Claude, Fourgoux and Jeanne Mihailov, La Normalisation en tant qu'instrument de la Sécurité des Consommateurs in Colloque des 6 et 7 Novembre 1986 organisé par le Centre de Droit des Obligations de l'Université de Paris 1, Patheon-Sorbonne.

Nanette, Pilkington, The Security of Transactions and Investment in Africa, in Proceedings of the OHADA Seminar held at the University of Buea, Cameroon, 18–19 September, 2003, pp. 28–41.

Ngwasiri, C., et al., The Informal Sector in Douala-Cameroon: A Survey of Street Vendors, Yaounde, 1997.

Roy, Goode, The Concept of Good Faith in English Law, Centro di Ricerche di Dritto Comparato e Straniero, Roma, 1993.

Internet Sources and Websites

www.cisg.law.pace.edu/cisg, (Last accessed on 10/4/2012)

www.confinder.richmond.edu:admin:docs:cameroon.pdf, (Last accessed on 20/10/2011)

www.heinoline.org, (Last accessed on 5/10/2011)

www.hrweb.org/legal/udhr.html, (Last accessed on 02/2/2012)

www.juriscope.org, (Last accessed on 11/4/2012)

www.jstor.org, (Last accessed on 21/11/2011)

www.ohada.com, (Last accessed on 10/4/2012)

www.unidroit.org, (Last accessed on 15/10/2010)

www.unilex.org, (Last accessed on 10/4/2012)